CHINA'S COMPLIANCE IN GLOBAL AFFAIRS

Trade, Arms Control, Environmental Protection,
Human Rights

Series on Contemporary China (ISSN: 1793-0847)

Published

Vol. 1
Legitimacy
Ambiguities of Political Success or Failure in East and Southeast Asia
edited by Lynn White

Vol. 2
China Under Hu Jintao
Opportunities, Dangers, and Dilemmas
edited by Tun-jen Cheng, Jacques deLisle & Deborah Brown

Vol. 3
China's Compliance in Global Affairs
Trade, Arms Control, Environmental Protection, Human Rights
by Gerald Chan

Series on Contemporary China – Vol. 3

CHINA'S COMPLIANCE IN GLOBAL AFFAIRS

Trade, Arms Control, Environmental Protection, Human Rights

Gerald Chan

Victoria University of Wellington, New Zealand

World Scientific

NEW JERSEY · LONDON · SINGAPORE · BEIJING · SHANGHAI · HONG KONG · TAIPEI · CHENNAI

Published by

World Scientific Publishing Co. Pte. Ltd.

5 Toh Tuck Link, Singapore 596224

USA office: 27 Warren Street, Suite 401-402, Hackensack, NJ 07601

UK office: 57 Shelton Street, Covent Garden, London WC2H 9HE

Library of Congress Cataloging-in-Publication Data
Chan, Gerald.
    China's compliance in global affairs : trade, arms control, environmental
protection, human rights / by Gerald Chan.
      p. cm. -- (Series on contemporary China; vol. 3)
    Includes bibliographical references and index.
    ISBN 981-256-504-3
    1. China--Foreign relations--1976–   . I. Title. II. Series.

DS779.27.C43 2006
327.51'009'0511--dc22

                                                                    2005053893

British Library Cataloguing-in-Publication Data
A catalogue record for this book is available from the British Library.

Typeset by Stallion Press
E-mail: enquiries@stallionpress.com

For Alice, Darwin, and Byron

Contents

Preface

This book has been a long time in the making. It began life in October 1999 when I was invited to give a paper at a conference held at the Australian National University (ANU) to mark the occasion of the 50th anniversary of the founding of the People's Republic of China. I was asked to give a paper on the relationship between power and responsibility in China's international relations. At first I was a bit hesitant to go, because I was not familiar with the concept of responsibility. However, the lure of visiting Canberra after a lapse of ten years and the challenge and opportunity of doing something new and exciting led me to look up the idea of responsibility in literature that crossed my desk and to consult my colleagues in International Relations at Victoria University of Wellington.

My subsequent visit to Canberra was all too brief, but I learned a lot from the conference, and that set me on my path to look for more. One of the conference organisers, Dr Zhang Yongjin, then a fellow of the Department of International Relations at ANU, in chairing my panel and introducing me to the audience, said that my paper represented "a Chinese view from inside out". That succinct remark has stuck in my mind since. The rather subjective tone of my "concept paper" pushed me to look for a more objective and empirical assessment of China's global responsibility. Since I have had a long-held interest in China's participation in international organisations, I turned quite naturally to this area to look for clues to make an assessment of China's global responsibility. The result of this pursuit led me to present another paper on China's global responsibility from the point of view of its participation in multilateral institutions, at the International Studies Association conference held in Hong Kong in July 2001, the New Zealand Political Studies Association conference held in Palmerston North in December 2001, and at a seminar at the University of Macau in January 2002.

Although the paper was well received, I felt that it didn't go much beyond what I was familiar and comfortable with — that is, China's participation in international organisations. I wanted to do something more. So I cast my mind a bit wider to try to find a way to measure China's global responsibility. My reading of books on international relations and law landed me on the idea of state compliance, which I thought would be useful to gauge China's global responsibility.

The concept of compliance in international relations opened up a new vista for my research, and I subsequently incorporated some of my preliminary understandings of compliance in my writings on China's global responsibility. Soon I began to realise that it is insufficient to discuss the concepts of responsibility and compliance in a general way; I needed to test those ideas against some empirical evidence. I felt it necessary to carry out some case studies where I could examine in detail China's compliance in some specific issues. Around that time, China's impending membership of the World Trade Organisation (WTO) was widely reported in the news, and I thought I could start with China's compliance in the WTO. Further readings on Chinese foreign policy and international relations revealed that I could also include China's compliance in the areas of arms control, environmental protection, and human rights.

An invitation to present a paper at a China conference organised by Hong Kong Baptist University gave me the opportunity to present a paper on China's WTO compliance in May 2002. Subsequently I presented revised drafts at the East Asian Institute of the National

University of Singapore in October 2002, the East Asian Institute of the University of Cambridge in November 2002, and the Universities Service Centre of the Chinese University of Hong Kong in February 2003.

I picked up China's compliance in environmental protection as my second case sometime in early 2003, partly as a response to a call for paper to a special issue on environmental protection organised by the editor of *Asia Pacific Viewpoint.* Of the two remaining cases, I mounted on the arms control issue first, as I had published a working paper on human rights before and thought that I could leave something easier to work on at the end. I spent a lot of time trying to catch up with my readings on arms control, disarmament, and non-proliferation until I forced myself to write up my first full draft when I was visiting the Academia Sinica in Taipei in the summer of 2004. Early versions of Chapter 5 on arms control were then presented at a seminar in the East-West Talks, held at Hong Kong Baptist University on 3 February 2005, and at another seminar held at the Chinese University of Hong Kong on 25 February 2005. My draft chapter on human rights was done in Hong Kong in early 2005 when I was visiting the Department of Government and Public Administration at the Chinese University.

I know of no better place than Cambridge in the UK to finish off my book manuscript, where its charm and tranquillity is so conducive to concentrate the mind. I retired to the solitude of my home, pace my rewriting, revision, and final editing. When I felt I had had enough, I turned to a cup of tea or coffee, or to my *Taiji* choreography, while immersing myself in the ambience of some light classical music. At times I felt like in heaven on earth. What a great and lucky way to sign off this book project!

St. Matthew's Gardens, Cambridge
June 2005

Acknowledgements

During the long period of gestation of this work, I have incurred a lot of debts to numerous people and institutions. First of all, I would like to thank my home institution, Victoria University of Wellington, New Zealand, for granting me an extended period of leave to take up a senior fellowship at the Centre of International Studies at Cambridge University and a visiting professorship at the Chinese University of Hong Kong. My colleagues at Victoria, Professor Stephen Levine and Dr Huang Xiaoming have been very supportive. Both of them, together with Drs Ray Goldstein and Rod Alley and Professor Ralph Pettman in the International Relations programme, have been instrumental in helping me to formulate my ideas about responsibility in international affairs.

While at Cambridge, on and off from October 2002 to June 2004, Clare Hall offered me a visiting fellowship, and thereafter elected me into life membership. I am grateful to the President and Fellows at Clare Hall for providing me a home away from home — a very stimulating environment for international and intellectual exchange and an eye-opening experience for me to the wider world of knowledge and fun beyond my little niche of expertise. At the Centre of International Studies where I coordinated a China project, my colleagues Professor James Mayall, Dr Philip Towle and Dr Charles Jones, have been most generous with their time and support in making me feel at ease with the intricacies of the Cambridge and College system. I enjoyed most of all our occasional conversations, on or off the fine wines and dining at various college halls.

The Chinese University of Hong Kong offered me twice a visiting professorship, in early 2003 and again from late 2004 to early 2005. I am grateful to Professor H.C. Kuan for hosting me in his Department of Government and Public Administration, and to colleagues in the department for welcoming me. Professor Ma Shu-yan opened doors for me to many interesting fields in China studies beyond my field of competence. The bulk of my literature research for this book was done on my many visits to the Universities Service Centre for China Studies at the Chinese University over the years, and I am grateful to the assistance extended to me by Ms Jean Hung and her many able staff.

In Hong Kong, my heartfelt thanks are due to Professor P.K. Lee of the Open University of Hong Kong. He has kept my research interest at heart and has kept feeding me with relevant information from time to time. His friendship, collegiality, and professionalism are much appreciated. I first floated my ideas of doing research on China's responsibility with a number of friends and colleagues and I am grateful to them for their suggestions: Professors Ting Wai, Herbert Yee and Richard Balme of Hong Kong Baptist University; Professors James Tang, Richard Hu and Kenneth Wang of Hong Kong University; and Professors K.K. Leung and Joseph Cheng of the City University of Hong Kong.

Beyond Hong Kong, a number of experts have shared their thoughts on various aspects of my research interest: Drs Philip C. Saunders and Yuan Jingdong of the Monterey Institute of International Studies; Dr Ann Kent of the Australian National University; Dr Yuan I of the Institute of International Relations, Taipei; Drs Zheng Yongnian and Zou Keyuan of the National University of Singapore; Professor Ng Ka-po of Aichi Bunkyo University, Japan; Professor Jia Qingguo of Peking University; Professor Zha Daojiong of the People's University of China; and

Ms Stephanie T. Kleine-Ahlbrandt, Programme Manager of the Asia-Pacific Unit of the United Nations Office of the High Commissioner for Human Rights, Geneva.

Professors P.K. Lee, Ng Ka-po, Zha Daojiong and Joseph Cheng have read earlier versions of some chapters and offered useful comments.

An earlier version of Chapter 1 has been published as a chapter entitled 'Power and responsibility in China's international relations,' in Zhang Yongjin and Greg Austin (eds), *Power and responsibility in Chinese foreign policy* (Canberra: Asia Pacific Press, 2001), pp. 48–68. An earlier version of Chapter 2 has been published as a chapter entitled 'Is China a "responsible" state? An assessment from the point of view of its multilateral engagements,' in Joseph Y.S. Cheng (ed), *China's challenges in the twenty-first century* (Hong Kong: City University of Hong Kong Press, 2003), pp. 217–246. An earlier version of Chapter 4 has appeared as an article entitled 'China and the WTO: the theory and practice of compliance,' *International Relations of the Asia-Pacific*, Vol. 4, No. 1 (February 2004), pp. 47–72. An earlier version of Chapter 6 has appeared as an article entitled 'China's compliance in global environmental affairs,' *Asia Pacific Viewpoint*, Vol. 45, No. 1 (April 2004), pp. 69–86. I am grateful to the publishers for permission to use the materials here.

Extracts of chapters in the book have been presented as papers in seminars and conferences in Hong Kong, Shanghai, Taipei, Canberra, Cambridge, Oxford, Nottingham, Sheffield, and elsewhere. I am truly grateful to the organisers and sponsors of these events and the participants for their comments and criticisms.

Words cannot express my love and gratitude to Alice for enduring the hardship of marrying to a roving scholar. Darwin our elder son (aged 14) has offered some technical help with computing, and Byron our younger one (11) has suggested some word changes to my typescript when I was doing proofreading. They all remind me that there is a world out there other than academic research. This book is dedicated to them.

List of Tables

List of Figures

List of Abbreviations

BWC	Biological and Toxin Weapons Convention
CBMs	Confidence-building measures
CWC	Chemical Weapons Convention
DSM	Dispute Settlement Mechanism
EU	European Union
GATT	General Agreement on Tariffs and Trade
IAEA	International Atomic Energy Agency
IGOs	Intergovernmental organisations
IMF	International Monetary Fund
INGOs	International non-governmental organisations
IOs	International organisations
MOFTEC	Ministry of Foreign Trade and Economic Cooperation
MTCR	Missile Technology Control Regime
NEPA	National Environmental Protection Agency
NGOs	Non-governmental organisations
NORINCO	China North Industries Corporation
NPT	Nuclear Non-proliferation Treaty
NSG	Nuclear Suppliers Group
OHCHR	Office of the United Nations High Commissioner for Human Rights

OPCW	Organisation for the Prohibition of Chemical Weapons
PRC	People's Republic of China
ROC	Republic of China
SARS	Severe Acute Respiratory Syndrome (atypical pneumonia)
SEPA	State Environment Protection Administration
TRM	Transition Review Mechanism
WMD	Weapons of mass destruction
WTO	World Trade Organisation
UN	United Nations

Introduction

There are only two types of people today, those who are talking about China and those who are not.

Former WTO Director-General Mike Moore, 2004[1]

The rise of China has thrown open many important and interesting questions: Will a strong China behave responsibly in world affairs, complying with the rules and norms of the "international community"? Or will it defy "universal standards", and fight instead for its own interests and those of the developing world, thereby posing a serious challenge to the global order dominated by the West?

This book takes a look at China's responsibility in world affairs by scrutinising its compliance with international rules and norms, embodied in the treaties that it has signed or ratified, especially in the areas of trade, arms control and disarmament, the protection of the environment, and human rights. The book examines China's compliance within the context of Sino-United States relations, as the US is heavily involved in monitoring China's compliance behaviour in world affairs.

---

[1] Mike Moore, former Prime Minister of New Zealand and former Director-General of the World Trade Organisation, *South China Morning Post*, 9 December 2004, p. A19.

1

Compliance is central to the long-term sustainability of a state's international obligations. Yet not much research has been done on the concept of compliance in international studies, much less on its impact on state behaviour, in view of the growing volume of international relations literature. There is close to nothing written on China's compliance in a comprehensive manner, despite China's growing importance in the global political economy. Two slight exceptions to this phenomenon are the works of Ann Kent and Wendy Frieman. Kent published in 1999 a judicious account of the limits of compliance in China's participation in United Nations human rights regimes in a book entitled *China, the United Nations, and human rights.*[2] It has remained the standard in this specific area of study, although new developments may warrant a thorough update. Similarly, Frieman published in 2004 a book entitled *China, arms control, and non-proliferation,*[3] giving a fairly up-to-date and pleasantly candid and balanced account of China's compliance behaviour, among other things. I draw some useful insights from this book to form the basis of some of my own analyses in Chapter 5 on arms control. Apart from these two books, there are other book-length treatments and journal articles which discuss one or more of the four issue areas covered in this book. However, they do not dwell specifically on the issue of compliance. For example, Elizabeth Economy's many writings on China's environment, including her book entitled *The river runs black,*[4] published in 2004, provide some stimulating thoughts. Also, books with chapters covering some of the issue areas discussed in this book include those written by Andrew Nathan and Robert Ross,[5] Iain Johnston and

[2] Ann Kent, *China, the United Nations, and human rights: the limits of compliance* (Philadelphia: University of Pennsylvania Press, 1999).

[3] Wendy Frieman, *China, arms control, and non-proliferation* (London and New York: RoutledgeCurzon, 2004).

[4] Elizabeth Economy, *The river runs black: the environmental challenge to China's future* (Ithaca and London: Cornell University Press, 2004).

[5] Andrew Nathan and Robert Ross, *The Great Wall and the empty fortress* (New York and London: W.W. Norton & Co., 1997).

Robert Ross,[6] Elizabeth Economy and Michel Oksenberg,[7] David Lampton,[8] and others.

This book is likely to be the first of its kind to take on as its central theme China's rule compliance in international relations covering the four crucial areas of trade, arms control, environmental protection, and human rights by a single author. It will be of interest to graduate students and specialists in contemporary Chinese affairs, international relations and law, world trade, security and strategic studies, environmental studies, and the studies of human rights.

How can we assess China's responsibility in global affairs? This question begs a close examination of China itself: it is the largest developing country in the world, currently undergoing a difficult transition from a socialist party-state to embrace a market-orientated economy. It is a country with a long history and civilisation, in an arduous process of integrating itself with the established global political-economic order largely designed, nurtured, and controlled by the liberal-democratic West. The stark contrast between China's worldview as an underdog in this global order and that of the West as the top dog can hardly be underestimated when assessing China's responsibility and compliance in world affairs.

In this book, I first of all define the terms "responsibility" and "compliance" in global affairs. I then assess China's global compliance by looking at its treaty accession, followed by an assessment of its compliance behaviour in the four specific areas of international affairs: arms control and non-proliferation, trade and economics, human rights, and environmental protection. These four areas represent important issues of security, trade, humanity, and ecology that form the core of international relations today. They also represent important areas of global activities in which China is increasingly

---

[6] Alastair Iain Johnston and Robert S. Ross (eds), *Engaging China: the management of an emerging power* (London and New York: Routledge, 1999), chapters 9 and 10.
[7] Elizabeth Economy and Michel Oksenberg (eds), *China joins the world: progress and prospects* (New York: Council on Foreign Relations, 1999).
[8] David M. Lampton (ed), *The making of Chinese foreign and security policy in the era of reform* (Stanford: Stanford University Press, 2001).

involved and in which other major countries in the world, the United States in particular, have a great stake in trying to maintain the status quo. The book concludes by suggesting that China's compliance behaviour in world affairs has shown some marked improvements, but much more work remains to be done if such behaviour is to meet the standards demanded by the West in general and the United States in particular.

In thinking through some of the issues discussed in the book, I have been agonising for some time over whether I should use the phrase "China's international relations" or "Chinese international relations". The former phrase gives the impression that China is a single political entity — the Chinese state in this case — whereas the use of the word "Chinese" in "Chinese international relations" opens up an array of entities to include not only the People's Republic of China (PRC) as a single political unit, but also Chinese thinking, Chinese style, Chinese political philosophy, and much more, apart from other Chinese political actors such as individuals, groups, and local governments. In my usage in the following analysis, the word "China" sometimes carries the wider connotation as to mean things "Chinese".

The book is organised in two parts. Part I, a theoretical part in the main, consists of three chapters. The first, Chapter 1, discusses the idea of responsibility from a Chinese perspective: how China perceives as its responsibility in global affairs. It explores China's understanding of its responsibility based on its national conditions: a huge population; a nuclear power; a permanent member of the UN Security Council; a participant in many international organisations; and a contributor as well as a recipient of foreign aids. Inevitably its recent history leaves an indelible mark on its perception. Chapter 2 defines the concept of responsibility, both from a Chinese perspective and from a Western perspective. It looks into China's participation in international organisations in some details, as a way to show that China's responsibility in global affairs can be seen from, among other things, its participation in the activities of international organisations. Chapter 3 moves from responsibility to compliance, a concept which has its origins in international law, but has now attracted the attention of an increasing number of political scientists. The chapter explains what is meant by compliance and assesses China's compliance in global affairs by scrutinising its accession to international treaties. This chapter provides an overview of China's involvement in the international treaty system, paving the way for a more detailed analysis of China's compliance in the four issue areas, discussed individually in the four chapters forming Part II.

Chapter 4 in Part II discusses the first case, China's WTO compliance. Potentially the world's largest trading nation, China has become a member of the World Trade Organisation since December 2001, pledging to abide by its rules. The extent to which it is willing to comply, and is capable of complying, with WTO rules has important implications for world trade. The chapter reveals the difficulties faced by China, as a professed responsible rising power, in trying to adjust itself to adhere to the global trading norm. It examines the theory of compliance in international relations from the perspectives of neo-realism, liberal institutionalism, and social constructivism, and tests these theoretical perspectives by examining the mechanisms used to gauge China's compliance, both bilaterally by the United States and multilaterally through the Dispute Settlement Mechanism and the Transition Review Mechanism of the WTO. The result of such an examination is mixed: different opinions exist as to how compliant China has been. On the whole, most monitors agree that China has made a lot of efforts in trying to comply with WTO requirements in various areas, but much more work remains to be done. The most severe tests will come in a few years' time when China's financial and service sectors will have to face fundamental changes to the way they operate.

As a nuclear power, how China behaves in arms control and disarmament will have a significant impact on the global strategic balance of power. Since the 1980s, the US has accused some Chinese entities, many of them state-owned enterprises, of selling weapons of mass destruction or their technologies to "rogue" states such as North Korea, Iran, Libya, and others, including due-use technologies which have both commercial and military applications. Chapter 5 looks into China's compliance in arms control, disarmament, and non-proliferation, especially in the areas of weapons of mass destruction: biological, chemical, and nuclear weapons, together with their delivery systems. It gives a historical background to China's nuclear weapon development and its participation in international arms control regimes. China's compliance behaviour in this area is complicated by the apparent move by the US away from multilateralism to unilateralism in arms control and other areas.

As the most populous country on earth with ten per cent of its rare species of flora and fauna, China's environmental practice is of global concern. Already the country is one of the most polluted places on earth. At least seven out of the ten most polluted cities in the world are located in China. It is the second largest producer of greenhouse gases after the United States, inflicting heavy, long-term casualties on its own public health and economic development as well as those of its close neighbours in the Asia-Pacific region. How to strike a right balance between environmental protection and fast economic growth will have an important impact on its modernisation outcome and its international standing. The country began to pay serious attention to environmental problems in the 1970s. Since the adoption of the reform and opening-up policy in the late 1970s, it has signed or ratified many international treaties dealing with environmental issues. By now, it has entered into many major international environmental regimes. Chapter 6 addresses these questions: How compliant is China with respect to commitments it has made, if any, to these regimes? How willing and capable is it in complying with international environmental norms and rules? What does sustainable development mean to China? How do red tape, fear, inexperience, and ignorance affect China's efforts to protect its environment? And how do inter-ministerial wrangling and the growth of green non-governmental organisations in China affect its compliance in environmental affairs?

The issue of China's human rights remains a bone of contention between China and the West. It has a negative spill-over effect on other issues and other aspects of China's bilateral relations with Western countries. China's views on human rights are at odds with those of the West. It stresses the importance of relativism, economic rights and developmental rights, in contrast to the West's emphasis on universal, civil, and political rights. It argues that the observance of human rights should take into account different stages of development of individual societies. Despite these and other differences, China none the less moves closer to embrace the universality of rights and has started to engage in numerous human rights dialogues with other countries. After a brief introduction to the growth of human rights awareness in the contemporary world and in China, Chapter 7 gives a background to the divergent views on human rights between China and the West. This introduction and background pave the way for a discussion of China's engagement with international human rights regimes, focusing on China's compliance or otherwise with the rules and norms embodied in those regimes. The chapter analyses China's bilateral human rights relations with the outside world, particularly with the US and the EU. It also takes stock of what China has done so far to further its human rights discourse.

The concluding chapter brings together the findings of previous ones and compares China's compliance behaviour across the four issue areas. China's overall compliance behaviour seems to be satisfactory, although a lot of work needs to be done in order to improve its compliance record and to meet the standards demanded by the West, especially by the United States. China's ability to make improvements depends on, among other things, its ability to tackle its many domestic problems.

The overall thrust of this book is to examine what China has done so far to comply with the treaties it has entered into in the four issue areas, including the submission of progress reports to relevant multilateral institutions, cooperation with outside inspection and scrutiny, the passing of domestic legislation to fall in line with international standards, and the setting up of institutions and procedures to cope with the required changes under its treaty obligations. Given the different nature of these four issues and the different priorities attached to them by different countries and organisations, the treatment of China's compliance behaviour in these areas will be somewhat uneven.

Central to any analysis of the compliance behaviour of a state are several basic questions: Who sets the rules and standards of global compliance? What are the mechanisms available to states and multilateral institutions to ensure state compliance? Who controls those mechanisms? And how fair and just are the rules and standards?

This book does not pretend to hold all the answers to the questions posed in this Introduction, but by offering a wholesome analysis of an area of growing importance and interest, I hope to be able to chart some of the main features in the field and to indicate some directions for future research. In the final analysis, this study aims to find out if China's compliance behaviour has anything to inform us or help us to improve our understanding of international relations in a globalised world.

Throughout the book, Chinese and Japanese personal names are presented with their surnames first, followed by their given names. The currencies cited are in US dollars unless otherwise stated.

Part I

Part 1

Chapter

1

The Idea of Responsibility: China Looking Inside Out

China could well be the second-largest, if not the largest, trading nation in the world, with greater weight and voice in international affairs. This is one vision of China in 50 years — modern, confident, and *responsible.*

Minister Mentor Lee Kuan Yew of Singapore[1]

Is China a responsible state in international society? This is an increasingly interesting and useful question, as China grows strong and as it plays an increasingly greater role in world affairs. To answer the question, it would be appropriate to consider first the following basic questions:

- What is meant by responsibility?
- How to assess the responsibility of a state?
- What is China's responsibility?
- To whom is China responsible?

---

[1] Quoted in Laurence J. Brahm, *China's century: the awakening of the next economic powerhouse* (Singapore: John Wiley & Sons (Asia) Pte Ltd., 2001), back jacket. Emphasis mine.

- What international society are we talking about?
- Why raise the issue of China's responsibility now?

WHAT IS MEANT BY RESPONSIBILITY?

According to *The concise Oxford dictionary*, the word "responsible" means:

1. liable to be called to account (to a person or for a thing);
2. morally accountable for one's actions; capable of rational conduct; and
3. of good credit, position, or repute; respectable; evidently trustworthy.

Seemingly the word "responsible" or "responsibility" carries legal, moral, as well as social connotations, and since legal, moral, and social standards vary across cultures, to a greater or lesser extent, the concept of responsibility would inevitably be laden with value judgements: responsibility refers to something ethical or desirable.

The word "responsibility" comes from the Latin word *respondeo*, meaning "I answer".[2] It is synonymous to answerability and accountability.[3] Its equivalent in Chinese is *zeren*. The first character, *ze*, carries a sense of burden, and the second character, *ren*, carries that of duty. In traditional China, duties and burdens are handed down or assigned by superiors and elders to their juniors and the young in a hierarchically-structured society. Duties and burdens also come with certain social and occupational positions within a family or in the wider community. There are certain duties that one is expected to perform and burdens that one has to shoulder. In other words, there are things that an individual, as a member of a family or community, *ought* to do. This word *ought* carries a

---

[2] L.R. Lucas, *Responsibility* (Oxford: Clarendon Press, 1993), p. 5, cited in Toni Erskine (ed), *Can institutions have responsibility? Collective moral agency and international relations* (Basingstoke: Palgrave Macmillan, 2003).

[3] Andrew Heywood, *Key concepts in politics* (New York: St. Martin's Press, 2000), p. 145.

moral conviction rather than a legal obligation. It has a strong ethical underpinning nurtured by centuries of culture and tradition.

Indeed morality plays an important part in Chinese foreign-policy behaviour, depending on the time and the circumstances in which events take place. As Shih Chih-yu has skilfully argued, Chinese leaders often "present themselves as the supreme moral rectifiers of the world order".[4] He gives the following examples in international politics during the Cold War to support his argument:[5]

- China's policy towards the Soviet Union was aimed primarily at shaming the Soviets for their betrayal of socialism;
- Its United States policy demonstrates China's anti-imperialist integrity;
- Its Japan policy blames the Japanese for a failed Asiatic brother-hood; and
- Its Third World policy is intended to be a model for emulation.

To the traditional Chinese mind, responsibility flows from something that one owes to others. The Chinese leaders today probably think that they owe little or nothing to the outside world or, for that matter, countries in the West. Rather, it is the West that owes them a huge "debt", because Western imperialists exploited China and humiliated the Chinese people for over a hundred years before 1949. Why then should China be responsible to the outside world, or to the West, since it does not owe them anything? On the contrary, it is the West which should be held responsible to China, for what Western powers had done to the country in the past. As a first step, Western countries should refrain from interfering in China's domestic affairs.

Some Western analysts have pointed out that Chinese leaders are using this kind of "victimhood" to drum up domestic support for their policies and to shore up their bargaining position with Western

---

[4] Shih Chih-yu, *China's just world: the morality of Chinese foreign policy* (Boulder, CO: Lynne Rienner Publishers, 1993), p. 243.
[5] *Ibid.*

powers by shaming them.[6] Some even suggest that the "culture of shame and humiliation" is a "nationalist myth".[7] However, to the many Chinese who have suffered enormously, physically or mentally, directly or indirectly, it was and is very real. The fact that the story of Western exploitation of China and the lessons to be learnt from it have been passed on from one generation to another as a painful reminder to the Chinese nation and people does suggest that it is a factor to be taken into account when dealing with China and in assessing its global responsibility.[8]

HOW TO ASSESS THE RESPONSIBILITY OF A STATE?

One common way to assess the responsibility of a state and hence its credibility is to scrutinise what it does rather than what it says. In other words, a state could be judged by its deeds and its actions. But who is in a position to pass judgement? Is the United Nations' Security Council, or its General Assembly, or its International Court of Justice in a good position to do so? Are countries in the West or those in the East in a better position to do so? Those in the North or in the South? Some powerful states? Or some form of international regimes? How valid are their judgements if they do pass them? We know that there is no complete consensus on these issues among states, not even among a group of like-minded states. We live in a world in which there are little completely accepted principles of international common law, except perhaps the UN Charter. But even some of the fundamental principles of the UN Charter are under

---

[6] Steven Goldstein, quoted in CNN news at http://cnn.com/SPECIALS/1999/china.50/asian.superpower/neighbors/

[7] Michael Yahuda, "China's foreign relations: the Long March, future uncertain," *The China Quarterly*, No. 159 (September 1999), p. 652. Ishihara Shintaro, a former right-wing Liberal Democratic Party member of the Diet (Parliament) and currently the Governor of Tokyo, once rejected outright the existence of the Nanjing Incident in 1937 as a fabrication. Ishihara is but one among many extreme right-wing nationalists in Japan.

[8] Chen Jie, "China's Spratly policy," *Asian Survey*, Vol. 34, No. 10 (October 1994), p. 894.

dispute. For example, member states of the UN are divided as to whether humanitarian intervention should override national sovereignty.[9] Some states choose to follow some rules while breaking others, whether they relate to human rights, trade, or political sovereignty. What is responsible to some may appear to be irresponsible to others. International responsibility is by and large a product of international civic awareness, but is very much grounded in and defined by local cultures and ideologies and is therefore severely contested.[10] If absolute or complete consensus is so difficult to achieve, then perhaps relative or near consensus may be achievable. Very often it is based on some sort of relative or near consensus that a group of like-minded states take collective action to tackle world problems. Sometimes it requires a strong power to take the lead to galvanise or forge a collective action.

To the Chinese mind, the linkage between power and responsibility depends on one's position in a scheme of things. It is utterly important to position oneself properly: only when one's position is properly established and "named" can one behave in a "correct" or righteous way.[11] The idea of *dingwei* or positioning therefore becomes significant in determining one's behaviour. Apart from positioning, the term *dingwei* can also mean the search for a place, the seeking of a proper role, or the going through of a process of negotiation to firm up one's position, thereby enabling one to avoid potential conflicts in the future. Because of the Chinese sense of history and collective memory, it is not inconceivable to assume that the idea of *dingwei* can be extended from China's domestic situation to its view of the world.

---

[9] Frank Ching, "UN: sovereignty or rights?" *Far Eastern Economic Review*, 21 October 1999, p. 40.

[10] Personal communication with Dr Ray Goldstein, School of Political Science and International Relations, Victoria University of Wellington, New Zealand, 8 October 1999.

[11] A traditional Confucian thought, deriving from the popular saying that *mingzheng, yanshun*, meaning roughly that "if one's name (meaning title) is properly given, then one's words can become righteous".

The Chinese sense of responsibility is very much tied to one's position of power, as indicated by the saying that *quanli yu yiwu jundeng*, which can be roughly translated as and represented by the following approximation:

$$\text{Duty} + \text{Burden} \approx \text{Power} + \text{Privileges}$$

where *yiwu* should be understood as "appropriate" work (i.e. duty + burden) in the traditional meaning of the term, rather than "voluntary" work.

It is useful to make a distinction between two forms of power: power as of right, which is derived from one's proper positioning in a social setting; and power as of might, which is an empirical substance. The wielding of power can therefore be righteous when exercised from a proper position, but can be hegemonic and imperialistic and therefore morally corrupt when exercised for the purpose of selfish gains without rightful entitlement according to some sets of moral principles. In this way, the conflict between China and the West may not be purely over material interests or relative power gains, but may also be over ideologies and moral principles, more so than most people would readily give credit to.

What is China's international position will therefore affect how it is going to behave, to exercise its power, and to fulfil its "responsibilities". To the Chinese thinking, China's position in the world is buttressed by its power relative to others, and hence there is a need to understand and to determine accurately its comprehensive national power and those of other countries so that China can know where it stands in relation to others and how it should relate to or behave towards them.[12]

Although the concept of comprehensive national power is difficult to define and its measurement lacks precision,[13] its utility, to

---

[12] Apart from Confucian influence, this line of Chinese thinking can also be attributed to the teachings of the famous Chinese strategist Sun Tze, author of *The art of war*: "Knowing well one's own situation and the situation of others, fight a hundred battles and be able to win them all."

[13] For a discussion of China's comprehensive national power, see Gerald Chan, *Chinese perspectives on international relations: a framework for analysis* (Basingstoke: Macmillan, 1999), pp. 30–33.

some Chinese analysts, lies in its ability to serve as a rough guide to assess one's position of strength in the world. One of the reasons why this concept has become so popular among Chinese analysts these days is that, since China is growing strongly, there is a need to take stock of its powers and evaluate its power base. Here of course we are dealing with something fuzzy rather than with something clear and precise, as the power of a state is difficult to measure and as the situation of the world constantly changes. Hard power, such as military hardware, is relatively more static and is easier to measure, while soft power, such as culture or morality, is more fluid and hence more difficult to measure.

WHAT IS CHINA'S RESPONSIBILITY?

If we follow the Chinese line of thinking about *dingwei di wenti* (the issue of positioning), then we need, first of all, to ask what China's global position is, before we attempt to make an assessment of its global responsibility. The mention of China conjures different images to different people, depending on their different standpoints. Some of the salient features of China's position may include the following:

- China has a huge population;
- It is a nuclear power;
- It is a permanent member of the Security Council of the United Nations;
- It is a member of many important international organisations; and
- It is a contributor as well as a recipient of aids.

Any assessment of China itself, let alone its responsibilities, must start with an understanding of China in the recent past, a China that had suffered for 100 years under Western imperialism,[14] followed by periods of internal strife, civil wars, and Japanese invasion, and then

---

[14] Michael Yahuda, "China's search for a global role," *Current History*, Vol. 98, No. 629 (September 1999), p. 266.

30 years of excesses under revolutionary, communist rule. It has only begun to open up to the outside world, more "voluntarily" than before, since the late 1970s, and has by now attained some degree of normality and stability. However, China faces many difficulties in its development path: apart from its huge population, on the whole it is still a relatively backward developing country in the midst of drastic and fundamental socioeconomic changes.[15] It is still a country suffering from, among other things, some sort of domestic political insecurity, arising out of crises of identity and legitimacy.[16] What can one expect of China's international behaviour?

A huge population. The task of feeding and sheltering the country's 1.3 billion people has not been easy. The government is determined to eradicate poverty, limit population growth, and raise the living standard of its people, to the extent that it argues that the rights to subsistence is more important than individual freedoms. Deng Xiaoping once reminded us that if the Chinese were starving and forced to flee their home country in search for food elsewhere, would it not cause problems for the neighbouring region and the world at large? The world therefore has an interest to see that China can lift its people out of abject poverty and that the country can remain stable. In a speech made at Cambridge University in October 1999, President Jiang Zemin said that "to ensure [the rights to subsistence and development] for our people is in itself a major contribution to the progress of the world's human rights cause".[17] To achieve the goals of modernisation and to raise the living standard of its people, China has opened its doors and adopted new economic measures since the late 1970s, including the establishment

---

[15] Jia Qingguo, "Economic development, political stability and international respect," *Journal of International Affairs*, Vol. 49, No. 2 (Winter 1996), pp. 573–576.
[16] Wang Fei-Ling, "Self-image and strategic intentions: national confidence and political insecurity," in Deng Yong and Wang Fei-Ling (eds), *In the eyes of the dragon: China views the world* (Lanham: Rowman & Littlefield Publishers, Inc., 1999), chapter 2. Some of Wang's ideas are further developed in Deng Yong and Wang Fei-Ling (eds), *China rising: power and motivation in Chinese foreign policy* (Lanham: Rowman & Littlefield Publishers, Inc., 2005).
[17] *Evening Post*, Wellington, 23 October 1999, p. 8.

of Special Economic Zones and the opening up of coastal and regional cities to foreign trade and investment. The joining of the World Trade Organisation in 2001 is another major step in this direction.

A nuclear power. China's successful testing of its first atomic bomb in 1964 boosted the morale of a people who had suffered and sacrificed so much. The depth of pride felt by its people, including those living overseas, that it could join the rank of nuclear powers, was hard to fathom. China prides itself not only as a nuclear power, but also as a country which has signed the Comprehensive Test Ban Treaty, in September 1996.[18] In the wake of the Pakistani and Indian missile and nuclear tests in April and May 1998, there were rumours that China might reconsider its treaty obligations and resume nuclear testing. China faces great strategic and military challenges, as it shares long borders with 14 countries on land and seven maritime neighbours. Of these, three are nuclear (Russia, India, and Pakistan), one declares it possesses nuclear weapons (North Korea), and three with potentials to develop them (Japan, South Korea, and Taiwan). On 3 June 1998, President Jiang Zemin pledged, in his first public reaction to the tests in South Asia, that "China has no intention of restarting its nuclear tests".[19] Either as a strategic move or as a responsible gesture to maintain world peace, China has also pledged not to use nuclear weapons first and has asked or even challenged other nuclear powers to do likewise. So far, it has not stationed a single soldier or held military exercises outside its

---

[18] China has yet to ratify it. The Treaty needs to be ratified by the 44 nuclear-capable states. Twenty-six have ratified, 15 have signed but not ratified, including the US, and three (India, North Korea, and Pakistan) have not even signed. See *Times* magazine, 25 October 1999, p. 20. As of May 2005, neither China nor the US has ratified, and India, North Korea, and Pakistan have not yet signed. See the website of the Comprehensive Test Ban Treaty Organisation, http://www.ctbto.org/ (accessed 14 June 2005).

[19] *South China Morning Post*, 4 June 1998. Earlier, an anonymous senior official of the Foreign Ministry in Beijing was quoted as saying that China would consider resuming tests if the nuclear arms tension between India and Pakistan worsened (*ibid.*, 2 June 1998).

claimed territorial boundaries,[20] apart from peacekeeping activities under UN auspices or limited drills with members of the Shanghai Cooperation Organisation.

As a regional power, China has initiated the Six-Party talks to find ways to end the conflict in the Korean Peninsula, especially North Korea's nuclear ambitions. It has joined and actively participated in regional security dialogues, such as the Asean Regional Forum and the Council for Security Cooperation in the Asia-Pacific, and in regional economic groupings, such as the Asia-Pacific Economic Cooperation forum and the Pacific Economic Cooperative Council. In the Asian economic crisis of 1997–98, it resisted temptations to devalue its currency, as devaluation might trigger off another round of crisis. Consequently, China had to endure temporarily a diminished share of its export market and a loss in economic competitiveness. It made financial contributions to help some neighbouring countries affected by the crisis.[21] In April 2005, it hosted the Boao Forum on Hainan Island to discuss economic issues and joined the Asia-African summit held in Jakarta. The summit resolved to enhance economic cooperation between countries across the two continents, to alleviate poverty, and to form a united front to tackle world trade negotiations.[22] One exception to this apparently responsible image of China is its policy towards Taiwan. It has steadfastly refused to give up the use of arms to reunify Taiwan. In March 2005, its Parliament, the National People's Congress, passed an anti-secession law to authorise the government to use force if Taiwan declares formal independence. Neighbouring countries are very worried that a war across the Taiwan Strait would seriously destabilise the Asia-Pacific region and disrupt its economic growth.

A permanent member of the UN Security Council. As one of the five permanent members with veto power, China can influence

---

[20] It was reported in May 2005 that China and Kirgyzstan held talks to set up a military base in Kirgyzstan, http://www.akipress.org.

[21] For example, China contributed one billion US dollars as part of an IMF effort to bail out Thailand's financial woe.

[22] Radio Hong Kong Channel 4 news, 24 April 2005.

world events in a significant way and can bargain with other powers from a position of some considerable strength. It speaks out on principles of non-interference thereby helping the world's poor resist the world's rich, since in most cases of foreign intervention in domestic affairs, it is the rich that intervenes in the affairs of the poor rather than the other way round. China's burgeoning involvements in UN peacekeeping activities since the mission in Cambodia in 1992 and operations in Kuwait, Palestine, Liberia, the Western Sahara, and Haiti have been seen as enhancing its image as "a good international citizen".[23] Its response to the East Timor crisis in 1999, by not exercising its veto after Jakarta agreed to the UN intervention, is seen as "responsible".[24] As the only developing country among the five permanent members of the Security Council, China can play a critical role in any major reform to the structure of the UN that affects China and the Third World.

A member of key international organisations. China is a late comer to the world of international organisations, even by Asian standards, when compared with countries like Japan and India. It was only since 1971 when China gained its seat in the UN General Assembly that it began to join more intergovernmental organisations (IGOs) and, since the adoption of the reform and opening-up policy in the late 1970s, that it began to join more international non-governmental organisations (INGOs). By now China is a member of some 304 IGOs and 2,786 INGOs,[25] including many UN specialised agencies such as the World Bank and the International Monetary Fund and other major universal organisations such as the International Red Cross and the International Olympic Committee. The reasons for joining these organisations are many, including China's concerted effort to gain or strengthen its international legitimacy in competition with Taiwan, the transfer of technology, the attraction of aids and investments, and so on. China's involvement

---

[23] J. Mohan Malik in *International Herald Tribune*, Internet ed., 8 October 1999.
[24] *Ibid.*
[25] *Yearbook of international organizations 2003–2004* (Munich: K.G. Saur, 2003), Vol. 2, p. 1,627.

in international organisations is very much a process of mutual legitimisation and mutual learning. It offers China an opportunity to learn more about international norms, practices, and expectations.[26] China's participation in and contributions to international organisations (IOs), though increasing steadily, are still limited or hindered by a number of factors:

- Tradition and ideology — that the global structure of international organisation is very much a product of Western experiences and that most Chinese find participation in a social setting on an open, equal, individual footing, as exemplified by China's participation in IOs, more alien than many other cultures;
- Power dominance — that the setting of goals and agendas in IOs are dictated by Western interests;
- Its own lack of civic awareness and of a general objective understanding of international affairs;
- The paucity of financial resources to allow it to fully participate in IO activities; and
- The use of the English language as the medium of communication in most IOs.

The giving and receiving of aids. The largest amount of aid that China gave was when it was relatively very poor, to African countries such as Tanzania and Zambia in the 1950s and 1960s, for reasons that have been viewed as ideological and strategic in nature. Now that China gets relatively richer, it still sporadically gives aids to countries in Africa and elsewhere in order to compete with Taiwan for diplomatic recognition. It also extends assistance to others to alleviate human sufferings when approached, increasingly

---

[26] For an incisive analysis of China's learning process of nuclear non-proliferation issues, see Hu Weixing, "Nuclear non-proliferation," in Deng and Wang (eds), *In the eyes of the dragon*, chapter 6. For some recent discussions on China's learning in international relations, see David M. Lampton (ed), *The making of Chinese foreign and security policy in the era of reform* (Stanford: Stanford University Press, 2001).

through the International Red Cross.[27] In the aftermath of the tsunami which struck countries bordering the Indian Ocean in December 2004, it joined international efforts to extend relief aids to the countries and people affected. It also joined many other countries in extending aid to the US after Hurricane Katrina struck America's Gulf coast in late August 2005. The terms of Chinese aids are usually very generous. More interestingly, China is not shy to ask for and receive international aids when it suffers from natural disasters. Apparently, the philosophy of aid-giving in China has changed from a purely strategic goal to a combination of strategic and humanitarian objectives. The fact that it is willing to accept humanitarian aids from a wide variety of agencies and countries shows that China has become more "normal" — that receiving aids from the outside is not regarded as a national shame, if it cannot maintain "self-sufficiency" temporarily.

Apart from the above features, more generally, China has cooperated with many other countries in certain areas of global concerns such as human rights, environmental protection, and arms control. It has ratified some 165 multilateral conventions,[28] and is currently involved in the codification and development of international law in a small way, with Chinese nationals serving as members in the International Law Commission of the UN, the International Court of Justice, the International Tribunal for the Former Yugoslavia War Criminals,[29] the Sub-Commission on Human Rights, and the Dispute Settlement Body of the World Trade Organisation.[30] China has been seen as doing its part in maintaining the smooth transition of Hong Kong in 1997 and of Macau in 1999 to Chinese sovereignty. It curbed

---

[27] For some discussions on the origins of China's shift from its strict adherence to self-reliance to its acceptance of international aids, see Gerald Chan, *China and international organisations* (Hong Kong: Oxford University Press, 1989), pp. 75–80.

[28] *Yearbook of international organizations*, p. 1,627. The website of the Chinese Ministry of Foreign Affairs lists 268 international conventions that China has signed from 1875 to 2003, see http://www.fmprc.gov.cn/chn/wjb/zzjg/tyfls/tfsckzlk/zgcjddbty/t70814.htm (accessed 26 April 2005).

[29] E-mail communication with Dr Zou Keyuan, research fellow, East Asian Institute, National University of Singapore, October 1999.

[30] *21st Century Economic Herald*, Internet ed., 15 March 2004.

excessive outbreaks of anti-American feelings as a result of the American bombing of its embassy in Belgrade in May 1999, and acted similarly to control the spread of anti-Japanese demonstrations (against the glossing over of Japan's wartime atrocities in new history textbooks) in April 2005. In an effort to make its government policies more transparent to its own people as well as to outsiders, the Information Office of the State Council started to publish White Papers in 1990.[31] So far (as of May 2005), some 45 White Papers have been published, on policy issues ranging from human rights, defence, to those relating to Taiwan and Tibet.[32] China's human rights record leaves a lot to be desired, but the country has signed the two major international covenants on human rights — the International Covenant on Economic, Social and Cultural Rights and the International Covenant on Civil and Political Rights — and has engaged in human rights dialogues with many countries and groups.[33]

The above points and cases are cited, not to suggest any direct causal relationship between China's sense of responsibility and its foreign-policy behaviour, but to indicate that China might be seen as behaving more responsibly these days than in those days of Mao Zedong some 30 years ago.

TO WHOM IS CHINA RESPONSIBLE?

If we put aside China's responsibility to its own people for the time being (see Chapter 7 on human rights), to whom is it responsible

---

[31] These White Papers are the products of the Bureau of Overseas Propaganda of the Chinese Communist Party's Central Propaganda Department. The Information Office of the State Council is under the dual leadership of the State Council and the Central Propaganda Department. See Wan Ming, "Human rights and democracy," in Deng and Wang (eds), *In the eyes of the dragon*, p. 102 and note 9.

[32] Soft copies are available at http://www.china.org.cn/e-white/ (accessed 15 September 2005). The exact figures are 1991 (2 papers), 1992 (2), 1993 (1), 1994 (2), 1995 (3), 1996 (3), 1996 (3), 1998 (3), 1999 (0), 2000 (6), 2001 (3), 2002 (3), 2003 (4), 2004 (5), 2005 (5, up to September), making a total of 45.

[33] China signed the economic, social and cultural covenant in 1997 and the civil and political covenant a year later. It ratified the former in 2001, but has yet to ratify the latter (as of May 2005). See Chapter 7 for further details and analysis.

outside the country? If we accept the Chinese thinking on its own terms that it owes little to the outside world, then this question will become a moot point. Also, centuries of development which inculcated an inward-looking mentality leaves little room for the growth of the spirit of voluntarism and adventurism that would otherwise have called for a greater sense of responsibility towards the outside world. As China grows strong and is more interactive with the outside world, there arises an expectation, both within and outside China, that the country should shoulder greater responsibility to international society. Also, as China becomes "normal" and its sense of victimhood becomes less acute, then its sense of responsibility towards the outside world is likely to become more intense.

WHAT INTERNATIONAL SOCIETY? IS CHINA IN OR OUT?[34]

The international society as we understand it today is, like it or not, dominated by the West, especially by the United States. The existing set of international laws, rules, and norms are very much the product of Western experiences. To try to tie China to international society basically means, therefore, to bring China to adhere to the rules of the game played by Western powers. To what extent should China be involved in such a system? Or should it make an effort to change or redefine the system? These are some of the issues that China has to face since it came into substantive contacts with the outside world. The process of interdependence and multilateralism is not new, only that the actors involved in such an international system are changing, so are the power distribution among them, their relationships, and the issues involved in such relationships.

---

[34] For some analyses in this area, see Alastair Iain Johnston, "Engaging myths: misconceptions about China and its global role," *Harvard Asia Pacific Review*, Vol. 2, No. 1 (Winter 1997/98), pp. 9–12; and Samuel Kim, "China in and out of the changing world order," Center of International Studies, World Order Studies Program Occasional Paper No. 21, Princeton University, 1991.

Underlying the idea and practice of bringing China into the system is the assumption that China is not in — it is out; it is the Other. This is basically a Western perspective. From China's own point of view, it has been part and parcel of international society since China began to interact with the outside world, only that it has not been a hegemonic power in the global sense, reaching out and setting rules for others to follow, but instead is an underdog of the system. China has been struggling through this system, wanting to get a better deal out of engagement with the system but without much success, mainly because it was weak. Now that it has become stronger and more confident, it wants to integrate more with the outside world and on better terms, demanding international respect and a rightful place that it thinks it deserves and making a presence that the West can hardly ignore.

The US policy towards China has been one of "congagement":[35] a combination of containment and engagement. During the Cold War, the policy consists of more elements of containment than engagement, but thereafter in the post-Cold War era, it has more elements of engagement than containment. Sometimes the US is not sure whether it should engage or contain China, as it is not certain whether China is in or out of international society. If China is in, then one set of rules should apply. If China is not, then another set of rules should.[36]

---

[35] The word "congagement" — a combination of containment and engagement — comes from a research team of scholars at Rand Corporation in California. See Zalmay M. Khalizad et al, *The United States and a rising China: strategic and military implications* (Santa Monica, CA: Rand, 1999), pp. 72–75. Gerald Segal, in his article "Tying China into the international system", suggests also that the West should contain China on one hand, but on the other, tying China into the world economic market at the same time. The rationale is that the more China is connected with the world, the less likely it will use force to settle disputes. (Thanks to Dr Huang Xiaoming and Ms Christina Chan of the School of Political Science and International Relations, Victoria University of Wellington, for their advice and help in tracing the sources.)

[36] For an interesting, short essay on the myths surrounding America's engagement policy towards China, see Johnston, "Engaging myths: misconceptions about China

Engaging China means socialising it into the existing system so that it may become one of Us — a responsible member, abiding by the rules and norms of the system. However, as pointed out by Wang Hongying,[37] a professor at Syracuse University, socialising China has its many limits: firstly, while China can learn to be more cooperative through participation in multilateral activities, it can also come to realise and to reassure itself of the expedience of the use of force in world affairs. In other words, China can become more realist (in the *realpolitik* sense) as well as more liberal. China had suffered tremendously under the so-called "gun-boat" diplomacy of the West in the past and has recently witnessed the use of force by the US in the Gulf War and in Yugoslavia. Chinese leaders were shocked when they saw on television the pin-point accuracy of the firing power of high-tech weapons and the scale of destruction caused. They realised how far behind their weapon system was and decided that their military modernisation must be speeded up.

Secondly, the process of multilateralism only affects a very small number of Chinese officials who deal with foreign affairs and trade. Their preference for multilateralism faces strong domestic opposition from the military as well as from the state industrial sector.[38] Moreover, the effects of individual learning of these officials have yet to be established empirically, not to mention the generally assumed spill-over effects from the individual level to the provincial and state levels.

---

and its global role." For a book-length treatment on engagement policy from the perspectives of some Asia-Pacific countries, see Alastair Iain Johnston and Robert Ross (eds), *Engaging China: the management of an emerging power* (London: Routledge, 1999).

[37] Wang Hongying, "Multilateralism in Chinese foreign policy: the limits of socialization," in Hu Weixing, Gerald Chan, and Zha Daojiong (eds), *China's international relations in the 21st century* (Lanham: University Press of America, 2000), pp. 71–91.

[38] Thomas J. Christensen arrives at a similar point. See his "Pride, pressure, and politics: the roots of China's worldview," in Deng and Wang (eds), *In the eyes of the dragon*, p. 246. He recalls from his research in China that "the foreign ministry (*Waijiaobu*) is so reviled in other sections of the government that it is now often referred to as the *Maiguobu* (translated as Ministry of Compradors or, perhaps, Ministry of Traitors!)." (p. 255, note 15)

Thirdly, the traditional world view based on Sinocentrism and on a hierarchically structured world order presents obstacles to the embracement of multilateralism. The Chinese realist school of thought tends to favour bilateral dealings rather than multilateral cooperation.[39] China's policy towards resolving the disputes over the Spratlys islands in the South China Sea is a case in point. Socialising is a slow and tortuous process, especially for an old and established civilisation like China. For most Western observers and decision-makers who expect quick results, socialising China can be a frustrating exercise, as China sometimes appears to be in and sometimes not: it sometimes seems to be responsible and sometimes not.

WHY RAISE THE ISSUE OF RESPONSIBILITY NOW?

The reason appears obvious: China is becoming strong, or has the potential to become very strong. In parallel with its growing strength, China is increasingly involved in world affairs. When China was weak and isolated, responsibility did not seem to figure much as an issue, especially when viewed from a Western perspective. At that time it was, for the West, a matter of trying to contain China, to confront it, to stop it from spreading its form of communism and revolution, and to use it as a lever to balance the power of other countries like the former Soviet Union. The assumption here is that a rising China should assume greater responsibilities in world affairs.

Whether China is a responsible power or not carried profound implications for US policy, according to Cheng Sijin, a Chinese national conducting research in the US: "If China behaves (or can be made to behave) responsibly, engagement might be the best way to

---

[39] A recently published book in China casts serious doubts on the benefits of the process of globalisation to China and sparks off heated debates among academics about the merits of China's active interactions with the outside world. The book, entitled *China's road: under the shadow of globalisation*, was co-authored by Wang Xiaodong and Fang Ning and published by the Chinese Academy of Social Sciences Press. It became a bestseller in the country. See *Far Eastern Economic Review*, 13 January 2000, pp. 16–18.

encourage Chinese cooperation. If it does not act responsibly, then containment may be a rational means to restrain China's irrationality and limit the damage it can do".[40]

Apparently, responsibility to international society does not seem to be a language commonly used by decision-makers in China.[41] Nevertheless, the meaning of responsibility has changed over time: in the revolutionary days, it meant responsibility to support and promote international struggles. Mao Zedong was of the opinion that it was responsible behaviour to help the proletariat of the world to revolt and overthrow the decadent, imperialist regimes and the "old world order".[42] Now the term means great power responsibilities. As pointed out by Jia Qingguo, a professor of international politics at Peking University, China opposed to military intervention in Yugoslavia, partly to fulfil its responsibility of upholding international law.[43] More generally, Chinese leaders have repeatedly said that the country will never become a hegemon (meaning a bully) even when it becomes rich. To them, this pledge is a responsible behaviour towards the attainment of world peace. Whether or not this Chinese pledge can be trusted is open to debate.[44]

The term "responsibility" is not much used by Chinese academics in their writings either. A check through a comprehensive and up-to-date Chinese encyclopaedia of international politics reveals the absence of any reference made to the term "responsibility".[45] On the

---

[40] Cheng Sijin, "Gauging China's capabilities and intentions under Deng and Mao," in Cathal J. Nolan (ed), *Power and responsibility in world affairs: reformation versus transformation* (Westport, Connecticut; London: Praeger, 2004), p. 106.

[41] Personal communication with Dr Huang Xiaoming, 13 October 1999.

[42] E-mail communication with Professor Ting Wai of the Department of Government and International Studies, Hong Kong Baptist University, 26 November 1999.

[43] E-mail communication with Professor Jia Qingguo, Associate Dean of the School of International Studies, Peking University, October 1999.

[44] For some discussions on this issue, see Gerald Chan, "Chinese perspectives on peace and development," *Peace Review*, Vol. 10, No. 1 (March 1998), pp. 35–41.

[45] Liu Jinji, Liang Shoude, Yang Huaisheng, et al (eds), *Guoji zhengzhi dacidian* [*A dictionary of international politics*] (Beijing: Chinese Academy of Social Sciences Press, 1994), contents page and index.

contrary and to be expected, the ideas of power and power politics are covered extensively; so are related topics such as national interest and national sovereignty.[46] By and large, Chinese literature on international relations dwells mainly on policy analysis at the state-to-state level.[47] When China exercised its veto against the sending of UN peacekeeping troops to certain countries which had diplomatic relations with Taiwan such as Haiti and Guatemala,[48] it was obviously trying to balance its national interest with its international obligation as a permanent member of the UN Security Council. When China negotiated its terms of entry into the World Trade Organisation, it was trying again to balance its national interest with its international obligations to adhere to the rules and regulations of the international (read Western) trading regime. The contradiction between realist and idealist aspirations,[49] although not clearly spelt out in the current academic literature, does seem to enter into the calculus of decision-makers in China nowadays.

CONCLUSION

Is China a responsible state? The answer to this question is elusive. Unless we have a commonly accepted set of standards to help us to make an assessment, we can hardly say for sure that one country is more responsible than another. Also, unless we make an international comparison across countries, we can hardly say conclusively that country A is more responsible than country B.

In the case of China, if we compare its present situation with its situation say 25 years ago, then we may reasonably conclude, by

---

[46] See also Yan Xuetong, *Zhongguo guojia liyi fengxi* [*Analysis of China's national interest*] (Tianjin: Tianjin People's Press, 1996).

[47] Gerald Chan, "A comment on an international relations theory with Chinese characteristics," (in Chinese), *Asian Review*, No. 8 (Autumn and Winter, 1998), pp. 176–184.

[48] See Wang Jianwei, "Managing conflict: Chinese perspectives on multilateral diplomacy and collective security," in Deng and Wang (eds), *In the eyes of the dragon*, pp. 80–81.

[49] Personal communication with Dr Huang.

using the correlation between position (*dingwei*) and behaviour as a yardstick, that China has become more responsible now than before. If Chinese leaders, by dint of their positions of power and authority in the country, do feel some strong sense of responsibility, then it is most likely to be a sense of responsibility towards their own families and eventually their nation and civilisation, rather than towards the outside world. After all, the "outer" world was, at least in the pre-modern days, unimportant to most Chinese, elites and commoners alike.[50] Things have changed, of course, especially as a result of globalisation, but tradition and culture still persist.[51]

Looking back over the 50 plus years of the history of the People's Republic of China, one can see, in general terms, that Mao Zedong is remembered in history as someone who established the People's Republic and who tried hard to maintain the ideological purity of his people through successive waves of revolutions and class struggles during the first 30 years; Deng Xiaoping is remembered as someone who opened China's door to the outside world in pursuit of stability and prosperity in the following 18 years; while Jiang Zemin, who lacked the credentials of the Long Marchers and who presided over the core leadership for about eight years or so, might be remembered as someone who tried, in addition to furthering Deng's policies, to enhance China's political image by reaching out to the outside world and by making China a more responsible member of the international community.

As China wishes to integrate fully into the world economy, it needs to abide by the prevailing international rules and norms. The West welcomes China to become a responsible state: stable and constructive. But as China continues to grow strongly, will it pose unwelcome challenges and cause serious troubles to the existing normative system which reflects, protects, and promotes in the main

---

[50] Richard J. Smith, *Chinese maps: images of "All Under Heaven"* (New York: Oxford University Press, 1996), p. 78.

[51] This is attested by the "anti-globalisation" book in China: *China's road: under the shadow of globalisation.*

Western values and interests?[52] The fourth generation of leadership under Hu Jintao and Wen Jiabao currently strives to make China a great power, but it also wants China to be seen as a responsible power. This is part of the reasons why the leadership has been making strenuous efforts to constrain the rise of extreme nationalism in the country. This is also the rationale behind the leadership's insistence that China can contribute to world peace: "A stronger China will be an important force for world peace".[53]

Francis Fukuyama is clearly right when he says that Asian values and Western values are increasingly merged through international communications and exchanges.[54] In the long run, the Chinese, through global learning and socialisation as a result of increasing interactions with the outside world, will acquire a greater sense of global responsibility, if not immediately apparent under the reign of Hu and Wen, then hopefully under their successors.

---

[52] E-mail communication with Professor Ting.
[53] E-mail communication with Dr Zheng Yongnian, Senior Research Fellow, East Asian Institute, National University of Singapore, October 1999.
[54] Francis Fukuyama, "Asian values and the current crisis," *Development Outreach*, The World Bank Institute, Vol. 1, No. 1 (Summer 1999), pp. 14–16.

Chapter

2

China's Responsibility in Global Affairs

With greater power comes greater responsibility.

Spiderman movie

As China grows strong, there is a heightened expectation, both within and outside the country, that it should shoulder greater responsibility in world affairs or behave more responsibly. Two assumptions seem to underlie this heightened expectation. The first is that China is at present not really behaving responsibly or, at most, it is negatively rather than positively responsible. That is to say, China is mainly reactive to international pressure when interacting with others rather than taking proactive actions when engaging with the outside world; it tries to refrain from disrupting the existing global order rather than to contribute positively to the common good.[1] This is basically an assumption held by Western observers, especially those in the United States. Is this assumption warranted? If the answer is yes, then what can the West do to make China behave

---

[1] The idea of negative rather than positive responsibility is used by Harry Harding in his review of Elizabeth Economy and Michel Oksenberg (eds), *China joins the world: progress and prospects* (New York: Council on Foreign Relations, 1999), *The China Quarterly*, No. 161 (March 2000), pp. 304–305.

more responsibly? If the answer is no, then how can we revise our understanding of China's responsibility in world affairs?

The other assumption is that a correlation exists between power and responsibility: the more powerful a country is, the greater should be its responsibility. Assuming that this correlation is valid, then China's power status will shape, if not determine, its own perception as well as the perceptions of others of its global responsibility. What is China's current power status then? Is it a great power, as is commonly assumed to be, or is it something else?[2]

This chapter does not pretend to hold all the answers to these questions. Neither does it attempt to make a direct judgement on whether or not China is a responsible actor in global affairs. Rather, it tries to analyse some relevant theoretical issues as well as examine some empirical evidence that might shed some light on the idea of responsibility in Chinese international relations. It starts by asking what global responsibility is. It then discusses some Chinese academic views on global responsibility. This is followed by a section on ways to assess global responsibility before we zero in on China's participation in multilateral institutions as a focus for making such an assessment. Towards the end of the chapter, we ask whether or not China's contributions made in multilateral diplomacy can constitute a case for arguing that China is increasingly responsible in global affairs.

WHAT IS GLOBAL RESPONSIBILITY?

The idea of global responsibility is a complex one, involving competing notions of values, order, justice, historical judgements, and other factors among the parties involved. The current international relations literature does not seem to shed too much light on this

---

[2] I do not want to dwell too much at length on these questions, as they have been dealt with quite sufficiently elsewhere, including the works of Samuel Kim, David Shambaugh, Alastair Iain Johnston, and others. For an updated analysis, see Cheng Sijin, 'Gauging China's capabilities and intentions under Deng and Mao,' in Cathal J. Nolan (ed), *Power and responsibility in world affairs: reformation versus transformation* (Westport, Connecticut; London: Praeger, 2004), pp. 103–126.

question.[3] Some legal experts in the West, however, have made some useful observations. One such observation suggests that the responsibilities of sovereignty should rest on three key elements:[4]

- Humanity, which is the *raison d'tre* of any legal system;
- The protection and development of the human dignity of the individual; and
- The maximisation of the benefits for individuals living within a state rather than the state itself, including such benefits as freedom of speech and elections, and freedom from hunger and the right to education.

These elements clearly highlight the ideals and principles of liberal democracy, to which even some countries in the West struggle to adhere. Non-liberal democracies, however, have different ideas about the proper relationship between state and society. Again, from a mainly Western perspective, the sovereignty of a state derives from three principal sources:[5]

- The degree of respect merited by an institution;
- The capacity to rule; and
- The recognition that the authority acts on behalf of and for the benefit of the people.

---

[3] Most discussions on responsibility centre on the domestic situation. See, for example, Andrew Heywood, *Key concepts in politics* (New York: St. Martin's Press, 2000), pp. 145–147.

[4] Richard B. Lillich, 'Sovereignty and humanity: can they converge?' cited in Louis Henkin et al, *International law: cases and materials*, 3rd ed (St. Paul, MN: West Publishing Co., 1993), p. 19. See Francis M. Deng et al, *Sovereignty as responsibility: conflict management in Africa* (Washington, DC: The Brookings Institution, 1996), pp. 4–5. Rod Alley and Russell Solomon also argue that the responsibility of states should be judged on participatory democracy within a rule-based framework, including the accountability of human rights and the protection of representational, constitutional and civil rights of individuals and groups. See Russell Solomon (ed), *Rights, rules and responsibility in international conduct* (Palmerston North, New Zealand: Dunmore Press, 2000), Introduction.

[5] Nicholas Onuf cited in Gene M. Lyons and Michael Mastanduno, 'Beyond Westphalia? International intervention, state sovereignty, and the future of international

In a similar vein, the *Concise Oxford dictionary of politics* defines a "responsible government" as one which is responsive to public opinion and accountable to people and their elected representatives.[6] Along this line of thinking, the state has certain fundamental responsibilities towards its citizens. If those responsibilities are not fulfilled, then outside intervention may be necessary to rectify the situation. Francis M. Deng goes a step further to say that some dominant powers "have been explicitly or implicitly charged with the responsibilities of enforcing the agreed norms of behaviour."[7] They must assume those "responsibilities that transcend parochialism or exclusive national interests. That kind of leadership serves the broader interests of the community and the human family beyond the barriers of sovereignty."[8]

This argument suggests that there is a linkage between domestic responsibility and international intervention. If a state fails miserably to fulfil its domestic responsibility, then outside powers can move in to intervene. This linkage forms the basis of "humanitarian intervention", a controversial subject in contemporary international politics.[9] Potentially more controversial is the recent development of the concept of "responsibility to protect", which grew out of some large-scale studies within the United Nations looking into the social and legal conditions under which international humanitarian intervention can be justified and therefore made. The concept arises out of at least two historical factors in the past decade or so: "One is the occurrence of many cases of 'humanitarian intervention,' as happened in Bosnia, Somalia, Kosovo, East Timor and other conflict areas.... The other factor is a post-Cold War shift from the traditional protection

---

society,' summary of a conference at Dartmouth College, 1992, p. 10. See Deng et al, *Sovereignty as responsibility*, p. 7.

[6] Iain McLean, *Concise Oxford dictionary of politics* (Oxford; New York: Oxford University Press, 1996).

[7] Deng et al, *Sovereignty as responsibility*, p. 5.

[8] *Ibid.*

[9] There is a growing volume of literature on the subject. For a recent succinct analysis, see Shashi Tharoor and Sam Daws, 'Humanitarian intervention: getting past the reefs,' *World Policy Journal*, Vol. 18, No. 2 (Summer 2001), pp. 21–30.

regime based on the rights of refugees and asylum seekers towards 'in-country' assistance."[10] The "responsibility to protect" would provide the rationale for the international community to act should sovereign states fail to fulfil its responsibility to protect its own citizens, resulting in genocide, ethnic cleansing, and crimes against humanity. According to Malcolm Shaw, a basic test of the nature of state responsibility consists of three factors: (1) an international legal obligation between states; (2) an act or omission which violates that obligation; and (3) resulting in loss or damage.[11]

In a study of the "international society" approach to international relations or the English school of international relations theory, Robert Jackson and Georg Sørensen put forward in clear conceptual terms three dimensions of responsibility in global affairs. They are national responsibility, international responsibility, and humanitarian responsibility.[12] National responsibility refers to the kind of responsibility directed towards one state's own citizens. For example, a state has the responsibility to safeguard the national and human security of its own citizens. International responsibility, on the other hand, refers to the kind of responsibility directed towards other states, resulting in the maintenance of international peace and order. And humanitarian responsibility is universal in nature, directed towards all people everywhere, for example, the protection and promotion of human rights. This kind of classification is based on a Western value system, which may not sit very well with understandings elsewhere. For instance, many Third World countries, including China, regard human rights as domestic affairs; they are relative rather than universal in nature, as they are closely related to the stages of social and economic developments of different individual countries. Furthermore, the rights and freedoms

---

[10] Yamashita Hikaru, 'Fighting terrorism and fighting humanitarian emergencies: two approaches to "elastic" sovereignty and international order,' *Cambridge Review of International Affairs*, Vol. 18, No. 1 (April 2005), p. 107.

[11] Malcolm N. Shaw, *International law*, 4th ed (Cambridge: Cambridge University Press, 1997), p. 542.

[12] Robert Jackson and Georg Sørensen, *Introduction to international relations*, 2nd ed (Oxford: Oxford University Press, 2003), pp. 158–160.

of individuals are subsumed under the collective needs of the community.

The elements of individualism, freedom, and democracy are fundamental to the Western thinking of responsibility. To protect and sustain these elements, rules have to be made and followed. When this line of thinking is extended to international relations, one can see that international order is by and large created and maintained by great powers in the West, which dominate the international system by designing the rules of transactions and by monopolising the process of adjudication, should disputes arise out of different interpretations of those rules. This is *the* international society, the so-called *civilised* one.[13] Those who wish to join this civilised society in the hope of reaping some benefits from it have to agree to abide by the rules and regulations so designed and controlled.[14] A latecomer to the world of international organisations,

---

[13] The September/October 2002 issue of *Foreign Policy* magazine, published by the Carnegie Endowment for International Peace in Washington, DC, included a special supplement on 'What is the international community?' This was in response to the US war against the Taliban regime launched in October 2001, in which President George W. Bush declared: "We are supported by the collective will of the world". For many observers, that collective will refers to the "international community" or "international society". Does such a community or society exist? If so, who is part of it? Who is not? Whose values does it reflect? And how does it work? How should it work? The magazine invited nine notable thinkers, activists, journalists, and policy makers from across the ideological spectrum to scrutinise the international community and to offer their views. In a recent publication, Edward Keene offers a distinctive, valuable critique of the idea of civilisation in Western, especially British, thinking in international relations. See his *Beyond the anarchical society: Grotius, colonialism and order in world politics* (Cambridge: Cambridge University Press, 2002). For a more empirical and cross-cultural analysis of the idea of civilisation in a globalised world, see Mehdi Mozaffari (ed), *Globalization and civilization* (London and New York: Routledge, 2002). For a closely related treatise, see Rosemary Foot, John Lewis Gaddis, and Andrew Hurrell (eds), *Order and justice in international relations* (Oxford: Oxford University Press, 2003).

[14] Martti Koskenniemi has developed an interesting and incisive view on the linkage between international law and hegemony in his article 'International law and hegemony: a reconfiguration,' *Cambridge Review of International Affairs*, Vol. 17, No. 2 (July 2004), pp. 197–218. In some ways, international politics is hegemonic politics, according to him.

like China, has little choice but to either join these organisations or stay away from them. Joining them would require it to play by the existing rules of the game that are largely unfair to developing countries. Staying away would mean that it would be isolated or ostracised by the wider community led by the West. China has to face this dilemma in its globalisation effort; it has to make the best use of a rather difficult and sometimes unfavourable situation in which it finds itself. Of course, China can stay in and lead a revolt, as it did in the 1950s to the 1970s, under the banner of creating a new international world order to protect the interests of the developing world, but to little avail. Now that China is growing strongly, it is tempted to initiate changes to some of the existing rules of the international game to its advantage. For example, at the WTO meeting in Cancun, Mexico, in September 2003, China sided with the developing world, including India and Brazil, and the Cairns Group of agriculture-producing countries to demand a fairer deal for farm trade by asking the rich countries, mainly the US and those in Western Europe, to cut their huge subsidies to their farmers.

GLOBAL RESPONSIBILITY: A CHINESE PERSPECTIVE

In the study of Chinese foreign policy, the idea of responsibility has just begun to attract some scholarly attention.[15] There is a growing interest — both within and outside China, in academic as well as policy-making circles — in China's global responsibility. Since the 1990s, questions have been raised as to whether or not China should shoulder greater responsibilities as a big power and, if it

---

[15] See, for example, Zhang Yongjin and Greg Austin (eds), *Power and responsibility in Chinese foreign policy* (Canberra: Asia Pacific Press, 2001). See also Zhu Kaibing and Qiu Guo, '*Lun guoji shehui de duili chongtu yu daguo zeren* [Antagonism and conflicts in the international society and the responsibilities of the big powers], *Guoji Guanxi Xueyuan Xuebao* [*Journal of the University of International Relations*], Beijing, No. 4 (2002), pp. 15–20; Xiao Huanrong, '*Zhongguo de daguo zeren yu diqu zhuyi zhanlue* [China's duty as a big power and the strategy of regionalism],' *Zhijie Jingji yu Zhengzhi* [*World Economics and International Politics*], Beijing, No. 1 (2003), pp. 46–51.

should, what sort of responsibilities it should carry.[16] Participating actively in the activities of international organisations such as the United Nations system and in regional institutions such as the Asia-Pacific Economic Cooperation forum and the ASEAN Regional Forum, and the sending of military and other personnel to perform peace-keeping duties[17] in various parts of the world can serve as indicators of its shouldering of global responsibility. Other indicators may include China's efforts to help to stabilise the volatile situation in the Korean peninsula and to discuss in multilateral forums ways and means to deal with disputes over the sovereignty of some islands with potentially rich resources of oil in the South China Sea. Still other measures may include China's approach, peaceful or otherwise, towards resolving inter-state disputes, especially in dealing with its own relationship with Taiwan. Despite these often popularised diplomatic activities, a survey of the international relations literature in China reveals very little cumulative, in-depth analysis as to what global responsibility is and what China's role in world affairs should be.

Nevertheless, a politics scholar in Beijing named Xiao Huanrong has offered some simple, but interesting, thoughts on great power responsibilities, perhaps analytically more thoughtful than most other Chinese scholars in this particular area of study.[18] Xiao puts these responsibilities into three separate groups (local responsibility,

---

[16] See Qiao Weibing, '*Nengzhanhou Zhongguo yu guoji jizhi de hudong guanxi* [Interactive relations between China and international regime after the Cold War],' in *Guoji Zhengzhi Yanjiu* [*Studies of International Politics*], Beijing, No. 1 (2001), pp. 137–143; Su Changhe, '*Zhongguo yu guoji zhidu* [China and international regimes],' *World Economics and International Politics*, No. 10 (2002), pp. 5–10; Xia Liping, 'China: a responsible great power'; and Bates Gill, 'Discussion of "China: a responsible great power",' *Journal of Contemporary China*, Vol. 10, No. 26 (February 2001), pp. 17–25 and 27–32.

[17] For a comprehensive Chinese source on China's international peacekeeping, see http://www.pladaily.com.cn/item/peace/index.htm. For an academic analysis, see Zhang Yongjin, 'China and UN peacekeeping: from condemnation to participation,' *International Peacekeeping*, Vol. 3, No. 3 (1997); and Pang Zhongying, 'China's changing attitude to UN peacekeeping,' *International Peacekeeping*, Vol. 12, No. 1 (2005).

[18] Xiao, 'China's duty as a big power and the strategy of regionalism.'

regional responsibility, and global responsibility), and examines three types of powers (general power, regional power, and super-power). Table 2.1 shows a resultant 3 × 3 matrix, with each cell showing the specific goals pursued by states in international politics, viewed under three different types of state responsibilities.

This table possesses some indicative and analytical values. "Strategic borders" in the table refer to the safe and secured boundaries with neighbouring countries. "Security circles", on the other hand, refer to the safe and secured buffer zones between countries. These zones may not be clearly demarcated in terms of geographical boundaries, but they can be established when neighbouring countries, sharing common interests, form multilateral organisations to promote those interests. An interesting correlation that can be deduced from the logics contained in the table is that the greater the power a country has, the greater its responsibility would be. This correlation carries a similar meaning to the Chinese saying *quanli yiwu jundeng* (power plus benefits are equal to duty plus burden) (see Chapter 1).

Xiao is of the opinion that China is basically a middle-ranging power, despite its huge physical size, its massive population, and its

Table 2.1 Three Levels of Responsibilities of Major Powers

	Local Responsibility	Regional Responsibility	Global Responsibility
General Powers	To *pursue* basic security and basic wealth	To acquire "strategic borders"	Little
Regional Powers	To *secure* basic security and basic wealth	To acquire "security circles"	Of growing importance
Super Powers	To *consolidate* basic security and basic wealth	To acquire spheres of influence	To dominate the global order

Source: Xiao Huanrong, '*Zhongguo de daguo zeren yu diqu zhuyi zhanlue* [China's duty as a big power and the strategy of regionalism],' *Zhijie Jingji yu Zhengzhi* [*World Economics and International Politics*], Beijing, No. 1 (2003), p. 48.

fast economic growth, because the country is beset with a host of developmental problems, which work against its rising influence. These problems include, among others: a low per capita GDP; a huge wealth gap between the urban rich and rural poor, and between the coastal areas and the hinterland; environmental degradation; fraud and corruption; a low level of basic education; a poor record of public health; the sovereignty problem with Taiwan; and territorial disputes with its neighbours. In short, China still struggles with its national development.[19] It does not possess the comprehensive capability to become a superpower in the near future.[20] What it can reasonably aspire to is to become a regional power, nurturing friendships with its Asian neighbours. Its limited global responsibility should therefore be contingent on the fulfilment of its local and regional responsibilities. According to Xiao and other Chinese scholars, China should concentrate on developing multilateralism in the Asia-Pacific region.[21] Apparently Xiao's understanding of state responsibilities, especially at the local level, is very much focused on state power, and differs markedly from similar understandings in the liberal-democratic West, where the internal responsibilities of a state are based on democratic principles of personal freedom, public accountability, and governance transparency. Her understanding is a kind of responsibility that stresses the importance of societal stability

---

[19] In a public lecture entitled 'Is China still a developing country?' held at the Hong Kong University of Science and Technology on 14 March 2003, Kerstin Leitner, Resident Representative of the United Nations Development Programme, was of the opinion that China is still a developing country, as it still needs outside help to deal with a host of problems in its development, including public health, environmental protection, rural poverty, unemployment, corruption, and others.

[20] Singapore's Minister Mentor Lee Kuan Yew said in the Boao Forum on Hainan Island in April 2005 that China needed 50 years to catch up with the power of the United States.

[21] Xiao's view that China should focus its attention on regional affairs in the Asia-Pacific region is shared by a large number of Chinese scholars. See, for example, the works of Pang Zhongying, '*Zhongguo de Yazhou zhanlue: linghuo de duobian zhuyi* [China's Asian strategy: flexible multilateralism],' *World Economics and International Politics,* No. 10 (2001), pp. 30–35; and Zhu and Qiu, 'Antagonism and conflicts in the international society and the responsibilities of the big powers.'

over the political and social well-being of individuals. It is, in short, a classic state-centric understanding.

In an article analysing rules, principles, and laws in international politics, Hu Zhongshan says a responsible state should strike a proper balance between realism and idealism. According to Hu, China should follow the basic principles set out in the UN Charter and the Five Principles of Peaceful Coexistence to achieve the democratisation, not the hegemony, of international relations.[22]

ASSESSING GLOBAL RESPONSIBILITY

How to assess a country's international responsibility becomes a crucial question. Making such an assessment is by no means easy, as it would involve measuring state behaviour against a certain standard. To establish a universally acceptable standard of state behaviour across the globe is extremely difficult, as state responsibility invokes different legal, moral, and social norms. We are far from establishing such a global benchmark of social behaviour. This state of affair is further complicated by the complex nature of social behaviour in different spheres of human activities. We are facing not only with one single benchmark but a series of benchmarks in a single sphere as well as across different spheres. Furthermore, world politics is in a constant state of flux. Norms and rules are changing across time and space, some rapidly, others slowly. What is legal may not be legitimate, and what is legitimate may not be legal. That said, it doesn't mean that there are no agreements among like-minded states to try to harmonise, if not standardise, certain behaviour of states. However, the international system is still in a situation of anarchy where states are the primary actors, where sovereignty is jealously guarded, and where there is no supranational government with jurisdiction over states comparable to those of national governments over their citizens.

---

[22] Hu Zhongshan, '*Lun guoji zhengzhi zhong de kuize, yuanze he faze* [On rules, principles, and laws in international politics],' 14 October 2004, on the website of China Politics, http://www.polisino.org (accessed 12 September 2004).

As a result, international responsibility remains a highly contested issue. What is responsible to some may be seen as irresponsible to others, and what is universal to some may be seen as hegemonic to others.[23]

The standards or benchmarks that come close to universality are perhaps those found in the United Nations system and programmes, where almost all nation-states of the world belong to or aspire to belong to as members. For all its tribulations and triumphs, the United Nations has been and will remain a battleground for states to fight for their national interests, a forum for governments to talk to each other, and an institution for establishing agreeable norms, rules, and programmes. Some of these norms and rules have become international laws when governments make treaties to that effect. The United Nations is of course more than just reacting to the needs and demands of states and the constituents that they represent, it is also capable of initiating actions to resolve global problems and to promote global welfare. Other major international organisations, either within and outside the United Nations system, try to do likewise. These international institutions help to set rules and standards for member states to follow.

Cheng Sijin suggests five indicators for gauging China's responsibility, although she does not seem to have given reasons to support the choice of these indicators:[24]

1. Collective governance;
2. Acceptance of the norms of the international community;
3. Awareness of security interdependence;
4. Management of regional balance of power; and
5. Non-initiation of conflicts.

---

[23] An interesting case, which serves to illustrate this point, is the deportation of the former Serbian leader, Slobodan Milosevic, to the International Criminal Tribunal in The Hague in July 2001. According to one commentator, "the tribunal is a subsidiary of Pax Americana", like many other international institutions, from the IMF to NATO. His deportation is "testimony not to the power of international law but to the power of the US." See Charles Krauthammer in *Time* magazine, 9 July 2001, p. 27.

[24] Cheng, 'Gauging China's capabilities and intentions under Deng and Mao.'

While non-initiation of conflicts is regarded as good international behaviour to be expected of all states, the management of regional balance of power has assumed greater urgency as a result of China's rise in its geo-strategic sphere of influence in Asia, and the awareness of security interdependence increases as it acquires greater understanding of international affairs. The acceptance of international norms is a matter of rule compliance (to be discussed in later chapters). The entry into collective governance, however, depends on China's increasing participation in multilateral regimes. In this light, it would be useful to examine China's responsibility through its multilateral engagements, especially its participation in international organisations and its accession to international treaties. This kind of approach is necessarily a macro approach aimed at obtaining an overview. It is in contrast to the micro approaches that have been used, very successfully, by scholars to examine China's relations with particular international organisations, such as the United Nations and some key international financial institutions, or China's involvement in such issue areas as trade, human rights, arms control, or the environment.[25] I choose this macro approach, partly to fill a gap in the existing literature on China and the world and partly to try to discern if a trend or pattern exists. I want to chart the contour of the forest, while not losing sight of some of the trees. To do this, let us start by examining, first of all, the current state of China's

---

[25] See Economy and Oksenberg (eds), *China joins the world*; Alastair Iain Johnston and Robert S. Ross (eds), *Engaging China: the management of an emerging power* (London and New York: Routledge, 1999), chapters 9 and 10; Andrew Nathan and Robert Ross, *The Great Wall and the empty fortress* (New York and London: W.W. Norton & Co., 1997); and selective chapters in David M. Lampton (ed), *The making of Chinese foreign and security policy in the era of reform* (Stanford: Stanford University Press, 2001). Ann Kent offers a book-length treatment on human rights issue in her *China, the United Nations, and human rights: the limits of compliance* (Philadelphia: University of Pennsylvania Press, 1999). Similarly, Wendy Frieman offers a book-length treatment on China's arms control in *China, arms control, and non-proliferation* (London and New York: RoutledgeCurzon, 2004). And Elizabeth Economy on the environment in *The river runs black: the environmental challenge to China's future* (Ithaca and London: Cornell University Press, 2004).

participation in international organisations, as a prelude to or a vehicle for assessing China's global responsibility in greater details in later chapters.[26]

CHINA'S PARTICIPATION IN MULTILATERAL INSTITUTIONS

According to the *Yearbook of international organizations*, there were 6,177 international organisations (IOs) in the world as of 2000, of which 241 were intergovernmental organisations (IGOs) and the rest of 5,936 were international non-governmental organisations (INGOs).[27] These are the major IOs in the world, called conventional international bodies by the *Yearbook*, consisting of four types: federations of international organisations (type A); universal membership organisations (type B); intercontinental membership organisations (type C); and regionally-oriented membership organisations (type D).

Of these 6,177 IOs, China is a member of 50 IGOs and 1,275 INGOs.[28] Table 2.2 shows how this membership size has grown since 1966, the year in which the *Yearbook* chooses as a starting year for comparison.

Three observations can be made from the table. First, China's participation in IGOs jumped from just one in 1966 to 21 in 1977. This great surge in participation can be attributed to China's entry into the United Nations in 1971, and subsequently, China was able to gain entry into many IOs affiliated with the UN system. A second observation

---

[26] I have not tried to examine China's domestic responsibility specifically here, as it deserves a research project of its own. Obviously there is a strong linkage between domestic and international responsibilities, as discussed in Chapter 7 of this book which deals with China's compliance in human rights affairs.

[27] *Yearbook of international organizations 2000–2001* (Munich: K.G. Saur, 2000), Vol. 2, Appendix 3, p. 1,465.

[28] Memberships of IGOs are based mainly on statehood, while memberships of INGOs are based mainly on private groups and individuals. There are also IOs of a hybrid type, consisting of states and non-states as members. Membership types are many, including full members, associate members, corresponding members, voting/non-voting members, observers, and so on.

Table 2.2 China's Membership
of International Organisations, 1966–2000

	1966	1977	1986	1997	2000
IGOs	1	21	32	52	50
INGOs	58	71	403	1,136	1,275
Total	59	92	435	1,188	1,325

Source: *Yearbook of international organizations 2000–2001*, Vol. 2, p. 1,468.

is that China's participation in INGOs has increased steadily over the years from 1966 onwards, which seems to be a reasonable progression. A third observation, which may not be apparent from the table,[29] is that since the adoption of a reform and opening-up policy in the late 1970s, China's participation in IOs, both IGOs and INGOs, has increased substantially over time up to this day.

Since Hong Kong is now a sovereign part of China and since Taiwan competes with China over participation in IOs, it would be interesting and revealing to compare China's current participation in IOs with that of Hong Kong and Taiwan (see Table 2.3).

The 11 IGOs of which Hong Kong is a member are:

1. Asia-Pacific Economic Cooperation;
2. Asian Productivity Organisation;
3. International Commission for Scientific Exploration of the Mediterranean Sea;
4. International Criminal Police Organisation;
5. International Institute of Refrigeration;
6. International Maritime Organisation;
7. International Organisation for Migration;
8. International Organisation of Legal Metrology;
9. World Customs Organisation;
10. World Meteorological Organisation; and
11. World Trade Organisation.

---

[29] This will become clearer later when we consider China's accession to international treaties.

Table 2.3 China, Taiwan, and Hong Kong in International Organisations, 2000

	China	Taiwan	Hong Kong
United Nations	Yes Admitted in 1971	No Left in 1971	No
IMF/World Bank	Yes	No	No
WTO	Yes, since 2001	Yes, since 2002 under "Chinese Taipei"*	Yes
Asian Development Bank	Yes Admitted in 1986	Yes Founding member since 1966 Participates as "Taipei, China" since 1986	Yes Admitted in 1969 Participates as "Hong Kong, China" since 1997

Asia-Pacific
  Economic
  Cooperation
  forum
	Yes
	Attended by
	President
		Yes
		Not attended
		by President
			Yes
			Attended by
			Chief Executive or
			Financial Secretary

International
  Olympic
  Committee
	Yes
	Normalised
	relations in 1979
		Yes
		Competes as
		"Chinese Taipei"
		since 1979
			Yes
			Competes as
			"Hong Kong,
			China" since 1997

Asian Games	Yes	Yes	Yes
FIFA**	Yes	Yes	Yes
Diplomatic relations	161 countries	29 countries	Nil
Membership of IGOs	50	10	11
Membership of INGOs	1,275	1,008	1,130

* The full name of Taiwan in the WTO is "Separate Customs Territory of Taiwan, Penghu, Kinmen and Matsu".
** FIFA: French acronym for International Federation of Football Association.
Sources: Updated from Gerald Chan, 'China and international organisations,' in Lo Chi-kin, Tsui Kai-yuen and Suzanne Pepper (eds), *China review 1995* (Hong Kong: Chinese University Press, 1995), chapter 7; *Yearbook of international organizations 2000–2001*, Vol. 2, pp. 1,468–1,469; various Internet sources.
Note: Data on the memberships of IGOs and INGOs are based on types A to D (the major IOs) listed in the *Yearbook of international organizations*.

Of these 11 IGOs, China was not (as of 2000) a member of the Asian Productivity Organisation and the International Organisations for Migration. Both China and Hong Kong are members of the other nine IGOs.

The 10 IGOs (in Table 2.2), of which Taiwan is a member are:[30]

1. Afro-Asian Rural Reconstruction Organisation;
2. Asia-Pacific Association of Agricultural Research Institutions*;
3. Asia-Pacific Economic Cooperation*;
4. Asian Productivity Organisation;
5. Asian Vegetable Research and Development Centre;
6. International Cotton Advisory Committee;
7. International Office of Epizootics*;
8. International Organisation of Legal Metrology*;
9. International Seed Testing Association*; and
10. World Trade Organisation*.

Of these 10 organisations, China is a member of six (marked with an asterisk*). The case of the Asia-Pacific Economic Cooperation, of which both China and Taiwan are members, is well known. So is the case of the World Trade Organisation, when both China and Taiwan were admitted in November 2001 (discussed further in Chapter 4). It would therefore be interesting to see why China and Taiwan can be accommodated in the other four IGOs, given the fact that China has consistently rejected Taiwan's admission into IGOs.

A look into these four IGOs reveals that they are largely science and technology organisations and are therefore much less politically orientated (see Appendix I for details). That explains in part why China tolerates (or pays relatively little attention to) co-existence with Taiwan in these organisations. Apart from that, Taiwan has to

---

[30] In fact, the *Yearbook of international organizations* gives 11 IGOs, including the Food and Agricultural Organisation of the United Nations, which is incorrect. Also, the government in Taiwan has a slightly different count of its membership of IOs. See *The Republic of China yearbook — Taiwan 2001*, Internet ed., at http://www.gio.gov.tw/taiwan-website/5-gp/yearbook/chpt09-1.htm (accessed 6 June 2001).

use such names as "Chinese Taipei" or "Taipei, China" to designate itself, or to accept its relegation to a lower level of membership such as associate member instead of full member. In the case of the World Trade Organisation, Taiwan's membership name is known as the "Separate Customs Territory of Taiwan, Penghu, Kinmen and Matsu".[31]

How active is China in participating in international organisations? Here some sort of comparison is required. Since Asian countries are late comers to the world of international organisations, it would not be very meaningful, for example, to compare China with advanced, industrialised countries in Europe. It would be more useful to compare China with say Japan, since they are close neighbours in Asia, both started to have substantial contacts with the outside world (the West) since the middle of the 19th century, and both are now major powers in the Asia-Pacific region (see Table 2.4).

Three observations can be made from Table 2.4. First, compared with Japan, China started with a very low base in its membership of both IGOs and INGOs in 1966, but gradually built up over the years to the present. Second, China's current membership size of IGOs is close to that of Japan's (China's 50 as compared to Japan's 63 in 2000). This is mainly because IGOs require statehood as a membership condition, and China is keen to join as many important IGOs as possible in order to establish its international legitimacy. However,

Table 2.4 Comparing China's Membership
of IOs with Japan's, 1966–2000

	1966	1977	1986	1997	2000
China's IGOs	1	21	32	52	50
Japan's IGOs	53	71	58	63	63
China's INGOs	58	71	403	1,136	1,275
Japan's INGOs	636	878	1,222	2,019	2,122

Source: *Yearbook of international organizations 2000–2001*, Vol. 2, pp. 1,468–1,469.

---

[31] See http://www.wto.org/english/thewto_e/countries_e/chinese_taipei_e.htm

China's membership size of INGOs still lacks very much behind that of Japan, especially when the population sizes of both countries are taken into account. One may conclude from this situation (as the third observation) that the development of China's civil society is very much behind that of Japan, as members of INGOs are in the main private individuals and groups. If Japan is regarded as a Westernised or even a Western country, then China's apparent active participation in IOs is not too far off from this Westernised or Western country.[32]

Of course membership of organisations is but one measure of participation in international organisations, and a rather crude one at that.[33] Other measures may include monetary contributions, personnel contributions, and policy input to these organisations. In terms of monetary contributions to international organisations, Japan is a major funding source to the UN system and other big international and regional organisations in Asia.[34] Apart from the United States, Japan's monetary contributions to the management of global affairs may be second to none. China's very modest monetary contributions to multilateral institutions have to be seen in the light of its economic conditions and policy preferences. In terms of personnel contributions, Japanese nationals had recently occupied top executive positions in the UN High Commission for Refugees (Ogata Sadako), the World Health Organisation (Nakajima Hiroshi),

---

[32] Alastair Iain Johnston and Robert S. Ross have given another interesting comparison: "The number of China's IGO memberships has gone from about 70 percent of the world average in 1977 to around 180 percent in 1996. By 1996, the number of its memberships approached 80 percent of the number for the United States." See Johnston and Ross (eds), *Engaging China*, p. 289. These statistics will be more meaningful if the types of IGOs are revealed.

[33] Some scholars call this nominal multilateralism, as opposed to qualitative multilateralism. See John Gerard Ruggie, 'Multilateralism: the anatomy of an institution,' *International Organization*, Vol. 46, No. 3 (Summer 1992), p. 566.

[34] For Japan's increasing contributions to the United Nations' regular budget from 1975 to 1999, in comparison with other major contributors like the United States, Germany and the United Kingdom, see Glenn D. Hook et al, *Japan's international relations* (London and New York: Routledge, 2001), Figure 19.5, p. 319.

the UN Transition Authority in Cambodia (Akashi Yasushi), and the Asian Development Bank (Chino Tadao and others). Despite these highly publicised positions, Japan in fact lags very much behind many Western countries in this respect. This is especially true in middle-ranking executive or professional posts.[35] Compared with Japan, China is further behind in personnel contributions to international organisations, although China has sometimes chaired the UN Security Council meetings due to the rotation of the chair among members of the Security Council. A Chinese national sitting in the International Court of Justice at The Hague is probably a reflection of its great-power status.[36] In terms of policy contributions, it is very difficult to measure. Scattered evidence suggests that China these days is more willing to discuss issues relating to human rights, trade, environmental protection, and arms control. Suffice to say that most policy programmes are initiated and led by governments in the West, the United States and major Western European powers in particular. Even in regional organisations in Asia, China lacks behind Japan and some ASEAN countries in policy input. The holding of the summit meeting of the Asia-Pacific Economic Cooperation forum in Shanghai in October 2001 and other associated activities involving government ministers, officials, and business executives from member countries represented a climax of China's contributions to this grouping.[37] However, China has begun to take proactive actions in establishing some multilateral institutions to rival those in the West and the United States. For example, China hosted the inaugural meeting of the Boao Forum for Asia on 27 February 2001 in Boao, Hainan province. It is a pan-Asian forum conceived in September 1998 by regional statesmen, including the then former Australian

---

[35] *Ibid.*, pp. 316–317.

[36] Judge Shi Jiuyong is one of the 15 member judges of the International Court of Justice. He is also serving as the President of the Court. The only other Asian sitting in the Court is a Japanese national, Judge Owada Hisashi. See http://www.icj-cij.org/icjwww/igeneralinformation/igncompos.html (accessed 27 April 2005).

[37] See http://www.apec-china.org.cn/.

Prime Minister Bob Hawke and Philippine President Fidel Ramos. The forum aims to give countries an opportunity to discuss their problems on their own terms. The inaugural ceremony was held in February 2002.[38] The latest annual gathering was held in April 2005 on Hainan Island.[39] Some observers see this as a counterpart, an alternative, or even a rival to the Davos-style annual World Economic Forum. Another example: in June 2001, Chinese President Jiang Zemin, Russian President Vladimir Putin and the leaders of four nations formed as a result of the collapse of the Soviet Union established a new bloc to fight Islamic militancy. The newly named Shanghai Cooperation Organisation replaces the so-called Shanghai Five. The leaders of the organisation, including those from Kazakhstan, Kirgyzstan, Tajikistan and Uzbekistan, hit out at US plans for a missile defence system as damaging to global security.[40] China is scheduled to hold the Olympic Games in Beijing in 2008 and the World Expo in Shanghai in 2010, events which may mark a new stage in its relations with the world.

MEAGRE CONTRIBUTIONS — SHIRKING RESPONSIBILITY?

Apart from monetary, personnel, and policy contributions, another way to assess China's integration with multilateral institutions is to take a look at the headquarters and secretariats of these institutions to see if they are physically located in China. This will serve as a measure of the commitment and the degree of involvement of China in the activities of these organisations. As of May 2001, China plays host to some 98 headquarters and 23 secretariats (the latter being offices of international organisations with headquarters based outside China), as indicated by the Union of International Associations in Brussels, the editorial office of the *Yearbook of international*

---

[38] See *South China Morning Post*, Internet ed., 27 February 2001; and *Xinbao* [*Hong Kong Economic Journal*], 28 February 2001, p. 11.

[39] See http://www.boaoforum.org.

[40] See *The Dominion*, Wellington, 20 June 2001, p. 13; and *Far Eastern Economic Review*, 28 June 2001, p. 12.

Table 2.5 Number of Headquarters and
Secretariats of IOs in China, May 2001

City/province	Headquarters	Secretariats
Beijing	64	20
Chengdu	3	0
Fujian	1	0
Guangzhou	2	3
Hangzhou	2	0
Hebei	1	0
Hubei	2	0
Jiangsu	2	0
Jingsu	1	0
Liaoning	1	0
Nanjing	2	0
Shandong	1	0
Shanghai	11	0
Tianjin	3	0
Wuhan	1	0
Yunnan	1	0
Total	98	23

Source: Adapted from the Union of International
Associations, www.uia.org (accessed 7 June 2001;
databases uploaded by the Union on 20 May 2001).
Note: This table does not include Hong Kong,
which maintains some 40 headquarters and 9 secretariats, as of May 2001.

organizations. Table 2.5 shows the distribution of these offices in various Chinese cities or provinces.

Table 2.5 shows that the vast majority of headquarters and secretariats are based in Beijing, while Shanghai comes in a distant second, which in turn leaves far behind other cities. This is not surprising, given the nature of Chinese politics and the structure of the Chinese political system, that power is concentrated in Beijing, the capital city, and in Shanghai, the most cosmopolitan commercial centre of the country. Hong Kong is of course in a different category.

It will be interesting to see what these headquarters and secretariats are.[41] Of the 23 IOs with secretariats in China, eight are associated with the United Nations system. Of the rest of 15, most are working in the areas of science and technology (five of them), and the others deal with education, culture, sports, and trade.

Of the 98 IOs with headquarters in China, many are in fact locally-based organisations with an international orientation, for example, the Asian Institute in Shanghai and the China Institute of Contemporary International Relations in Beijing. Some are associated with the promotion of Chinese culture and tradition, such as the Asian Xianqi Federation, the International Confucian Association, and the International Wushu Federation. If we put aside these organisations, we can obtain a short list of about 35 organisations with a more universal outlook and set-up, including, among others:

1. Asian-Pacific News Network;
2. Asian Rowing Federation;
3. Asian-South Pacific Association for Sport Psychology;
4. Association of Asia Pacific Physical Societies;
5. Federation of Asian Nutrition Societies;
6. International Centre of Climate and Environmental Sciences;
7. International Network on Small Hydro Power;
8. International Research Centre on Hydraulic Machinery; and
9. International Research and Training Centre for Rural Education.

An interesting pattern emerges out of these organisations with headquarters in China: They are mostly scientific organisations of one kind or another, with a few promoting sports. In other words, they are functional organisations dealing with issues of low politics. None of them are major IOs dealing with strategic issues of war and peace, or economic issues that affect the global financial structure. In terms of geographical spread, most of these organisations are regional in nature, mainly confined to the Asia-Pacific region. As such, China is far from being a dominant power in international

---

[41] For details, see http://db.uia.org/scripts/sweb.dll/sweb_uiae (accessed 22 May 2001).

Table 2.6 A Comparison of the Number
of Headquarters, Secretariats, and IO Membership
of Some Asian Countries, 2001

	Headquarters	Secretariats	Members
Japan	615	119	5,801
South Korea	288	67	4,180
Singapore	138	46	2,710
Hong Kong	132	17	2,653
China	98	23	3,456
Taiwan	57	12	2,268

Note 1: ranked in descending order of the number
of headquarters.
Note 2: All types of IOs are considered, not restricted
to types A to D (in the *Yearbook of international
organizations*).
Source: Extracted from the website of the Union of International
Associations, http://db.uia.org/scripts/sweb.dll/
sweb_uiae (accessed 7 June 2001).

organisations or governance. Although its comprehensive power is
rising, it is still a minor player in global governance trying to
increase its influence.

How does China's involvement in IOs through the establishment
of headquarters and secretariats compare with its Asian neighbours?
Table 2.6 offers a comparison with Japan and the so-called four Little
Dragons in Asia: South Korea, Taiwan, Hong Kong, and Singapore.

The table suggests that China is less involved in the world of
international organisations than Japan, South Korea, Singapore or
Hong Kong. It is ahead of Taiwan, for the simple and obvious reason that China exerts political pressure on international organisations not to accept Taiwan as a member and on other countries not
to join organisations set up by Taiwan. It is fair to say that, compared with the countries and region under consideration, China is
the latest comer to the world of international organisations. Its membership of IOs, though increasing rapidly in the last 20 years or so,
still trails behind most other countries, especially when calculated
on a per capita basis.

The generally low level of participation of Asian countries, including China, in international forums must be seen in a broader context. This includes the cultural differences between the East and the West, the degree of pluralism in social behaviour, the level of technological know-how, and the wealth of the country concerned. As observed by Johan Galtung, one reason why there are so few Chinese in international organisations is conceptual: "The very idea of detaching an individual from his or her habitat and placing that individual in the context of a conference room is an idea which is highly compatible with individualising Western civilisation, but not necessarily so compatible with the thinking, concepts and traditions as developed elsewhere."[42] Seen in this light, China's relatively low level of participation in multilateral institutions may not be taken as to mean that China deliberately shirks its responsibility in global participation.

CONCLUSION

Let us consider our central question again: Is China a responsible state? From an official Chinese perspective, it is certainly a responsible state, so far as its strict adherence to the letter of international law is concerned.[43] In any case, it is now more responsible than the China of 1949 to 1978: it is less authoritarian, less revolutionary, and less destructive to society; it is more open, pragmatic, and constructive. Domestically, it has made substantial progress in raising the living standard of its people and in strengthening its legal system,[44] while admitting that there are defects, which need to be

---

[42] Johan Galtung, 'The role of transnational universities in the future growth of transnational organisation,' in *The future of transnational association from the standpoint of a new world order* (Brussels: Union of International Associations, 1977), p. 75.

[43] The adherence to the spirit is often subject to debate and further investigation.

[44] Reservations have to be made for the distribution of growth and wealth, and for the scope and limits of legal reform. The legal development in China has been aptly described as a "bird in a cage" by Stanley B. Lubman, *Bird in a cage: legal reform in China after Mao* (Stanford: Stanford University Press, 1999).

fixed. Externally, it has signed a large number of international treaties and participated in an increasing number of multilateral institutions. It has also tried hard to abide by the rules and norms of the global society, and has engaged in dialogues with other countries and groups on human rights, trade issues, arms control, and environmental issues. Since 1991, it has published some 45 White Papers to explain its policies on various issues.

From a liberal-democratic perspective, especially from an American perspective, China is not yet a responsible state: witness the many human rights abuses in the country, the curtailment of religious and other freedoms, threatening behaviour towards Taiwan, unfair trade practices, and "illegal" sales of arms. Although China is increasingly involved in multilateral institutions and treaties, it is not doing enough: it is not actively taking part in their programmes by contributing sufficient money, personnel, or policy input. It seems to be "inside", and yet is "outside" of the world of international organisation.[45] At most it is negatively responsible rather than positively responsible.[46] It has *adapted* (referring to behavioural change as a tactic) rather than *learned* (meaning internalised) the rules and norms of the "international community".[47]

Whether China has learned or has just adapted is open to debate.[48] Certainly China has learned useful lessons through

---

[45] This apparent ambivalence has been captured well by Samuel S. Kim, *China in and out of the changing world order* (Center of International Studies, Princeton University, 1991).

[46] Harding's review on Economy and Oksenberg in *The China Quarterly*.

[47] Western scholars and politicians have often used the term "international community" without really defining it. To me, they refer to the "international community" whose power, rules, and norms are largely those dominated by the West, especially the US. One scholar has suggested that the term "international community" be eliminated from public policy discourse because of its imprecision. See Thomas G. Weiss, 'Researching humanitarian intervention: some lessons,' *Journal of Peace Research*, Vol. 38, No. 4 (July 2001), p. 424.

[48] Alastair Iain Johnston, 'Learning versus adaptation: explaining change in Chinese arms control policy in the 1980s and 1990s,' *China Journal*, No. 35 (January 1996).

globalisation and participation in multilateral organisations and treaties. The learning may be selective, it may be voluntary or forced, it may be moving in different speeds at different times, and in some cases it may be "counter-productive" in the sense that it may acquire some Western ways of using force for the sake of expediency in international affairs.[49] Yet the more China is engaged, the more it is exposed to the influence of different worldviews and ideologies. Through comparison, China (or Chinese elites who deal with external affairs, to be more exact) learns to be aware of the different choices of actions and their consequences. Furthermore, it is not only China that learns in the process, the outside world too learns about China's thinking and behaviour. It is this type of mutual learning that is useful in building trust and confidence, and in reducing tension and settling disputes in a mutually satisfactory way.[50]

Apparently, by using a more absolutist conceptualisation of responsibility to gauge China, the West, especially the United States, finds its behaviour deficient, and repugnant, at times. China, on the other hand, by using a more relativist conceptualisation of responsibility, refutes the criticisms of the West that China is somehow irresponsible. In the absence of a universally accepted standard of measurement, any judgement is likely to be controversial. Assuming that there is a certain universal standard out there, then every country in the world is, in fact, in a relative position along a scale with absolute responsibility at one end and

---

Some scholars have reservations about the distinction between adaptation and learning, viewing them as somewhat intertwined. See Lampton's arguments in his edited book, *The making of Chinese foreign and security policy in the era of reform*, pp. 32–33 and 225–228.

[49] See Wang Hongying's discussions on the limits of socialisation in 'Multilateralism in Chinese foreign policy,' in Hu Weixing, Gerald Chan, and Zha Daojiong (eds), *China's international relations in the 21st century* (Lanham: University Press of America, 2000), pp. 81–85.

[50] Mutual learning may not be "balanced learning" in the sense that both sides devote more or less the same amount of energy in learning from each other, and mutually satisfactory may not be "equally satisfactory".

absolute irresponsibility at the other. Some countries, because of their history and tradition, can be found to be more "responsible" than others. As every country is arguably in a transitional stage of responsibility, they should be encouraged to be more responsible, through acts of appreciation, or peaceful means of admonition, or assistance in capacity building. In this sense, the outside world should continue to persuade China to reform and become more responsible. China, on the other hand, should make its system and operations more transparent and subject itself to greater scrutiny. It should, however, be given a fair chance to find its own way to achieve greater responsibility, while not losing sight of its overall responsibility to balance between change and continuity, disruption and stability, domestic constraints and international pressure.

Mutual learning between China and the West will continue to reveal their cognitive dissonance about human values and aspirations. Outbreaks of conflicts over values and interests are inevitable. There is a need to recognise their differences and find ways to reconcile them in a non-violent way, moving beyond the rather simplistic notions that China and the US are "strategic partners", "strategic competitors" or "strategic collaborators".[51]

Beyond the expectation that China should shoulder greater responsibility in world affairs, there is little common understanding, both inside and outside China, as to what and how China should do to be more responsible. In general, at the global level, China stresses the importance of the adherence by all nations to the UN Charter and to the peaceful settlement of disputes through the UN system as the guiding principle of international relations. It also stresses the importance of the preservation of state sovereignty,

---

[51] In the latter part of the Clinton administration, the US regarded China as a "strategic partner". In his presidential election campaign, George W. Bush said that China was a "strategic competitor". After his visit to Beijing in July 2001, Secretary of State Colin Powell used the term "constructive cooperation" to describe the state of US-China relations. In the global campaign against terrorism after 9/11, China became a "strategic partner" again.

the equality of states, the non-interference in the domestic affairs of others, and the freedom to choose one's developmental path. At the regional level, there is a general recognition among many Chinese international relations scholars that China should play a greater role in promoting peace, stability and prosperity in Asia.[52]

[52] See Ye Zicheng, '*Zhongguo shixing deguo waijiao zhanlue shizai bixing* [Strategy of great-power diplomacy is imperative for China — some problems in China's diplomatic strategy],' *Shijie jingji yu zhengzhi* [*World Economics and Politics*], Beijing, No. 1 (2000), p. 10; Pang Zhongying, '*Zai bianhua de shijieshang zhuiqiu Zhongguo de diwei* [To establish China's status in a changing world], *World Economics and Politics*, No. 1 (2000), p. 38; and Chen Quansheng and Liu Jinghua, '*Quanqiu zhong de Zhongguo yu shijie* [China and the world under globalisation],' *Zhongguo waijiao* [*Chinese Diplomacy*], No. 3 (2000), p. 4.

3

China's Compliance in Global Affairs

China needs to follow "the rule of law and to be exposed to the powerful forces of free enterprise systems and democracy".

US Secretary of State Colin Powell, 2001[1]

The United States wants to become both rule maker and arbitrator of the game.

China Daily, 2001[2]

Closely related to the idea of responsibility is the idea of compliance, a concept lying at the very heart of international relations and international law. Originally coming from legal studies, it has now attracted the attention of many political scientists,[3] as the role played by international institutions in world affairs gains in importance after the Cold War. This chapter starts by defining first of all the concept of compliance and then examines China's accession to international treaties, thus providing a prelude to an analysis of China's compliance with the rules and norms embodied in those treaties covering the four issue areas in the following chapters in Part II.

---

[1] Quoted in *Asiaweek*, 30 March–6 April 2001, p. 38.

[2] Quoted in the *People's Daily*, Internet ed., 22 February 2001.

[3] See the growing number of articles on compliance in such academic journals as *International Organization* and the *American Political Science Review*.

WHAT IS GLOBAL COMPLIANCE?

Compliance is an act of implementing and enforcing agreements made. It is a correspondence between behaviour and agreed rules.[4] As a result of globalisation and interdependence of one kind or another among states and non-state actors, a growing body of rules and norms is made to govern international behaviour. Some of these rules and norms are set in formal ways. Others, in increasing numbers, are informal or "soft" in nature, like declarations, communiqués, and memoranda of understanding. In comparison, these rules are more fluid and less well-defined than "hard" laws such as treaties. Abraham Chayes and Antonia Handler-Chayes are among the earlier groups of scholars who argue that absolute state sovereignty has been checked by the growth of regimes in that states increasingly find it necessary to comply with the rules of these regimes, rules that set limits to their independence and freedom of action.[5] Other scholars, like George Downs and his associates, probe the idea of compliance further and find that there is a correspondence between deeper compliance and greater enforcement.[6] That is to say, greater

---

[4] Individual compliance in social life can be traced to classical philosophy in the West. Friedrich Kratochwil puts classical theories into three groups: the first group is the Hobbesian or realist position which derives compliance with norms from force or the threat of force. A second group explains compliance in terms of the long-term utilitarian calculations of actors, a perspective perhaps best identifies with Hume's argument about the nature of conventions. The third group is the idealist position of Durkheim, who conceptualises norms and rules as "social facts" existing objectively and constraining individual choices. Cited by Isao Miyaoka, 'State compliance with international legitimate norms: wildlife preservationist pressures on Japanese fishing,' paper presented at the 41st Annual Convention of the International Studies Association, Los Angeles, 14–18 March 2000, in Columbia International Affairs Online, http://www.ciaonet.org/isa (assessed 3 March 2003).

[5] Many of the early writings by Chayes and Chayes on international regimes that appear in *International Organization* have been collected and published in Abraham Chayes and Antonia Handler-Chayes, *The new sovereignty: compliance with international regulatory agreements* (Cambridge, MA: Harvard University Press, 1995).

[6] George W. Downs, 'Enforcement and the evolution of cooperation,' *Michigan Journal of International Law*, Vol. 19, No. 2 (1998), pp. 319–344; George W. Downs, David Rocke, and Peter Barsoom, 'Is the good news about compliance good news about cooperation?' *International Organization*, Vol. 50, No. 3 (1996), pp. 379–406.

enforcement by regimes is necessary to exact state compliance in areas of deep integration and cooperation, because there is always a tendency for domestic actors to foul compliance rules, for example, in setting up trade barriers against free trade. Assessing compliance is difficult, as states dispute over what really makes compliance, especially when the rules are not very clear-cut due to the vagueness of the meanings of the terms used, as in many "soft" rules. In addition, concepts such as "political will", "trust", and "negotiation posture", upon which compliance decisions are made and based, are very difficult to measure.[7] Hence the degree of state compliance is often open to different interpretations.

Furthermore, most international treaties and organisations have little or no teeth with which to enforce their rules, and so rule compliance in many instances becomes a gentlemen's agreement.[8] Even in the case of the rulings of the World Court (the International Court of Justice), states can choose to ignore its rulings as they are non-binding. In general, some states choose to comply with some rules in some issues at some times, while others do not. As a result, state behaviour varies across time and space. Inevitably scholars have disputed over the extent of state compliance. Some, like Louis Henkin, argue that probably *"almost all nations observe almost all principles of international law and almost all of their obligations almost all of the time* [emphasis in original]".[9] Other scholars, like Marc Busch and Eric Reinhardt, found evidence to the contrary. They found, for example, that the total non-compliance with GATT (General Agreement on Tariffs and Trade) panel rulings approached

---

[7] Jana von Stein, 'Do treaties constrain or screen? Selection bias and treaty compliance,' *American Political Science Review*, forthcoming, quoting the works of James Vreeland.

[8] Peter Brookes, Senior Fellow, The Heritage Foundation, speaking at the "China 2020 Vision" conference held at the Royal Institute of International Affairs, The Chatham House, London, 30 March 2004.

[9] Louis Henkin, *How nations behave: law and foreign policy*, 2nd ed (New York: Columbia University Press, 1979), p. 47, cited in Kal Raustiala and Anne-Marie Slaughter, 'International law, international relations and compliance,' in Walter Carlsnaes, Thomas Risse, and Beth A. Simmons (eds), *Handbook of international relations* (London; Thousand Oaks; New Delhi: Sage Publications, 2002), p. 540.

30 per cent, and almost 60 per cent of rulings failed to elicit full compliance.[10]

The picture of global compliance is uneven and rather complex, since the nature of international politics is largely anarchical, meaning the absence of a central government at the global level comparable to governments at the national level. There is no one in an authoritative position to make a definitive judgement that would be acceptable to, let alone binding on, all states or even the majority of states. Consequently, what is compliance to some may not be regarded as such by others. Seen in this light, the nature of compliance and the standards for measuring compliance are by and large relative rather than absolute.

Why do states sometimes choose to comply then? In general, states are induced to do so because, in their overall strategic assessment, positive outcomes resulting from compliance outweigh negative ones. It is on the whole a rational calculation, rational in the sense that states would weigh the pros and cons carefully, based on information available to decision-makers. It is, however, a limited rationality. The fundamentals upon which calculations are made can change over time and over different issues when perceptions change or when new information is made available to decision-makers. In addition, decisions to comply or not to comply are in the main based on a combination of domestic and international factors.[11] The domestic factors may include the democratic form of government, leaders' commitment to certain course of action that favours compliance, and administrative and economic capacity. It is generally assumed that the more democratic a country is, the more compliant it will be with international rules and norms. This correlation is based on the observation that the general public and NGOs

---

[10] Cited in Raustiala and Slaughter, 'International law, international relations and compliance,' p. 549.

[11] Peter M. Haas, 'Choosing to comply: theorizing from international relations and comparative politics,' in Dinah Shelton (ed), *Commitment and compliance: the role of non-binding norms in the international legal system* (Oxford: Oxford University Press, 2000), pp. 43–64.

are able to put pressure on governments to comply. However, exceptions to this observation exist, as instances can be found in which authoritative governments can marshal enough resources in order to adhere to specific rules and norms that they see as beneficial to their countries. The administrative and economic capacity relates to the resources and technological know-how that a country can muster in order to comply. The administrative capacity is closely related to the level of education and training of bureaucrats. The international factors, on the other hand, may include the number of states involved in any compliance issue, the distribution of power among those states, and the influence of regimes on states,[12] such as the strength of the regimes' monitoring and verification process.[13]

How to deal with a country if it does not comply with international agreements? Two major ways have been suggested: one, called the "legalistic" school, stresses the importance of legal compliance of states. If states do not comply, then legal pressure should be brought to bear on their non-compliance, including the use of sanctions of various kinds available to complaining states to get redress. The other is liberal in nature and can be named the "liberal" school,[14] which calls for a flexible, diplomatic solution to resolve complaints arising out of non-compliance. These two schools represent two opposite ways of dispute settlement. They spring from two different philosophical approaches to dealing with the issue of compliance: enforcement and managerialism. Managerialism is

---

[12] Michael Faure and Jürgen Lefevere, 'Compliance with international environmental agreements,' in Norman J. Vig and Regina S. Axelrod (eds), *The global environment: institutions, law, and policy* (Washington, DC: Congressional Quarterly, 1999), pp. 141–144. For a study of international courts as regimes affecting state compliance, see Karen J. Alter, 'Do international courts enhance compliance with international law?' *Review of Asian and Pacific Studies*, Seikei University Center for Asian and Pacific Studies, Japan, No. 25 (July 2003), pp. 51–78.

[13] See also Edith Brown Weiss, 'Conclusions: understanding compliance with soft law,' in Shelton (ed), *Commitment and compliance*, pp. 535–553.

[14] Supachai Panitchpakdi calls these two schools the "litigation route" and the "policy route" respectively, in his public lecture at the University of Hong Kong, 21 May 2002.

based on "the premise that states have a propensity to comply with their international commitments."[15] When left alone, states are inclined to comply and can manage well their compliance behaviour. However, enforcement theorists think otherwise:[16] external pressure is required to bring about state compliance.

Teall Crossen, a law researcher at the University of Calgary in Canada, has compiled a useful bibliography on the compliance literature.[17] Apart from the two major schools of thought mentioned above — managerialism and enforcement, there are other theories which help to explain compliance behaviour of states. These include fairness theory, transnational legal process, reputational theory, and international relations theory, among others. According to Thomas Franck,[18] fairness in law, based on legitimacy and equity, encourages compliance. On the contrary, unfair laws are likely to complicate the issue of compliance. Although international relations theory, especially the neo-liberal school and constructivism,[19] also pays attention to the legitimate concerns of compliance issues, the mainstream neo-realist school, however, puts much greater emphasis on interests, reputations, and institutions, especially when power, wealth, and position (position in the international system with regard to states, and offices for individuals) are at stake.[20] From the perspective of foreign office officials, the promotion of state interests and the preservation of state integrity are far more

---

[15] Raustiala and Slaughter, 'International law, international relations and compliance,' in Carlsnaes, Risse, and Simmons (eds), *Handbook of international relations*, p. 542.

[16] Raustiala and Slaughter, pp. 542–544.

[17] Teall Crossen, 'Responding to global warming: a critique of the Kyoto Protocol compliance regime: an annotated bibliography,' a paper accessed through the Internet, April 2005.

[18] Thomas Franck, *Fairness in international law and institutions* (Oxford: Oxford University Press, 1995).

[19] Haas, 'Choosing to comply: theorizing from international relations and comparative politics,' in Shelton (ed), *Commitment and compliance*, pp. 43–64.

[20] Robert O. Keohane, 'International relations and international law: two optics,' *Harvard International Law Journal*, Vol. 38 (1997), pp. 487 ff.

important than a strict adherence to legal norms.[21] Reputational theory, proposed by Andrew Guzman,[22] suggests that states do care about potential damage to their reputation as a result of treaty violation, as well as the possibility of being censured. States, however, have multiple reputations, meaning that defection under one agreement may not affect their observance of and their reputation under another.[23] Transnational legal process, however, is a process through which an international law or rule, being deliberated at international forums, is subsequently internalised into domestic law through the actions of transnational actors.[24] There is, therefore, a need to study the social, political, and legal processes through which this process of internalisation works and the various actors involved, be they diplomats, academics, NGO advocates, or political leaders.[25]

Most, if not all, of these theories are subject to how states or their representative actors interpret compliance. A study of compliance has reviewed that different states may rely on different standards of evidence, types of information, and varying definitions of what constitutes "significant" non-compliance.[26] Examples of different standards of evidence may include such hard evidence as a "smoking gun", or sufficient information so that the non-compliance situation is "beyond reasonable doubt", or soft evidence such as "a preponderance of evidence". Types of information may

---

[21] Richard B. Bilder, 'Beyond compliance: helping nations cooperate,' in Shelton (ed), *Commitment and compliance*, pp. 67–73.

[22] Andrew T. Guzman, 'A compliance-based theory of international law,' *California Law Review*, Vol. 90, No. 6 (December 2002), pp. 1,823 ff.

[23] George W. Downs and Michael A. Jones, 'Reputation, compliance, and international law,' *The Journal of Legal Studies*, Vol. 31 (2002), pp. 95 ff.

[24] Harold Hongju Koh, 'Why do nations obey international law?' *Yale Law Journal*, Vol. 106, No. 8 (June 1997), p. 2,599.

[25] Harold Hongju Koh, 'Bringing international law home,' *Houston Law Review*, Vol. 35 (1998), p. 623.

[26] Michael Moodel and Amy Sands, 'Introduction: new approaches to compliance with arms control and non-proliferation agreements,' The *Nonproliferation Review*, Vol. 8, No. 1 (Spring 2001), Internet printout, p. 6.

range from nationally collected intelligence, which is a source of information gathering preferred by the United States, to open resources. And "significant" non-compliance can mean any of the following five categories of violations:[27]

1. Minor technical or inadvertent problem;
2. Different interpretations or gaps in treaty language;
3. Significant, detected, overt violations;
4. Significant, detected, but covert violations; and
5. Suspected covert violations of possible significance.

The application of different standards, on the other hand, can be attributed to imprecise language, divergent texts or honest differences of interpretation. The prejudice and ignorance of state actors also contribute towards differences in opinion about compliance.[28]

How to test these divergent theories against China's compliance behaviour? Detailed case studies are in order. As a first step towards answering this question, it is necessary to examine China's treaty accession in order to realise the extent to which China is involved in rule compliance, rule interpretation, rule adjudication, and rule making.

CHINA'S TREATY ENGAGEMENT

Although China's entry into international agreements is a primary measure of its global responsibility, there is a difference between signing a treaty *per se* and adhering to the spirit of the treaty.[29]

---

[27] *Ibid.*

[28] Luke T. Lee, *China and international agreements: a study of compliance* (Leyden: A.W. Sijthoff; Durham, NC: Rule of Law Press, 1969), p. 9.

[29] Ann Kent has provided a useful list of ways to measure China's compliance in human rights issue. See her *China, the United Nations, and human rights* (Philadelphia, PA: University of Pennsylvania Press, 1999), p. 7. Another recent publication has also provided a general framework for assessing compliance. See Shelton (ed), *Commitment and compliance*, especially the chapter by Haas, 'Choosing to comply.'

(The latter is, of course, an interesting and complex issue, but lies beyond the immediate concern of this study.)[30] Nevertheless, the signing of a treaty (and its subsequent ratification) represents an elementary yet fundamental step towards treaty compliance. As of 2003, China is party to 266 international treaties, covering a wide range of issues, from politics to economics, social to cultural, and science to sports. An examination of the timing of China's accession to these agreements reveals several interesting features (see Figure 3.1).

Firstly, the People's Republic of China (PRC) only started to engage substantially with the multilateral treaty system since 1971, the year in which it gained its seat in the United Nations. Before that, from its establishment in 1949, China had only acceded to six treaties, five in 1952 and one in 1958. The five treaties acceded to in 1952 were the Protocol for the Prohibition of the Use in War of Asphyxiating Poisonous or Other Gases, and the four Geneva Conventions relating to certain humanitarian conducts during military conflicts.[31] The single treaty acceded to in 1958 was the Convention for the Unification of Certain Rules Relating to International Carriage

---

[30] There are, however, quite a lot of useful studies of China's legal system and legal culture. See, for example, Randall Peerenboom, *China's long march toward rule of law* (Cambridge: Cambridge University Press, 2002); Pitman B. Potter, *The Chinese legal system: globalization and local legal culture* (London; New York: Routledge, 2001); Karen Turner, James V. Feinerman, and R. Kent Guy (eds), *The limits of the rule of law in China* (Seattle: University of Washington Press, 2000); and Stanley B. Lubman, *Bird in a cage: legal reform in China* (Stanford: Stanford University Press, 1999).

[31] These are the Geneva Convention Relative to the Treatment of Prisoners of War, the Geneva Convention for the Amelioration of the Condition of the Wounded Sick and Shipwrecked Members of Armed Forces at Sea, the Geneva Convention Relative to the Protection of Civilian Persons in Time of War, and the Geneva Convention for the Amelioration of the Condition of the Wounded and Sick in Armed Forces in the Field. The People's Republic of China declared in 1952 their recognition of those Conventions, but only ratified them in 1956 by the Standing Committee of the National People's Congress. The document signifying the ratification of these Conventions was deposited with the Red Cross authorities in Switzerland later that year. For a detailed analysis of China's relations with the International Red Cross, see Gerald Chan, *China and international organisations* (Hong Kong: Oxford University Press, 1989), chapter 5.

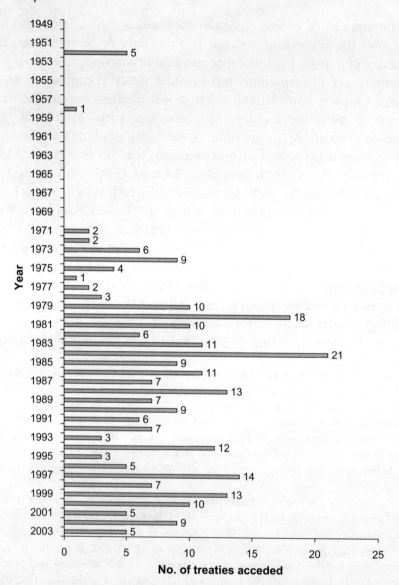

Figure 3.1 China's Accession to International Treaties, 1949–2003

Source: Compiled from the website of the Ministry of Foreign Affairs of the PRC ('China's participation in multilateral treaties', in Chinese) http://www.fmprc.gov.cn/chn/wjb/zzjg/tyfls/tfsckzlk/zgcjddbty/t85211.htm (accessed 30 April 2005).

Note 1: The word "accession" is used here to refer to the signing of the treaty, its recognition, ratification, or its becoming effective in and applicable to China. The year indicates, in most cases, the year in which China signed the treaty or the treaty became effective in China.

Note 2: The total number of treaties acceded = 266.

by Air. Hence, for two decades from 1949 to 1970, China was more or less outside the international treaty system.

Secondly, the year 1971 marks a watershed in China's engagement with the multilateral treaty system. Subsequent to its admission to the UN, the country steadily gained entry into other specialised agencies of the UN system. The treaties signed between 1971 and 1979 largely reflected China's increased participation in that system. For example, the United Nations Educational, Scientific and Cultural Organisation was the first specialised agency to recognise the PRC, on 29 October 1971, four days after it was admitted into the UN. In 1972, the Constitution of the World Health Organisation became effective in and applicable to China. This was followed by others, including the Food and Agriculture Organisation, the Universal Postal Union, the World Meteorological Organisation, and the International Maritime Organisation, all in 1973; and the Convention on International Civil Aviation and various subsequent Protocols relating to the Amendments to the Convention in 1974.[32]

Thirdly, the surge in engagement with the multilateral treaty system happened only after China adopted its reform and opening-up policy. The year 1979 marked the first year in which China became heavily involved in accession to international treaties, signing ten of them that year followed by 18 a year later, reaching a peak of 21 in 1984. Many of the treaties recognised by the PRC in 1984 related to workers' rights of various kinds under the purview of the International Labour Organisation.[33] In fact, the 1980s witnessed a golden decade in China's accession to international treaties. The Tiananmen Incident of 1989 did not seem to have dampened China's enthusiasm in gaining entry into the multilateral treaty

---

[32] For the dates on which most of the UN specialised agencies recognised the PRC subsequent to its admission to the UN, see Samuel S. Kim, *China, the United Nations, and world order* (Princeton, NJ : Princeton University Press, 1979), p. 347.

[33] The government of the Republic of China (the Nationalist government) signed these treaties in 1936. And the PRC recognised them in 1984 and they became effective in mainland China since then. See the website of the Ministry of Foreign Affairs of the PRC (under "Multilateral Treaties", in "Treaties and Law") http://www.fmprc.gov.cn/chn/premade/24475/dabian.htm (accessed 11 March 2003).

system, although the tempo since then seems to have slowed down somewhat. This slowdown is due probably to the fact that there are fewer treaties to be concluded at the global level, since the "easy" topics on which there is widespread consensus among nation-states have been largely completed.[34] All in all, the bulk of China's multilateral treaties has been signed since 1979, some 231 out of 266, representing about 87 per cent of all treaties that it has acceded to since its establishment in 1949.[35]

Figure 3.2 indicates that China has increased substantially its accession to international treaties and hence its participation in international organisations since the 1970s, although there was a small plateau between 1975 and 1979, coinciding with the death of Mao Zedong and the political turmoil surrounding the rise and fall of the so-called Gang of Four.[36] From the point of view of rational decision-making, it would be safe to assume that Chinese leaders could have estimated that the benefits derived from an increase in accession and participation must have outweighed the costs involved. The costs obviously vary according to the terms of the treaties concerned and the commitments that China has to make as a treaty member. Nonetheless China's behaviour in this respect indicates the progress made in its national development, its readiness

---

[34] See Shelton (ed), *Commitment and compliance*, p. 555.

[35] The calculation is based on Figure 3.1. A full list of the treaties can be found in the Ministry of Foreign Affairs website. According to the UN, about 40,000 multilateral treaties and international agreements have been deposited with the UN Secretary-General. Some 520 of them are major ones. See the UN Treaty Collection, http://untreaty.un.org (accessed 11 May 2005). The Fletcher School of Law and Diplomacy at Tufts University in Maryland, USA, maintains a project on multilateral treaties in the Internet called Tufts Multilaterals Project (http://fletcher.tufts.edu/multilaterals.html). Its chronological index collects the major treaties since 1899 together with some historical documents. It would be interesting, as a separate project, to compare China's involvement in the multilateral treaty system with similar involvements of other countries. Such a comparative assessment could take into consideration a country's political, economic, social and legal developments.

[36] They were Jiang Qing (Mao's wife), Wang Hongwen, Zhang Chunqiao, and Yao Wenyuan.

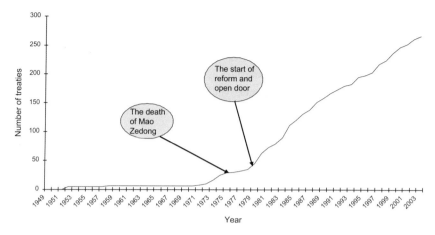

Figure 3.2 China's Accession to International Treaties, 1949–2003 (Cumulative Sum)

to open up itself to international scrutiny, and its willingness to shoulder some global responsibilities and to subject itself to certain compliance tests.

In reviewing the study of international law in China, Zou Keyuan, a Chinese legal expert based in Singapore, has identified three periods of development: the socialist approach (1949–1965); the three-world approach (1966–1977); and the international approach (1978 to the present).[37] In the current period of international approach, the study of international law has become "normalised", although traces of influence from the two earlier periods can still be found. This current period coincides with the reform and opening-up period in which China has acceded to or ratified a large number of international treaties. The period represents a significant break from the earlier revolutionary periods. One major problem that China faces today is how to reconcile its international obligations with its domestic law, especially in the areas of human rights, trade, environmental protection, and arms control. How to turn

---

[37] Zou Keyuan, 'Chinese approach to international law,' in Hu Weixing, Gerald Chan, and Zha Daojiong (eds), *China's international relations in the 21st century* (Lanham: University Press of America, 2000), p. 188.

international law into domestic legislation has become a long-term ongoing process of legal modernisation.

Two scholars at the Georgetown University Law Center in Washington DC, James Feinerman and Daniel Chang, have complied a record of China's compliance with some international obligations and treaties, which shows that China's compliance behaviour is rather mixed but has made improvements. At least it is not worse than those of many other developing countries at a similar stage of development.[38]

SUMMARY

This chapter has discussed the concept of compliance in some details and has indicated the difficulties involved in assessing the compliance of states based on a host of domestic and international factors, as well as different understandings of what constitutes compliance among the states and international regimes involved. China's accession to international treaties, as analysed here, serves as a good entry point to an assessment of China's global compliance behaviour, which needs to be examined in greater details using in-depth case analyses, to be discussed in the following chapters.

---

[38] James V Feinerman and Daniel Chang's project on Chinese practice of international law in the post-Mao era, cited by, among others, A.S. Bhalla and Qiu Shufang, *The employment impact of China's WTO accession* (London and New York: RoutledgeCurzon, 2004), p. 163.

Part II

Part II

4

China's WTO Compliance

China, as a full member of the WTO,... will have the right and responsibility to fashion and enforce the rules of open trade.

US President George W. Bush, 2002[1]

China will build the WTO into "an open, fair, transparent and rational mechanism."

China's Trade Representative, Ambassador Sun Zhenyu, 2002[2]

Never in the history of the world has a country committed so much to change, largely on a voluntary basis, as China has done to adhere to the rules of the World Trade Organisation.[3] China's entry into the

---

[1] President Bush speaking at a news conference in Beijing on 21 February 2002. See http://biz.yahoo.com/rf/020221/pek91398_1.html (accessed 27 February 2002).

[2] Quoted in *Taipei Times*, Internet ed., 29 January 2002. Sun is China's first Trade Representative to the WTO in Geneva. Before that, he was a Vice-Minister of the Ministry of Foreign Trade and Economic Cooperation and a member of the GATT/WTO leading small group. See Margaret M. Pearson, 'The case of China's accession to GATT/WTO,' in David M. Lampton, (ed), *The making of Chinese foreign and security policy in the era of reform* (Stanford: Stanford University Press, 2001), p. 348.

[3] In July 2002, the China Security Review Commission of the United States-China Commission issued a report to the US Congress, chapter 3 of which is entitled

world body in December 2001 signals the beginning of a shift in global political and economic order. Not only is the world's most populated country and potentially its largest market now a member of the WTO, China's entry also marks a milestone in its global behaviour — from one based mainly on power and ideology to one based largely on commonly accepted rules.[4] In addition, not only has the power balance within the WTO been drastically altered,[5] but also how global political economy is going to be governed. This is an event that goes beyond the immediate concerns of business-people to the way in which international relations in general, and international political economy in particular, is going to change.

This chapter analyses China's international behaviour shortly before and after its entry into the WTO, focusing on the ideas of responsibility and compliance. The General Agreement on Tariffs and Trade (the predecessor of the WTO), together with the World Bank and the International Monetary Fund, made up the post-war Bretton Woods architecture designed largely by the United States to build its cherished global economic order. At present, the US

'China and the World Trade Organization'. On p. 8 of that chapter, the report says, "China's accession documents are unprecedented within the WTO or its predecessor, the General Agreement on Tariffs and Trade (GATT), in terms of their complexity, range of specific commitments, and number of deviations permitted at the time of accession." For a soft copy of the report, see http://www.uscc.gov/ch3-02.htm (accessed 16 July 2002).

[4] On the successful conclusion of negotiations on China's membership of the WTO in September 2001, the Director-General of the WTO, New Zealander Mike Moore, said: "With China's membership, the WTO will take a major step towards becoming a truly world organisation. The near-universal acceptance of its rules-based system will serve a pivotal role in underpinning global economic cooperation." See http://www.wto.org/english/news_e/press01_e/pr243_e.htm (accessed 28 February 2002).

[5] According to European Union Trade Commissioner Pascal Lamy, China's entry into the WTO sparks off a major shift in the balance of power within the global trade body. The United States and the EU have been the dominant players in the WTO, with Japan and the developing world competing to get their issues on the agenda for discussion. This sort of four-corner power game has changed to a five-corner game with the inclusion of China. Associated Press World Business news, 15 February 2002 (accessed through Yahoo, 27 February 2002).

is overwhelmingly dominant in this global economic order. Now that China is a member of the WTO, many of its trade partners, especially the United States, will closely watch how responsible its trading behaviour is going to be and how compliant it would be with the rules of the WTO.

The rest of this chapter is divided into five sections:

- The first section gives a brief history of China's bumpy ride on the road to become a WTO member. It provides a context against which to better understand China's predicament in turning itself from a centrally-planned economy to a market-orientated one, including the numerous difficulties it faces in turning itself into a rule-based system compatible with the global system.
- The second section discusses and in some ways retraces the idea of responsibility in China's international behaviour and the concept of compliance in China's participation in international organisations, especially in the WTO. It lays a theoretical foundation for the analysis in the next section.
- The third section analyses the monitoring mechanisms used by the WTO and the United States to monitor China's WTO compliance.
- The fourth section examines what China has done so far to fulfil its duties and obligations under the rules of the global trading regime, as a way to comply with its entry requirements.
- In the final section, I offer some of my own thoughts on China's WTO compliance, looking briefly into the near future and the dilemma faced by its trade partners.

THE BUMPY RIDE TO THE WTO: FROM REJECTION TO RECEPTION

The history of China's relations with the WTO started with the formation of the General Agreement on Tariffs and Trade (GATT), shortly after the Second World War.[6] The Republic of China (ROC)

---

[6] The historical narrative in the following paragraphs draws from materials found on China's Ministry of Foreign Affairs website http://www.fmprc.gov.cn, Taiwan's

became a contracting member when it signed the Final Act of Geneva on 30 October 1947, and subsequently one of the 23 founding members of GATT on 21 May 1948. The ROC formally withdrew from GATT in early 1950, amidst confusion resulting from the move of its seat of government to the island of Taiwan upon the establishment in Beijing of the People's Republic of China (PRC) in October 1949.[7] For a time, neither the ROC nor the PRC was represented in GATT. The PRC initially had little interest in trading with non-communist countries and thus little need for GATT membership. In any event, it is unlikely that GATT would have welcomed the PRC's membership at that time either, because of China's socialist, closed system of trading and its anti-capitalist and anti-American stance. In the tense and difficult years after its move to Taiwan, the ROC did not regard GATT membership as a high priority. However, in the 1960s, as Taiwan began to establish itself as an important trading power, interest in GATT participation returned. In 1965, the ROC began attending GATT meetings as an observer.

A major change came about in October 1971 when the PRC was formally admitted into the United Nations, while the ROC was forced to leave the world body. Subsequently, China acquired membership of a large number of specialised agencies affiliated with the UN system, forcing Taiwan to leave them. These agencies included the United Nations Educational, Scientific and Cultural Organisation, the World Health Organisation, the Food and Agriculture Organisation, and others. In the case of GATT, as a result of China's insistence on a "de-recognition" of the ROC upon its admission to the UN, Taiwan lost its observer status in November 1971. During the 1970s, China was not ready for GATT membership. It was only after the adoption of the reform and opening-up policy in the late

---

Ministry of Foreign Affairs website http://www.mofa.gov.tw, and the WTO website http://www.wto.org/english/news_e/press01_e/pr243_e.htm (accessed 27 February 2002).

[7] Taiwan withdrew from GATT at the urging of the US, which was worried that the PRC might replace Taiwan in GATT, thus circumventing the US trade embargo on China as a result of China's entry into the Korean War.

1970s that China's external trade began to grow rapidly and subsequently there was a felt need to enter GATT.

In the early 1980s the PRC gained observer status in GATT and eventually membership of the Multi-Fibre Agreement, a sub-group of the world trading system devoted to textile trade. China formally applied for membership of GATT in 1986, triggering a long process of negotiations with the GATT secretariat as well as with China's trade partners. The Tiananmen Incident of 1989 set back China's effort to normalise and improve its trade links with the outside world, as many countries in the West applied trade sanctions of one kind or another against China. In 1990 Taiwan began its own effort to rejoin GATT and became an observer again in 1992. Both China's and Taiwan's applications were transferred to the WTO in 1995, when it was formed to replace GATT. Because of China's political insistence, an agreement was reached so that China would enter the WTO ahead of Taiwan and that Taiwan's membership name in the WTO should read "Separate Customs Territory of Taiwan, Penghu, Kinmen and Matsu", or "Chinese Taipei" for short.

After 15 years of tough negotiations on the terms and conditions of membership,[8] China was finally admitted into the World Trade Organisation in November 2001 as a developing country and became its 143rd member in December 2001 upon completion of the process of ratification and accession. One day after China was admitted into the WTO, Taiwan also gained admission, but as a developed country under the long and winding name. Although Taiwan was unable to enter the organisation under its official state name, its newly acquired membership was a great victory for the Taipei authorities, as this was the first major inter-governmental organisation that Taiwan was able to gain entry into for more

---

[8] Part of the reasons why it took so long was because of the procedural changes from GATT to the WTO. The WTO is more legalistic than GATT; its functions are more comprehensive, covering both trade and non-trade issues; and China was required to enter into trade agreements with all the major trading nations, which were time-consuming to reach. Public lecture delivered by Supachai Panitchakdi, Director-General designate of the WTO, at the University of Hong Kong, 21 May 2002.

Table 4.1 Timeline of China's and Taiwan's Accession to the WTO

	China	Taiwan
1947 October 30		Republic of China signs the Final Act of Geneva for the creation of GATT
1948 May 21		Becomes founding member of GATT
1949 October 1	People's Republic of China established	
1958		Withdraws from GATT
1965 March 16		Becomes an observer
1971 October 25	*The UN adopts a resolution to admit China*	
1971 November 19		Loses observer status
1986	Applies to join	
1990 January 1		Submits application to rejoin
1992 September		Becomes observer again
1995 January 1	*WTO replaces GATT*	
1995 July 11	Becomes an observer	
2001 November 10	Entry approved	
2001 November 11		Entry approved
2001 December 11	Accession completed	
2002 January 1		Accession completed

Sources: Adapted from information found on China's Ministry of Foreign Affairs website http://www.fmprc.gov.cn and Taiwan's Ministry of Foreign Affairs website http://www.mofa.gov.tw (accessed 27 February 2002).

than ten years.[9] Chinese Taipei became the 144th member in January 2002, under the same terms and conditions as for many other members and on an equal footing with them. The outcome is seen as a win-win solution for all parties concerned. Table 4.1 summarises the relationship among China, Taiwan, and the WTO (and GATT prior to its formation).

---

[9] Before the WTO, the other "major" international organisation that Taiwan was able to acquire membership of was the Asia-Pacific Economic Cooperation forum in 1991 under the name "Chinese Taipei".

With membership of the WTO secured, China becomes a full-fledged member of the Bretton Woods system, having joined the World Bank and the International Monetary Fund in 1980. This event marks a new stage in China's transition from socialism to a largely market-driven economy and in China's arduous process of opening up and reform started more than two decades ago. China's integration with the global economy is near complete.[10]

---

[10] What are the implications of China's entry into the WTO for China and the world? Although this question is not the focus of this chapter; it is an important area to note. Several trends are discernible at this stage, concerning domestic consequences and international implications. They carry both challenges and opportunities.

Despite its significance, China's entry into the WTO continues to stimulate debates within China, between the conservatives and the reformers. (This two-camp categorisation, though crude, is heuristic.) While the reformers stress the importance of membership and the political and economic benefits that may flow from it, the conservatives warn that China's economy will face severe competition, domestic breakdown and foreign control. The possible negative impacts include: Firstly, the agriculture sector in which cheap foreign imports will leave many traditional farms out of work. The resultant unemployment in the vast rural area, together with existing unemployment in the cities, may create social tensions and unrest that might lead to instability and even chaos in society. (It has been estimated that the size of unemployment can reach 47 million. See testimony of William H. Overholt before the US-China Commission, 18 January 2002, at http://www.uscc.gov/tesove.htm, accessed 8 March 2002. A Chinese White Paper on employment and social welfare issued in April 2002 puts the number of registered urban unemployed at 6.8 million at the end of 2001, with about 150 million surplus rural labourers. It also indicates that the number of urban jobless may rise to more than 20 million over the next four years. See *South China Morning Post*, 30 April 2002, p. 1.) Secondly, the many state-owned enterprises will not be able to compete with the outside world. Many will collapse unless greater government subsidy is available, which is currently in short supply. Thirdly, foreign companies will expose China's financial and service industries — like banking, insurance and telecommunication — to severe competition and possible take-overs. These and other reservations, though not entirely groundless, must be balanced by benefits which may accrue from a more open international market for Chinese products and from other opportunities, such as investment attractions and political goodwill.

The prospect of cheap Chinese products flooding the international market is the major concern of many China's trade partners, including those in the developing world which are competing with China for exports. However, for consumers in many parts of the world, it can be seen as a blessing because they will be able to enjoy cheap Chinese products. On balance, countries around the world welcome China's entry into the WTO, because that will help booster two-way trade, to the benefit of the global and local economies. The fact that many of China's major trade partners concluded trade agreements with it before its accession to the WTO testifies to the merits of engaging China rather than isolating it from the global economy. Trade frictions between China and its trade partners will not diminish, however, but the gratifying aspect is that these frictions will now have a new channel for resolution, that is, through the rule-based Dispute Resolution procedures in the WTO, rather than to seek redress through bilateral trade retaliations. Many of the fears harboured initially by China's trade partners in neighbouring countries proved to be excessive, as exports of East Asian economies grew by 5.3 per cent in 2002. Of these, exports to China, including Hong Kong, jumped by 32.7 per cent. See *South China Morning Post*, 20 February 2003, p. 9.

China's entry into the WTO provides an opportunity for the Chinese government to enhance its legitimacy before the eyes of the Chinese people, if the transition is handled smoothly and results in improved living standard. The opposite can also be possible, that is, the government may lose its legitimacy, if the transition proves to be detrimental to the overall health of the economy or leads to social instability. Either way, the process of increasingly opening up and reform is likely to lead to a greater demand for political change and openness as a result of increasing public awareness of civil rights.

Another opportunity is the possible spill-over effect of membership of the WTO of both China and Taiwan to greater communication and integration between the two. The trade offices of China and Taiwan based in Geneva, the site of the WTO headquarters, provide an additional channel for dialogue on trade matters, either in a bilateral or multilateral way. Taiwan hopes that this will lead to a more formal way of starting a dialogue on trade across the Taiwan Strait and to more direct or indirect communications of one kind or another, based on equality in negotiation status. Much depends on the goodwill on both sides to make good use of this opportunity. At the moment, it seems to depend more on the Beijing side than the Taipei side as to whether or not to limit the new-found channel to trade matters or to expand it to cover other matters. It also depends on whether Beijing prefers to continue to shut the door, requiring Taiwan to accept the "one-China" principle before meaningful talks can begin. As of early 2003, the trade offices of both China and Taiwan in Geneva have agreed to talk to each other on some trade disputes between the two, but disagreements over Taiwan's official status in Geneva remain to be settled.

In any case, membership of both in the WTO opens a window of opportunity for easing tensions across the Strait and for providing a mechanism for dispute resolution, which might be built upon to increase mutual understanding and trust.

RESPONSIBILITY AND COMPLIANCE: "WESTERN INSTRUMENTS, CHINESE APPLICATION"?[11]

China's membership in the WTO carries onerous duties and responsibilities, laid down in detail in a legal document some 900 pages long.[12] In essence, China has committed:[13]

- To provide non-discriminatory treatment to all WTO members.
- To eliminate dual pricing practices as well as differences in treatment accorded to goods produced for sale in China in comparison to those produced for export.
- To remove price controls for protecting domestic industries or services providers.
- To implement the WTO Agreement in an effective and uniform manner by revising some of its domestic laws and enacting new legislation fully in compliance with the WTO Agreement.
- To allow all its enterprises to import and export all goods, and trade with them throughout the customs territory with limited exceptions, within three years of accession.
- To stop maintaining or introducing any export subsidies on agricultural products.

Many of the restrictions that foreign companies have at present in China will be eliminated or considerably eased after a three-year phase-out period. In other areas, like the protection of intellectual property rights, China will have to implement the TRIPS (Trade-related Aspects of Intellectual Property Rights) Agreement in full

---

[11] The sub-heading draws its idea from "Chinese learning as essence, Western learning as instrument", a phrase popularised during the May Fourth Movement of China in 1919 when China was debating about the path of its development and modernisation.

[12] China's WTO commitments are documented in (1) Protocol on the Accession of the People's Republic of China, which contains the terms of membership; (2) Report of the Working Party on the Accession of China; and (3) annexes containing market access commitments.

[13] http://www.wto.org/english/news_e/press01_e/pr243_e.htm (accessed 28 February 2002).

from the date of accession. In simple terms, China has to adopt
non-discriminatory practices and to increase transparency in business
transactions in accordance with WTO rules and regulations.
However, it reserves the right of exclusive state trading for some
products such as cereals, tobacco, fuels and minerals, and maintains
some restrictions on transportation and distribution of goods inside
the country, under some safeguard rules.

How do we evaluate China's responsibility as a member of the
WTO? The idea of responsibility in personal affairs is not new,[14] as
its importance in human relationships has been stressed from time
immemorial, in China as in other parts of the world. In the study of
international relations, it seems to have attracted the attention of the
"Cosmopolitan" or "International Society" school of thought, which
is a stream of thought closely associated with the "English School"[15]
of international relations. Mainstream international relations
approaches, such as the Realist school or the Liberalist school, do
not pay as much attention to the idea of responsibility. Still, the
English School has little to say about the idea of responsibility in
international affairs, relative to the growing volume of literature on
global politics. In a way, the idea of responsibility in international
relations is under-developed, and is overshadowed by considerations of power and interests. For instance, the English School, as
had been pointed out by one of its leading proponents, Hedley Bull,
suggests that great powers in world affairs have a special responsibility in seeing that there is a modicum of order in a largely anarchical world,[16] where a central authoritative enforcement agency
comparable to a national government within a state is missing. In

---

[14] For an explanation of the concept of responsibility, including personal responsibility, see Andrew Heywood, *Key concepts in politics* (New York: St. Martin's Press,
2000), pp. 145–155.
[15] The "English School" has a website, hosted by the Department of Politics and
International Relations at the University of Kent, see http://www.ukc.ac.uk/
politics/englishschool/. See also http://www.leeds.ac.uk/polis/englishschool/.
[16] Hedley Bull, *The anarchical society: a study of order in world politics*, 3rd ed
(Basingstoke and New York: Palgrave. 2002), pp. 212–220.

other words, great powers have a role to play in managing world affairs, in setting up rules of engagement, and in maintaining the status quo largely in their favour. This view, of course, is under-pinned by power politics, and is therefore disputed by the Liberalists and strongly challenged by the Structuralists or Marxists, not so much on the ground of the exercise of power *per se*, but on the ground of the resulting inequality and injustice. The idea of responsibility is therefore contested and its importance subject to different interpretations.

China's decision to join the WTO must have gone through cautious and even agonising considerations by its leaders, for there are obviously pros and cons associated with membership. In the long run, more gains are likely to accrue than losses. The task ahead for the Chinese leaders, therefore, is to minimise as much as possi-ble the risks involved while trying to maximise the opportunities. By signing the documents of accession, China has accepted extraordi-nary responsibilities of changing the ways it used to work. Will China become a responsible member of the WTO? No one can say for sure, despite the assurances given by its top leaders, including Premier Zhu Rongji and Vice Premier Wen Jiabao (who has assumed premiership since early 2003),[17] that China will. Its trade partners are, however, not so certain: they are rather sceptical, and they begin to take steps to monitor China's compliance with the rules it has agreed to follow. Hence monitoring China's compliance has become a major way to assessing China's global responsibility. The fact that China decided to enter the WTO shows that the country is at least prepared to subject itself to compliance tests.

Despite China's willingness to comply with WTO rules, is it capable of doing so? This is the sort of question that sticks in the minds of many of China's trade partners. Peter M. Haas, a professor at the University of Massachusetts at Amherst, has pointed out that for a country that is willing to comply but lacks the capacity to do so, what others can do is to monitor, assess, and enforce compliance

---

[17] *South China Morning Post*, 18 February 2003, p. 7.

on the one hand and, on the other, to assist that country to build the necessary capacity to do so.[18] This is precisely what China's largest trading partner, the United States, has begun to do, on its own as well as in coordination with other countries and international organisations. From a theoretical point of view, the United States' approach is basically a Neo-Realist one, coupled with elements of Liberal Institutionalism and Social Constructivism.[19] A Neo-Realist view suggests that state behaviour is based on material capacity, that the US is prepared to use its power to monitor and to ensure that China complies, and that the US will not shy away from exerting pressure on China to achieve such an outcome. This kind of approach is aimed at promoting America's commercial interests. A Liberal Institutionalist view, however, suggests that state behaviour is shaped by international regimes — rules, norms, and principles of international institutions. From this perspective, the US plans to work closely with the WTO, and other like-minded countries, to monitor and assess China's compliance behaviour. Finally, a Social Constructivist approach stresses the importance of shared knowledge and a common understanding in shaping state behaviour. To achieve this, the US works with liberal government officials, academics, businesspeople and groups in China to promote the idea of free trade and to help this "epistemic community"[20] to strengthen China's capacity to comply. In the main, the United States takes a two-pronged approach towards China: while trying to negotiate issues of non-compliance at an early stage and in an amicable way as far as possible, it is prepared to use unilateral retaliatory actions as well as to invoke the Dispute Settlement Mechanism of the WTO to get what it wants.

---

[18] Peter M. Haas, 'Choosing to comply: theorising from international relations and comparative politics,' in Dinah Shelton (ed), *Commitment and compliance: the role of non-binding norms in the international legal system* (Oxford: Oxford University Press, 2000), pp. 47 and 60.

[19] Haas, 'Choosing to comply,' pp. 51–64.

[20] David M. Lampton (ed), *The making of Chinese foreign and security policy in the era of reform* (Stanford: Stanford University Press, 2001).

HOW EFFECTIVE ARE THE MONITORING MECHANISMS?

No country is more concerned about China's WTO compliance than the United States, as the US is the world's largest trading nation and China the fourth largest, after the US, Japan, and the European Union (in 2001).[21] To the US, China is its third largest trading partner. And to China, the US is its largest trading partner. In 2004, bilateral trade reached a record of US$232 billion,[22] up from $191.7 billion in 2003,[23] representing a huge increase from $116 billion in 2000 and a far cry from $5 billion in 1980. The US registered a record trade deficit of $162 billion with China in 2004, and this has become a major source of trade conflict between the two. The US provides China with the largest source of foreign investment after Hong Kong and Taiwan, with US$44.29 billion actually invested in China between 1979 and 2003, and US$4.2 billion in 2003 alone, following a peak of US$5.4 billion in 2002.[24] Other trade partners that are concerned about China's compliance behaviour include the European Union, Japan, Canada and Australia. China's Asian neighbours, especially those in Southeast Asia, are more concerned about its increasing economic competitiveness and its ability to divert foreign investments away from them, while benefiting from increasing volumes of trade with China.

The US monitors China's WTO compliance via three ways: unilateral actions, intergovernmental coordination, and multilateral

---

[21] According to WTO senior economist Karl-Michael Finger. See *South China Morning Post*, 3 May 2002, Business, p. 1. In 2000 China was the seventh leading exporter and eighth largest importer, according to *WTO News*, Press 243, 17 September 2001. For a comparison of the major economic statistics of the world's 46 major trading nations, see *Guoji wenti yanjiu* [*International Studies*], Beijing, No. 2 (2002), pp. 54–55.

[22] *The Standard*, Hong Kong, 8 April 2005, p. A61.

[23] The US-China Business Council, at http://www.uschina.org/statistics/tradetable.html and http://www.uschina.org/statistics/fdi1979-03.htm (accessed 3 December 2004); Robert A. Kapp, Testimony to the Subcommittee on Trade, Committee on Ways and Means, US House of Representatives, 10 July 2001, at http://www.uschina.org/public/testimony/testimony12.html (accessed 7 March 2002).

[24] US-China Business Council.

arrangements. Of these, America's own unilateral effort is the most significant. Its monitoring mechanism is massive. In fact, it is the largest of any trade agreement,[25] involving many staff posted in Washington DC, Geneva, and some major cities in China. At the heart of this mechanism is an inter-agency group called the Trade Policy Staff Committee (TPSC), in particular its Sub-Committee on China's WTO Compliance, formed by the Bush administration. This inter-agency group, chaired by the US Trade Representative Office's Deputy Assistant, brings together representatives from some 20 different agencies in the US government, including the Departments of Treasury, Commerce, State, Agriculture, and Labor.[26] It held its inaugural meeting in December 2001 and is scheduled to meet every month to consider China's obligations, steps that China has taken, and ways that the US should respond.[27] Its mandate is to coordinate US government efforts to ensure that China complies with its WTO commitments. Additional meetings of various sub-groups are also scheduled regularly.[28] The TPSC is required to submit annual reports to the government on China's WTO compliance, the first one being made towards the end of 2002 (to be discussed later).

---

[25] Charlene Barshefsky, 'China's WTO accession; America's choice,' Speech to the National Association of Counties, Washington DC, 6 March 2000.

[26] It is interesting to point out that, as of March 2002, the US Trade Representative Office had 178 full-time staff and a budget of US$26 million. This budget was in fact not much more than what the Defense Department spent on stationery each year. With this budget, the Office addressed US$2 trillion in US trade with the world (See Barshefsky, 2000). In view of China's entry into the WTO, funding for agencies with responsibility for trade agreement compliance and administration of US trade laws was increased by $22 million and full-time staff by 100 (Commerce News, United States Department of Commerce, 31 March 2000, at http://www.ita.doc.gov/media/CommerceNews/TPCC00.html (accessed 28 February 2002).

[27] Robert B. Zoellick, Speech given to the US-China Business Council, Washington DC, 31 January 2002.

[28] Shaun Donnelly, Testimony before the US-China Commission's Public Hearing on WTO Compliance and Sectoral Issues, 18 January 2002, http://usinfo.state.gov/regional/ea/uschina/donnelly.htm (accessed 28 February 2002).

The TPSC is one of the three layers that make up the hierarchical structure responsible for dealing with China's compliance. While the actual monitoring and processing of incoming information takes place at the TPSC level, significant questions of policy are taken up by the deputy-level Trade Policy Review Group. The highest, decision-making layer in this structure is the cabinet-level National Economic Council, headed by the chief economic adviser to President Bush.[29] (See Table 4.2.)

In monitoring China's WTO compliance, the TPSC acts as a clearing house for information collected by US businesses operating in China as well as by US government agencies that monitor and analyse events as they unfold in the Chinese economy. As individual US businesses have the most extensive insights into how well the Chinese government and business perform in this regard, the Bush administration is working closely with the American Chamber of Commerce in Beijing and Shanghai, the US-China Business Council, and the US Chamber of Commerce.

In terms of monitoring and putting pressure on China to fulfil its WTO obligations, the Department of State coordinates a network of groups to carry out surveillance in the field. Four Department of Commerce compliance officers are posted in the US Embassy in Beijing.[30] The Embassy has established a WTO Implementation Coordination Committee chaired by its Economic Minister. The aim of this committee is to coordinate WTO monitoring, compliance, technical assistance, and outreach efforts of several officials. These include State Department Economic, Environment, Science and Technology, and Public Affairs officers, as well as Foreign Commercial Service officers, Foreign Agricultural Service officers, and Customs attachés. The committee is responsible for tracking and analysing changes in laws and regulations, maintaining regular dialogues with US government officials on WTO commitments,

---

[29] 'Business Alert — US', Issue 25, Hong Kong Trade Development Council, 17 December 2001, at http://www.tdctrade.com/alert/us0125.htm (accessed 7 March 2002).

[30] 'Business Alert — US,' 17 December 2001.

Table 4.2 The Three-Tier Structure of the US Monitoring Mechanism

Tier/Role	Actors	Functions
Decision making	US President National Economic Council	"The buck stops here." • Cabinet level • Advises the President
Policy review	Trade Policy Review Group	• Sub-Cabinet level • Chaired by Deputy US Trade Representative (USTR)
Information gathering and analysis	Trade Policy Staff Committee Sub-committee on China WTO Compliance	• Made up of representatives from 20 or so agencies, including Departments of State, Treasury, Commerce, Agriculture, Labor, etc. • Chaired by Deputy Assistant USTR • Initiates position papers • Meets monthly • Sub-group meetings
	• Government agencies • Interest groups • Businesspeople and companies	• Trade-related staff in Washington DC, Geneva and major cities in China • Embassy and consulates in China • Interest groups: US Chamber of Commerce; US-China Business Council; American Chamber of Commerce; American Federation of Labor-Congress of Industrial Organizations (AFL-CIO); etc. • Functions: monitoring, consultation, enforcement, capacity building

Sources: Various Internet sources.
Acknowledgement: Thanks to Professor Ming K. Chan of Hoover Institution, Stanford University, for some useful suggestions in upgrading this table.

undertaking outreach programmes for Chinese government and other audiences, and meeting regularly with members of the private sector and other diplomatic missions to assess progress and to identify possible problems. The five consulates in Shanghai, Guangzhou, Chengdu, Shenyang and Hong Kong also play key roles on the front lines in these monitoring and coordinating efforts.[31]

The US government realises that China faces a mammoth task in fully implementing and enforcing WTO rules, a task that affects in numerous ways in which the Chinese government works, including the proper coordination between the central government in Beijing and provincial governments. To monitor and put pressure on China is one thing, but to help China to understand the way WTO rules work in practice within the country is quite another. To undertake the latter task, the US government has organised, in coordination with the business sector, multilateral institutions, and the Chinese government at various levels, numerous seminars and workshops in some major cities in China in the past few years.[32] Areas discussed cover the rule of law, financial services, protection of intellectual property, and trade standards. Other countries like Europe, Germany, Canada, Japan and Australia also run similar training and capacity-building exercises.[33]

---

[31] Donnelly, Testimony before the US-China Commission's Public Hearing on WTO Compliance and Sectoral Issues, 18 January 2002.

[32] Although China entered the WTO in December 2001, training related to TRIPS (trade-related intellectual property rights) was in place in 1995 to prepare China for its need to provide TRIPS-compliant enforcement. See David Quam, Testimony before the US-China Commission, 18 January 2002, fn 2, at http://www.uscc.gov/tesqua.htm (accessed 8 March 2002).

[33] For some details about foreign-supported WTO training facilities for China, see Brian L. Goldstein and Stephen J. Anderson, 'Foreign contributions to China's WTO capacity building,' *The China Business Review*, January–February 2002. According to Christian Murck, chairman of the American Chamber of Commerce in Beijing, the EU has been actively assisting China for almost a decade. Their funding is at the level of about US$10 million a year. Germany comes in second as a major player in the field. The German Technical Assistance agency has trained MOFTEC's lawyers in trade law and WTO compliance. Next to Germany comes Canada as a significant player. See Christian Murch, Statements made at a hearing of Congressional-Executive Commission on 'WTO: Will China keep its promises? Can it?' on 6 June 2002, http://www.cecc.gov (accessed 28 August 2002).

In terms of dealing with China's compliance, the Department of Commerce has a five-point plan:[34]

1. To concentrate on enforcement efforts;
2. To help China to reform;
3. To address promptly market access-problems;
4. To give US companies a head start; and
5. To monitor aggressively trade flows.

To carry out these tasks, the Department has set up a Market Access and Compliance unit, which aims to "obtain market access for American firms and workers and to achieve full compliance by foreign nations with trade agreements they sign with [the US]."[35] Within this unit, a Trade Compliance Center works with American traders who have compliance complaints against other countries, including China. In March 2002 the Department opened a Trade Facilitation Office in Beijing to support and coordinate compliance activities in both Beijing and Washington DC, and to act as an "early warning" system.[36]

In addition to the efforts made by the executive branch of the US government, the Senate Finance and the House Ways and Means Committees have asked the General Accounting Office to conduct a four-year investigation into China's WTO compliance.[37] (This Office is the investigative arm of Congress. It exists to support Congress in meeting its Constitutional responsibilities.)

Apart from its unilateral effort in monitoring China's compliance, the US government also initiates collaboration with like-minded

---

[34] William H. Lash III, Testimony before the US-China Commission's Public Hearing on WTO Compliance and Sectoral Issues, 18 January 2002, at http://usinfo.state.gov/regional/ea/uschina/lash.htm (accessed 8 March 2002).

[35] *Ibid.*

[36] Grant Aldonas, Testimony before a hearing of Congressional-Executive Commission on China on 6 June 2002 to consider China's WTO compliance, http://www.cecc.gov/pages/hearings/060602/ (accessed 28 August 2002).

[37] 'WTO: Will China keep its promises? Can it?' Hearing before the Congressional-Executive Commission on China, 6 June 2002, p. 9, at http://www.cecc.gov.

trading countries such as the UK, Germany, Japan, Canada and Australia, although at present this kind of collaboration seems quite limited. The US also cooperates with international agencies such as the World Bank, the Asian Development Bank, and other private foundations and universities in organising trade capacity-building programmes in China. For example, for four weeks in early 2004, the Asian Development Bank trained 200 Chinese judges and 80 legal experts in order to improve China's compliance with the WTO.[38] The amount of aids used to help China in this way is, however, very small compared with similar kinds of aids extended to countries in eastern Europe and the former Soviet Union during their transition from a communist to a market system.

Ultimately, the US can rely on the Transition Review Mechanism and the Dispute Settlement Mechanism of the WTO to get redress from China if it fails to comply. The Transition Review Mechanism (TRM) is an *unprecedented* measure requiring China to provide detailed information to WTO members and to give them the opportunity to raise questions about Chinese compliance with its WTO commitments.[39] China's trading practice is to be reviewed annually, in terms of its laws, regulations and programmes, in the first eight years after its accession to the WTO, followed by a final review during the ninth to the tenth year. In this TRM process, the 16 subsidiary bodies of the WTO that have mandates covering China's commitments,[40] such as the Council for Trade in Goods,

---

[38] Andrew K. Collier, 'Legal system taxed by WTO,' *South China Morning Post*, Internet ed., 21 April 2004. China has 300,000 judges and 19,000 senior judges — a huge logistical challenge for the country as it reforms its courts to keep pace with the demands of its entry into the WTO.

[39] Lash III, Testimony before the US-China Commission's Public Hearing on WTO Compliance and Sectoral Issues, 18 January 2002. China has made a commitment to subject itself to the review process, under Article 18 of its Protocol of Accession.

[40] Testimony of Jon M. Huntsman, Deputy US Trade Representative, at a hearing of Congressional-Executive Commission on China on 6 June 2002. The TRM process had been activated, and committee and council meetings were underway in September 2002 to review China's performance.

the Committee on Subsidies and Countervailing Measures, the Committee on Anti-dumping Measures, will review China's compliance. China is under obligation to provide relevant information "in advance" of these reviews. The results of these reviews will then be reported to the WTO General Council, which will then conduct the final review. China's accession Protocol gives a detailed list of specific information it must provide, including economic data in ten fields ranging from foreign exchange to pricing policies, as well as copies of laws and regulations on issues ranging from import licensing to government procurement.[41] The US will no doubt participate actively in the TRM process and to study these reviews very carefully to make sure that China complies with WTO rules. Initially, the US has not been entirely satisfied with the result of the process, and is determined to work hard with other like-minded states to strengthen the TRM's monitoring power. The idea of this mechanism is to exert peer pressure on China to meet its obligations.

The Dispute Settlement Mechanism is, on the other hand, available to member countries of the WTO to invoke if they feel that they have not been fairly treated by other member countries. The general rule is that the complaining country can ask the target country to discuss the issue involved. If the result is not satisfactory, the complaining country can take the case to the WTO for settlement before a tribunal. If the targeted country fails to act upon the advice of the tribunal, then the complaining country can take retaliatory measures against it. The process usually takes a few years to run its course, during which countries in conflict would impose trade sanctions of one kind or another on the other. In most cases, bilateral agreements and compromises are made before the dispute is to be decided by a trade tribunal. Going through this dispute settlement process is not entirely an ideal way to resolve possible trade conflicts with China. The US intends to help or to put pressure on China to change before reaching such a stage, but as many

---

[41] Report to Congress of the US by the China Security Review Commission, July 2002, chapter 3, p. 13.

American officials have reiterated time and again, the US will not shy away from using this legal mechanism if necessary.

Besides the Transition Review Mechanism and the Dispute Settlement Mechanism, some safeguards built into China's accession Protocol and its WTO membership can also be used by the United States to protect itself. These include non-market economy anti-dumping methods,[42] product specific safeguards, textile safeguards, and national security-related exceptions.[43] Some of these safeguards may be used to curb the sudden surge of Chinese textile and clothing products into the US and EU markets as a result of the lifting of a worldwide quota system in January 2005. Table 4.3 summarises the theory and practice of the US effort in monitoring China's WTO compliance.

Table 4.3 The Theory and Practice of the US Monitoring of China's WTO Compliance

Theory	Key Concepts	US Practice
Neo-Realist	National interest; Material capacity	Unilateral monitoring; Enforcing compliance through sanctions
Liberal Institutionalist	Rules; Regulations; Regimes	Making use of WTO's TRM and dispute settlement mechanism; Multilateral coordination
Social Constructivist	Shared knowledge; Socialisation; Learning	Capacity building; "Epistemic community" nurturing

---

[42] Under WTO rules, governments are allowed to impose anti-dumping duties on imports that harm domestic industries, provided they prove they are sold at artificially low prices. The burden of proof is virtually eliminated in cases involving non-market economies. China is treated as such an economy, and so it suffers from a lot of potentially unfair complaints because of its many cheap productions. See Kevin Watkins, 'An unwise, and unfair, assault on China's markets,' *International Herald Tribune*, 7 November 2003, p. 10.

[43] For details of the workings of these safeguards, see Report to Congress of the US by the China Security Review Commission, July 2002, chapter 3, pp. 14–15.

HOW ENDURING IS CHINA'S COMPLIANCE?

Three questions are central to a discussion of the strength
or otherwise of China's compliance. What has China promised to do
to meet its compliance commitments? What has it done so far to
meet these commitments? And, is what it has done so far enough?
What China has promised to do to comply with WTO rules can be
seen from the lengthy documents that it has signed to complete
its membership application. These documents include several
protocols laying down China's promises after accession. They
include various ways to bring China's trade practices into line with
the global practice of trade liberalisation, such as reducing tariffs,
increasing transparency, cutting government subsidies, enacting
necessary legislation, and instituting administrative organs to enforce
the legislation. Copies of these documents can be found on the
websites of the WTO, China's Ministry of Foreign Trade and
Economic Cooperation (reorganised and renamed as the Ministry of
Commerce since 2003), and the US Department of Commerce,[44] and
in many printed publications. A brief account of China's promises
can also be found in a booklet entitled *China in the WTO: what
it means for US business*,[45] distributed by the American Embassy in
Beijing to US businesspeople.[46] The booklet gives useful summaries
of phase-in schedules for tariff cuts across various sectors of industries. It also provides useful links to various sources relating to WTO
compliance.

What has China done so far to meet its commitments?
To prepare for the enormous task ahead, China started to introduce

---

[44] See, for example, China's WTO accession document published by the Ministry of
Foreign Trade and Economic Cooperation, which can be viewed and downloaded at
http://www.moftec.gov.cn/moftec_cn/wto/wtolaw.html, or http://www.chinawto.
gov.cn/databank/ since MOFTEC has been reorganised and renamed as the Ministry
of Commerce, in early 2003.

[45] Distributed by the American Embassy in Beijing and cleared by the Office of the
US Trade Representative, October 2001.

[46] A soft copy can be downloaded from the Embassy's website at http://www.
usembassy-china.org.cn/fcs/pdf/wto.pdf (accessed 9 July 2003).

various reforms during the final phase of its entry negotiations in the late 1990s. By the end of year 2000, a year before its entry, the Ministry of Foreign Trade and Economic Cooperation had reviewed over 1,400 laws, regulations, and other similar documents, including six statutes (of which five were revised), 164 State Council regulations (of which 114 were to be repealed and 25 amended), and 887 of its own ministry regulations (of which 459 were to be repealed and 95 amended). In addition, the Ministry had signed 191 bilateral agreements, 72 bilateral investment treaties, and 93 tax treaties.[47] In the first two months of the year 2001, various ministries and commissions of the State Council were reported to have reviewed some 2,300 laws and regulations, of which 830 were identified as in need of repeal and 325 as in need of revision.[48] As of mid-2004, the number of local government rules and regulations that had been revised or repealed amounted to some 190,000.[49] The legislative changes relating to WTO compliance are on-going.

Five national WTO centres have been established since January 2000, one each in Beijing, Hainan and Shenzhen, and two in Shanghai. As of mid-2001, more than 54 websites and 41,438 webpages relating to WTO existed on the Chinese Internet portal Sina. Yahoo also offered 15 such websites and 113,000 WTO webpages.[50] In addition, numerous private centres have been set up to provide instructions relating to the WTO and the impact of China's entry. Key government departments have established WTO committees to review industry-specific laws under the supervision of the State Council. To meet public demands, a lot of books of various qualities about the WTO have been published and are put

---

[47] Nan Xianghong, 'WTO: *fa de chongxin guojia* [WTO: the restructuring of law],' *Nanfang zhoumo* [*Southern Weekend*], 25 October 2001, quoted in Statement made by Donald C. Clarke before the US-China Commission's Public Hearing on WTO Compliance and Sectoral Issues, 17 January 2002.

[48] *Ibid.*

[49] Zhang Xianchen, '*Zhongguo jiare WTO liannianban de weigu he sikao* [Retrospection and thinking after China's entry into the WTO for two and a half years],' in *Zhanlue yu guanli* [*Strategy and Management*], Beijing, No. 3 (2004), p. 14.

[50] *Asian Wall Street Journal*, 20–22 July 2001, p. 3.

on prominent display in major bookstores across the country. All in all, an unprecedented massive learning is going on, more active in the cities than in the countryside.

The *China Business Review,* a periodical published by the US-China Business Council, provides some useful information about the changes adopted by the Chinese government to comply with WTO rules.[51] Stewart and Stewart, a US law firm, has been hired by the US-China Commission[52] to prepare a study that will set benchmarks for future efforts to monitor and assess China's WTO compliance. Its managing partner, Terence P. Stewart, in a testimony before the Commission in January 2002, gave some detailed information about measures taken by China in complying with WTO rules up to December 2001.[53]

In the end, the greatest challenge to China is the building of a legal system that would be compatible with the WTO.[54] Many observers are worried that China, given its rudimentary legal system,[55] may not be able to live up to the standard of responsibility of a normal state and to the compliance standard expected in international trade rules. Indeed China needs time to learn about the

---

[51] For details of the Review's assessments of China's compliance from June 2001 to September 2004, see http://www.uschina.org/public/wto/#wtocompliance (accessed 3 December 2004).

[52] The Commission was created on 30 October 2000 through Congress legislation. Its purpose is to study, investigate, assess and report to Congress on the economic and security implications of the bilateral economic relations between the US and China. Its works include any actions taken by the Chinese government in the context of the WTO that is adverse or favourable to the national security interests of the US. See http://www.uscc.gov/txhome.htm (assessed 15 March 2002).

[53] http://www.uscc.gov/tesste.htm (accessed 8 March 2002).

[54] Yang Jingyu, '"*Rushi*" *yu woguo de fazhi jianshe* ["WTO entry" and the building of our country's legal system],' *Qiushi* [*Seeking Truth*], March 2002, pp. 32–37.

[55] The low qualifications of China's judges go a long way to expose the country's weak legal system. For example, in 1995, only 5 per cent of its judges nationwide had a four-year college degree in any subject (let alone in law). As of mid-2002, it is estimated that about 10 per cent of judges have four-year college degrees in law. A study in 1998 of nine basic-level courts (the lowest level) in a major provincial city revealed that only 3 per cent of the judges had a bachelor's degree in law and

rules and to play by those rules. Its trade partners may or may not be willing to give it the necessary time to make the required adjustments. Already China has continued to publicise the consequences of its entry into the WTO to the general public, including the impact arising from the passing of so many rules and regulations to comply with the global trading norm. In December 2001, the Ministry of Foreign Trade and Economic Cooperation (MOFTEC) established two WTO-related departments: the Department of WTO Affairs; and the Fair Trade Bureau for Imports and Exports. The Department of WTO Affairs is made up of six offices, each staffed by four to eight people. It stems from an office under MOFTEC's Department of International Trade and Economic Affairs which was responsible for China's bilateral and multilateral negotiations in its bid to become a WTO member over the past 15 years before its entry. The new department is in charge of China's multilateral negotiations in the new round of trade liberalisation talks of the WTO. The main tasks of the department are to make sure that China carries out its promises in the WTO's goods trade and services trade agreements and that the country lays down laws and rules in line with WTO principles. Two offices under the department are responsible for answering WTO's enquiries into China's trade policies and for notifying the WTO of China's policies, laws and rules on trade and investment.[56]

The Fair Trade Bureau, consisting of eight offices with a total of about 40 staff members, is responsible for conducting investigations into imports and for determining whether or not anti-dumping, anti-subsidy and protective measures are applicable. The bureau guides and coordinates local companies in responding to foreign charges of dumping and subsidy. It also investigates other countries' discriminatory trade policies towards China and ensures that

---

that the "great majority" had had other types of jobs in the court administration such as bailiff, clerk, or driver before being promoted to the rank of judge. See Donald Clark, Testimony at a hearing of Congressional-Executive Commission on China on 6 June 2002 to consider China's WTO compliance, at http://www.cecc.gov/pages/hearings/060602/ (accessed 28 August 2002).
[56] 'WTO departments begin work,' http://www.xinhuanet.com, 27 November 2001.

Chinese companies enjoy fair trade in the global market through negotiations and consultations with other countries.

To protect its home industries, the State Economic and Trade Commission established in early 2001 an agency called the Investigation Bureau for Domestic Industry Injury to monitor the damage to domestic enterprises due to possible surging imports. This bureau is restructured from the commission's Anti-dumping and Countervailing Office. It is to decide, together with the Ministry of Commerce's Fair Trade Bureau, whether to take anti-dumping, anti-subsidy or protective measures against importers. Interestingly, the first case of trade dispute between China and the US after China's entry into the WTO originated from the US, not from China. On 20 March 2002, the Bush administration announced the imposition of tariffs of up to 30 per cent on imported steel products, in order to protect the country's ailing steel industry. China filed a complaint on 26 March with the WTO against the US decision.[57] Other steel-exporting countries, like Japan, South Korea, Australia, New Zealand, the United Kingdom and Brazil had either filed similar complaints or demanded consultations with the US government.[58] In March 2003, the WTO made an interim decision against the US, saying that the tariffs imposed were illegal. Eventually the US backed down by lifting some of the tariffs or by phasing in the tariffs of some products over a period of time. On the other hand, since China joined the WTO in December 2001, the US has been able to resolve several trade disputes with Beijing through negotiation, including the lifting of barriers to US cotton and soybean sales, the opening of China's market for US car finance companies, and the phasing out of subsidies to semiconductor manufacturers in China.[59]

Premier Zhu Rongji, in a government report to the National People's Congress on 5 March 2002, said that, starting from

---

[57] *Far Eastern Economic Review*, 4 April 2002, p. 25.
[58] *Asia Times*, 7 March 2002.
[59] Edward Alden, 'Washington to file WTO complaint against China,' *Financial Times*, Internet ed., 17 March 2004.

1 January 2002, China's general tariff level had dropped from 15.3 per cent to 12 per cent, and the reduction involved over 5,300 taxable items.[60] A Chinese trade official said that China's tariffs dropped from 42 per cent in 1992 to 15.6 per cent in 2001, 11 per cent in 2003, and then 10.4 per cent in 2004,[61] and would be further reduced to 10.1 per cent in 2005 and to 10 per cent in 2008. Such rate cuts far exceed those of many countries.[62]

Finally, is what China has done so far enough? To be sure, how well China's efforts will measure up to outside expectations in the end has yet to be determined. Already many observers are skeptical about their effectiveness when the new trade policies adopted by the central government are being filtered down to provincial levels and below, where the hardships of change are expected to be felt most severely. Full implementation will take time, and the process in the coming years will be a long-term work-in-progress, during which the US-China Commission will review the situation annually, and submit reports to the legislative and executive branches of the US government for their consideration. The WTO too will review annually the situation under the Transition Review Mechanism, as discussed before. Will China be able to deliver in the near, if not the long-term, future? This question can only be answered in a speculative way at this stage. In general, many US academics, taking a long-term view and considering China's behaviour in international financial institutions such as the World Bank and the International Monetary Fund in the past 20 years or so, are optimistic that China will largely comply with WTO rules.[63] In reviewing China's WTO compliance behaviour one year into China's membership, Margaret Pearson, a political science professor at the University of Maryland,

---

[60] The full text of Zhu's report can be found at FBIS (Foreign Broadcast Information Service) Translated Text.

[61] China's WTO commitment was to cut tariff rates to 11.5 per cent in 2003 and 10.6 per cent in 2004, so in legal and technical terms, China has fulfilled its promise well within target.

[62] Zhang, '*Zhongguo jiare WTO liannianban de weigu he sikao*,' p. 12.

[63] Margaret M. Pearson, 'China's track record in the global economy,' *China Business Review*, Internet ed., January–February 2000.

said that China's behaviour is "cooperative" and within the bounds of "legitimate actions in the WTO". She was, however, careful to make a distinction between "cooperative behaviour" and "adherence to the agenda of the United States".[64] US traders, demanding quick, maximum returns from their investments, are generally less optimistic. They tend to focus on their specific areas of trade and are generally more stringent in their assessment of China. US government officials, on the other hand, take a position somewhere in between, giving China certain leeway to adjust initially,[65] while keeping a close eye on China's compliance record, preparing for tough negotiations,[66] and standing ready to put unilateral and multilateral pressures on China when they are called for. While holding up long-term prospects, the US can expect shocks in the near future as China experiences the pain of change, which may severely test bilateral relations in trade and other areas.[67]

CONCLUSION

China's entry into the WTO is arguably *the* most important peaceful change in the global political economy in the post-Cold War era. As a new member with a socialist tradition, a lot of work remains to be done in many areas to bring it in line with the liberal trade system,

---

[64] Written testimony of Margaret M. Pearson in a hearing on 'Is China playing by the rules? Free trade, fair trade, and WTO compliance,' before the Congressional-Executive Commission on China, 24 September 2003, http://www.cecc.gov (accessed 20 October 2004).

[65] The Asian division vice-president of the US Chamber of Commerce, Myron Brilliant, said that US companies may be tolerant initially but would be less so if the same problems in trade persist for three or four years. See 'China rebuked for failing promises,' *South China Morning Post*, 13 September 2002.

[66] A glimpse of the structure and constraints of this kind of trade negotiations with China can be seen from Liang Wei, 'China's WTO negotiation process and its implications,' *Journal of Contemporary China*, No. 33 (November 2002), pp. 683–719.

[67] Pei Minxin, 'Future shock: the WTO and political change in China,' *Policy Brief,* Carnegie Endowment for International Peace, Washington DC, 1 (3) (February 2001).

including the strengthening of its legal system, better protection of intellectual property rights,[68] and the phasing out of agricultural subsidies.[69] In the US review of China's WTO compliance in early 2005,[70] the issue of the currency peg of the Chinese yuan to the American dollar figured prominently.[71] On the whole, China seems to have passed its compliance test in the first three years of membership pretty well.[72] The future years may prove to be crucial as many of the more painful reforms start to bite, such as the ending of restrictions on many kinds of distribution by foreign retailers and the adoption of financial reforms to allow foreign banks to compete on an equal footing with Chinese banks.[73]

---

[68] According to the US Chamber of Commerce, Chinese piracy and counterfeit products cost American industries more than US$20 billion a year, and the issue has become acute in Sino-US trade disputes. This amount contributes significantly to the US trade deficit with China in 2004, amounting to US$162 billion (against the total US trade deficit with the world amounting to US$617 billion). See *International Herald Tribune*, 23–24 April 2005, p. 16.

[69] China's membership in the WTO is still quite new and many of its most far-reaching obligations will not be phased in until several years later. However, as of July 2002, a US government report has pointed out several areas in which China has failed to meet its commitments, including those covering the Information Technology Agreement, tariff-rate quotas, genetically-modified organisms, insurance services, courier services, and export subsidies. See the report to Congress of the US by the China Security Review Commission, July 2002, chapter 3, pp. 12–13.

[70] US-China Economic and Security Review Commission report on 'China and the WTO: assessing and enforcing compliance,' 25 March 2005, http://www.uscc.gov (assessed 26 March 2005).

[71] Whether the currency issue falls within the ambit of the WTO or not has yet to be tested by the US lodging a compliant against China in the WTO. Some observers suggest that the issue should come under the purview of the IMF rather than that of the WTO.

[72] For example, Robert Kapp, president of the US-China Business Council, lauded Beijing's moves to introduce tariff reductions in 70 per cent of the categories mandated by the WTO, causing the average tariff rate to drop to 12 per cent from 15.3 per cent since accession (*Far Eastern Economic Review*, 5 December 2002). So did Robert Zoellick, the US Trade Representative, during his visit to China in February 2003 (*The Standard*, 20 February 2003, p. A-6).

[73] *Far Eastern Economic Review*, 5 December 2002.

As the volume of trade between China and the outside world grows, trade frictions are bound to increase. Based on an analysis of some statistics on trade disputes brought before the WTO, two Chinese researchers have arrived at three interesting findings. Firstly, the number of trade disputes is in direct proportion to the volume of trade. Secondly, the number of respondent cases in the WTO trade disputes is also in direct proportion to the market maturity and the rate of increase in trade of the respondent country. Thirdly, the US and European Union governments are far more conversant than developing countries with the mechanics of the WTO's dispute settlement, and as a result developing countries are often left in a defensive, reactive mode. Furthermore, developed countries are more inclined to use WTO mechanisms to lodge complaints about trade issues than developing countries. Statistics show that 60 per cent of complaining countries are in the developed world.[74] Based on these findings, it is likely that China will face an increasing number of trade disputes with the US and Europe.[75] Indeed, recent developments have largely confirmed these findings. As exports grow, China's manufacturers have become the targets of numerous anti-dumping and protectionist complaints,[76] including the looming

---

[74] Zhang, '*Zhongguo jiare WTO liannianban de weigu he sikao,*' p. 20.

[75] Zhou Xiaoshi and Jin Minli, '*Maoyi zhengduan fengxian wenti de sikao* [Probing into trade dispute risks after China's entry into the WTO],' *International Economics and Trade Research*, Guangzhou, No. 1 (2002), p. 32.

[76] Before 1979, China's exports totalled less than US$10 billion, with no anti-dumping at all against the country (*Faji shibao* [*Legal Daily*], 23 October 2002, p. 7). Since 1979, about 33 countries have initiated 544 investigations and taken action against 4,000 Chinese export products. In 1993, China surpassed Japan as the main target of anti-dumping complaints. From 1993 to 2003, one in every six global trade disputes involved a product or company in China. In 2001, 17 countries filed a total of 67 cases against companies in China, 55 for allegedly dumping products on the market at cut-rate prices and 12 for selling products beyond agreed quotas. In total, a record US$1.14 billion worth of goods were involved. In 2002, following China's accession to the WTO a year earlier, 18 countries filed 60 complaints with the trade body over disputed goods worth a total of US$1 billion. Chief among the complainants was the United States, which filed 14 of the complaints, and India,

conflict over China's surging textile and clothing exports to the US and EU.[77] This situation arises mainly out of mistrust among trading nations of each other's intentions and of the conscious need to protect and promote one's own trading and industrial interests, including the job security of factory workers.

Whether or not China can live up to the expectations of the outside world in the long run remains to be seen. Inevitably, a gap would remain between outsiders' expectations and China's ability to meet those expectations. How to reconcile this difference poses a serious challenge to political leaders on all sides and provides a testing ground for the managerialist and enforcement theorists in compliance studies. For China's trade partners, a right balance has to be struck between a "hard" approach to China's WTO compliance and a "soft" one. Too hard an approach is likely to provoke China's defiance and plays into the hands of its conservative leaders, many of whom are sceptical of China's speedy opening up. Too soft an approach, however, may not be able to satisfy the demands of the domestic constituencies of China's trade partners.

---

which filed 13. Disputed products included Chinese steel, vehicle windshields, cigarette lighters, machinery parts and various agricultural products (*South China Morning Post*, 5 February 2003, p. 5).

[77] On 10 June 2005, the EU and China reached an agreement to limit the rise in Chinese exports of textiles and clothing for three years, thus averting a trade war between the two. They two sides agreed to limit growth rates of 10 categories of clothes to about 10 per cent through to 2008. This agreement is expected to give European textile and clothing manufacturers time to adjust. EU imports of T-shirts rose by 157 per cent in the first quarter of 2005, but pullovers and men's trousers lept even more, by more than 400 per cent. See *The Independent*, London, 11 June 2005, p. 47. As of mid-June 2005, the Chinese and US governments also conducted negotiation to try to avert a trade war between them along the China-EU agreement. See *International Herald Tribune*, 18–19 June 2005, p. 14.

China's Compliance in Arms Control and Non-Proliferation

> While all nuclear weapons states should agree to no first use, the United States, as the sole superpower, should take lead on this issue.
>
> *Former US President Jimmy Carter, 2005*[1]

> When the United States insists that nuclear weapons are vital to its own security but harmful to the security of others, it becomes hopelessly lacking in credibility.
>
> *Tad Daley, 2002*[2]

The year 1964 marks the beginning of a new era in the strategic relations among the world's big powers. Not only has China become a nuclear state since, but also the two superpowers at the time — the United States and the Soviet Union — have to start to take the Chinese nascent nuclear capabilities into serious account when

---

[1] Jimmy Carter, 'Erosion of the Nonproliferation Treaty,' *International Herald Tribune*, 2 May 2005, p. 8. China, in fact, is the first and only nuclear power so far to declare no first use.

[2] Tad Daley, 'America's nuclear hypocrisy,' *International Herald Tribune*, Internet ed., 21 October 2002.

considering their strategic moves. The domestic turmoil associated with the Cultural Revolution from 1966 to 1976 isolated China from the rest of the world and from the global arms control and disarmament regimes initiated by the two superpowers. At the height of the Cold War, the amount of nuclear weapons owned by either superpower was sufficient to destroy the world's infrastructure many times over.[3] China chastised both countries for monopolising the production and possession of nuclear arms. In the 1960s, it even declared its support for nuclear proliferation as a means to "break the hegemony of the superpowers."[4] The issue of compliance in arms control and disarmament that we witness today has been shaped in the main by the confrontations, negotiations, and bargaining between the two superpowers. However, since China began to reform and open up to the outside world in the late 1970s, it has taken great strides in engaging with the international treaty system and in participating in the activities of many international organisations. Beginning in the late 1980s and the early 1990s, China has become a significant player in global arms control and disarmament, although the size of its initial involvement was small. The end of the Cold War and the demise of the Soviet Union brought about a major shift in the US strategic calculation. As Russia was preoccupied with the reconstruction of its political and economic system, many of its huge stocks of weaponry, including nuclear weapons, were left unattended and some lying to rust. On the other hand, China's military power grew steadily in strength. As a result, the US started to shift part of its strategic focus from Russia to China. The terrorist attacks on the US in September 2001 and the subsequent "war on terror" have highlighted the importance of China's non-proliferation

---

[3] See David C. Gompert et al, *Nuclear weapons and world politics: alternatives for the future* (New York: McGraw-Hill, 1977). See also Walter C. Clemens, Jr. 'China,' and Gloria Duffy, 'Arms control treaty compliance,' both in Richard Dean Burns (ed), *Encyclopedia of arms control and disarmament* (New York: Charles Scribner's Sons, 1993), pp. 59–74 and 279–295.

[4] Robert Einhorn, 'China and non-proliferation,' *In the National Interest*, Vol. 2, Issue 13 (2 April 2003), p. 1.

policy and practice. While China sides nominally with the US in the global campaign against terrorism, the country has a record of selling nuclear materials and technologies to countries like Pakistan, Iran, Libya and North Korea. Such proliferation of weapons of mass destruction has threatened the national security of the US and its allies. Hence, China's non-proliferation diplomacy has attracted the increasing attention of the West, especially the US.

This chapter aims to assess China's compliance diplomacy in the area of arms control, disarmament, and non-proliferation. It looks specifically at weapons of mass destruction: chemical, biological, and nuclear weapons, together with their delivery systems. To provide a background, the next section gives a brief account of the history of China's nuclear-weapon development and its participation in international arms control regimes. This is followed by another section discussing the interest of the US in China's compliance behaviour. The chapter then turns to China's compliance diplomacy in the four specific areas covered by the Biological and Toxin Weapons Convention, the Chemical Weapons Convention, the Nuclear Non-Proliferation Treaty, and the Missile Technology Control Regime. Together, these areas highlight the importance in dealing with weapons of mass destruction, which form the core US security concern. The chapter concludes by making an overall assessment of China's non-proliferation behaviour.

CHINA'S ARMS CONTROL POLICY: A BRIEF OVERVIEW

From 1964 when China conducted its first atomic test to 1997 when it halted its nuclear testing, China had conducted 45 nuclear-weapon tests,[5] a number equalled to that of Britain's but was far less than

---

[5] Of these 45 nuclear-weapon tests, 23 were atmospheric and 22 underground. They ranged in yield from about one kiloton to about four megatons. China first tested underground on 23 September 1969. Its largest atmospheric test was four megatons, conducted on 17 November 1976, and its largest underground test was 660 kilotons, conducted on 21 May 1992. See http://www.nti.org/db/china/testpos.htm (accessed 22 July 2004).

America's 1,030.[6] After its adoption of the reform and opening-up policy in the late 1970s, the country began to join international arms control and disarmament efforts. Before 1978, China had entered into only two sets of major international treaties dealing with arms control and disarmament: the Geneva Protocols in 1952; and the Treaty of Tlatelolco (for the prohibition of nuclear weapons in Latin America) in 1973. The entry into the Geneva Protocol, which prohibits the use of poisonous gases in inter-state conflicts, was mainly for the purpose of trying to establish the international legitimacy of the newly-formed government of the People's Republic of China. Its ratification of the Protocols was also due to the legacy of the Second World War, when Japan experimented with chemical and biological weapons in China. The signing of the Treaty of Tlatelolco could be seen as China's initial and isolated attempt to engage with an international arms control issue, especially when the issue was in connection with a part of the Third World far away from its homeland. Both treaties are, however, tangential to the testing of China's compliance behaviour in the current regimes of arms control and non-proliferation. In the 1970s, China signed about 10 to 20 per cent of all arms control agreements it was eligible to sign. By the late 1990s, however, the percentage had jumped to 85 to 90 per cent.[7]

China's participation in international non-proliferation and arms control regimes can be divided into three time periods: (1) the period of self-imposed isolation from 1964 to the late 1970s;[8] (2) the period of partial participation in the 1980s, when it began to engage selectively and in a limited way with some of these regimes; and (3) the period of full participation, beginning in the early 1990s and

---

[6] Brad Roberts, Robert A. Manning, and Ronald N. Montaperto, 'China: the forgotten nuclear power,' *Foreign Affairs*, Vol. 79, No. 4 (July/August 2000), pp. 53–63.

[7] Michael D. Swaine and Alastair Iain Johnston, 'China and arms control institutions,' in Elizabeth Economy and Michel Oksenberg (eds), *China joins the world: progress and prospects* (New York: Council on Foreign Relations Press, 1999), p. 101.

[8] Despite China's international isolation during this period, it did not stop developing its nascent nuclear capability.

continuing up to this day.[9] In the first two periods, China can be regarded as a "unique nuclear state", in the sense that it was still suspicious of the nuclear intentions of the two superpowers at that time, whereas in the third period, it can be regarded as a "normal nuclear state", in the sense that it began to fully integrate itself with these regimes, like most other states in a comparative stage of development. It is, however, a normal nuclear state with a difference, as it behaved quite differently from countries in the West due to differences in political history, political system, political culture, and national interests (to be elaborated later).

The 1990s saw China taking a number of major steps in increasing its non-proliferation commitments. A month after it had promised to abide by the Missile Technology Control Regime in February 1992, it acceded to the Nuclear Non-proliferation Treaty (NPT). In January 1993, it signed the Chemical Weapons Convention, as one of the early signatory parties, and in 1995 it published its first White Paper on defense,[10] which discussed, among other things, its arms control and disarmament efforts. In May 1996, the Chinese issued a statement promising to make only safeguarded nuclear transfers. Two months later, the country began a moratorium on nuclear testing and, in the following September, signed the Comprehensive Test Ban

---

[9] I borrow the idea of these three periods (with modifications) from Zhou Baogen, 'A constructivist analysis of China and international nuclear non-proliferation regime,' (in Chinese) *Shijie Jingji yu Zhengzhi* [*World Economics and Politics*], Beijing, No. 2 (2003), pp. 23–27.

[10] In December 2004, China issued its fifth defence White Paper. A copy can be downloaded from the *People's Daily* at http://english.people.com.cn/whitepaper/defense2004.html (accessed 9 January 2005). The second, third, and fourth were published in 1998, 2000, and 2002. Also, in December 2003, the State Council published its first 'White Paper on China's non-proliferation policy and measures'. A full text can be downloaded at http://www.chinadaily.com.cn/en/doc/2003-12/03/content_287061.htm (accessed 7 February 2005) or found in *Zhongguo waijiao* [*China's foreign affairs*] (Beijing: World Knowledge Press, 2004), pp. 289–421. In September 2005 it published another White Paper entitled 'China's endeavors for arms control, disarmament and non-proliferation,' downloadable at http://www.china.com.cn/english/features/book/140416.htm (accessed 15 September 2005).

Treaty. The signing of this treaty was of great significance,[11] because it marked a change from China's long-held demand that the two super-powers — the US and the Soviet Union/Russia — should make deep cuts in their nuclear arsenals first before China would consider stopping its testing.[12] In April 1997, China deposited its instrument of ratification of the Chemical Weapons Convention. In the following October, it joined the Zangger Committee. (Named in honour of its first chairman Claude Zangger, this committee is also known as the NPT Exporters Committee. It consists of some 36 member states which are parties to the NPT as of August 2004.[13] It has met regularly since 1971 to develop a common strategy to deal with the implementation of safeguard requirements for nuclear exports.) In August 2002, China finally released detailed regulations controlling the export of missile-related technology, fulfilling a pledge it had made to the United States two years earlier.[14] So far, China has participated in some 29 arms control and non-proliferation agreements, organisations and regimes.[15] In terms of its membership size in these treaties, China can be regarded as a full participant in the global arms control and disarmament network. (See Appendix II for a list of major international arms control and non-proliferation treaties that China has signed.)

---

[11] As of 19 February 2005, 175 countries have signed the Comprehensive Test Ban Treaty, of which 120 have been ratified. Both China and the US signed on 24 September 1996 but both have yet to ratify. The Russian Federation, however, ratified on 30 June 2000. See the Preparatory Commission for the Comprehensive Nuclear-Test-Ban Treaty Organisation website, http://www.ctbto.org (accessed 19 February 2005).

[12] In an agreement reached in Moscow in May 2002, the US and Russia agreed to reduce their strategic nuclear warheads from about 6,000 on each side to a level of 1,700 to 2,200 by 2012. See a fact sheet issued by the White House on 24 May 2002, at http://usinfo.state.gov/topical/pol/arms/02052414.htm (accessed 24 March 2003).

[13] One of which is an observer — European Commission. See the Zangger Committee website, http://www.zanggercommittee.org (accessed 9 August 2004).

[14] *Far Eastern Economic Review*, 5 September 2000, p. 11.

[15] For a comprehensive list of these agreements, organizations and regimes, see *The EANP Factsheets*, Center for Nonproliferation Studies, Monterey Institute of International Studies, April 1999. For details, see the website of Nuclear Threat Initiative at http://www.nti.org/db/china/regimes.htm.

US INTERESTS IN CHINA'S COMPLIANCE

The US is most concerned with China's nuclear policy and practice, as China is seen as a strategic competitor and a potential challenger to its power supremacy. Some US officials have accused China of exporting weapons of mass destruction or their technologies to such countries as Pakistan and Iran, especially in cases involving dual-use technology (materials that have both civilian and military uses), including vibration test equipment, high-strength aluminium, uranium isotope separation equipment, implosion systems, and heavy water production equipment.[16] Some American analysts say that certain Chinese transfers of nuclear materials have violated China's own international commitments. Others argue, however, that even if no laws or treaties are violated, China's transfer serves to undermine the national security and the global interests of the US. In addition, the US suspects that China has continued to develop biological weapons, in contravention of its commitments to the Biological and Toxin Weapons Convention.[17]

Although China has made substantial progress in its non-proliferation policies over the past decade or so, a big gap still remains in its full and transparent compliance with America's non-proliferation demand, due to differences in perceptions, interests, policy goals, mutual mistrusts, and so on. To better understand the Sino-US divide over this issue, the non-proliferation record of any country should be viewed against the context of its military defence. The weapon development programmes of many countries are shrouded in secrecy, and those of China and the United States are no exception. No one in the public domain knows quite well what sort of new weapons are being developed or produced unless and until they are tested or used in battlefields. Examples include the

---

[16] 'China's nuclear exports and assistance,' http://www.nti.org/db/china/nexport.htm (accessed 23 July 2004).

[17] It is interesting to point out that although the US has signed the 1993 Chemical Weapons Convention, it has developed substantial quantities of chemical weapons since then. See Martin Griffiths and Terry O'Callaghan, *International relations: the key concepts* (London and New York: Routledge, 2002), p. 7.

cluster bombs, the "bunker buster", and the so-called MOAB (mother of all bombs)[18] developed or used by the US in its war against Iraq in March/April 2003, some of which can penetrate thick layers of concrete and cause extensive damage and destruction, far beyond the destructive power of many heavy conventional weapons. Speaking in a ceremony to commemorate the 59th anniversary of the Hiroshima bombing in August 2004, Akiba Tadatoshi, the city's mayor, accused the US of continuing to research and develop nuclear weapons to make them smaller and "usable", such as "mini-nukes" and "bunker busters", flying in the face of international law and the UN.[19] Also, the US is developing weapons in space which can be used for defence as well as for offensive purposes. For these and other reasons, it is very difficult to make an objective assessment of the compliance of a country in non-proliferation, especially when it comes to big powers. Although Russia's nuclear capability is far more menacing than China's, Russia is generally seen as a declining power relative to the height of its military might during the Cold War era, and so the US, in planning strategically, has shifted part of its attention from Russia to a rising China. Although China has become at least a nominal partner of the US in the global campaign against terrorism, its proliferation practice in recent years has begun to haunt the United States. According to US reasoning, if China's nuclear export is not properly checked or controlled, it could pose a security threat, especially if the related technologies, materials, or knowledge fall into the hands of terrorists.

Compared with the US and Russia, China is a latecomer to the world's nuclear club, and many of the existing rules governing arms control were made between the two superpowers during the Cold War. These rules have inevitably been used or modified to be used to gauge China's compliance record in arms control and disarmament. In general, a country's compliance in this area is affected by various

---

[18] 'US tests massive bomb,' CNN.com, 11 March 2003.

[19] International Community Radio Taipei, 6 August 2004; *Taipei Times*, 7 August 2004; *International Herald Tribune*, 7–8 August 2004, p. 3. For a media report on current US efforts to develop smaller but more powerful nuclear warheads, see *International Herald Tribune*, 8 February 2005, p. 3.

factors. These include the content of treaty provisions, the mechanisms of verification, domestic oversight of treaty compliance, unintentional military errors, and the international context of the arms control regime.[20] The content of treaty provisions refers to whether the terms of the treaty are clearly spelt out or not, and therefore whether they are easily enforceable or not. The mechanisms of verification can range from the use of satellites or other technologies to surveillance such as espionage or human intelligence. Domestic oversight relates to a country's capacity to comply, in particular the strength of its legal system to enforce compliance. And the international context refers to the architecture of the international system and the existence or otherwise of peer examples and pressures.

Most disputes arising out of non-compliance with arms control and disarmament measures, as in many other global issues of conflict, are dealt with on a bilateral, consultative basis, but if bilateral efforts fail to resolve them, then a complaining country can take one or more of the following actions against the non-complying or violating country[21]:

- Do nothing;
- Make the violation public;
- Suspend the treaty signed by the complaining and the non-complying countries;
- Take military steps to counteract the significance of the violation, which may also violate the treaty;
- Violate the treaty in the same manner as the original violator;
- Adopt sanctions to punish the violator that are unrelated to the treaty or the specific violation; and
- Refer the case to international bodies such as the UN.

Multilateral arms control and non-proliferation regimes are in general less effective in enforcing compliance than bilateral regimes because of the nature of international anarchy and the lack of

---

[20] Gloria Duffy, 'Arms control treaty compliance,' in Richard Dean Burns (ed), *Encyclopedia of arms control and disarmament* (New York: Charles Scribner's Sons, 1993), pp. 281–289.

[21] Duffy, 'Arms control treaty compliance,' p. 293. The last point in the dot-point list is mine.

Table 5.1 Costs of Multilateral Verification, 2000

Treaty	Personnel*	Inspectors	Annual Cost (US$ Million)
Non-Proliferation Treaty	600	200	88
Chemical Weapons Convention	470	211	90
Comprehensive Test Ban Treaty	250	50	120
Biological and Toxin Weapons Convention	100	N.A.	40

* The number of personnel here includes the number of inspectors.

Source: Slightly modified from F.R. Cleminson, 'Multilateral on-going monitoring and verification (OMV) of compliance: nurturing cost-effectiveness,' the Sixth ISODARCO Beijing Seminar on Arms Control, Shanghai, 29 October–1 November 1998, p. 9.

human and financial resources in most multilateral regimes to verify compliance (see Table 5.1). Within multilateral regimes, some are more stringent than others in enforcing compliance. For instance, the Non-Proliferation Treaty "has no formal internationally-recognized verification regime attached to it" and the International Atomic Energy Agency "cannot effectively measure compliance with the treaty."[22] However, the Comprehensive Test Ban Treaty is supported by a rather sophisticated verification system consisting of an International Monitory System and an International Data Centre. Also, the Chemical Weapons Convention is stricter than the Biological and Toxin Weapons Convention in applying its verification process. The major powers of the world, especially the declared nuclear powers in the West, are more ready to enforce the compliance of others. Of these major powers, only the United States has the resources and political will to enforce compliance, in most cases, in accordance with American standards or American interpretations of the terms of arms control and non-proliferation. Russia is a power in relative decline, and Britain and France do not yet have

[22] Wendy Frieman, *China, arms control, and nonproliferation* (London and New York: RoutledgeCurzon, 2004), p. 35.

the necessary resources or the urgent desire to monitor the compliance behaviour of others.

On many occasions, the US has applied trade sanctions on Chinese entities and even the Chinese government as a way to punish Chinese acts of non-compliance. The Bureau of Verification and Compliance, set up in December 1999 and became fully operational in February 2000 within the Department of State, is responsible for checking the compliance of other countries, including China. Headed by an Assistant Secretary,[23] it prepares the US President's Annual Report to Congress on the compliance record of the US as well as those of other countries of concern, with respect to arms control, disarmament, and non-proliferation. In such a report entitled 'Adherence to and compliance with arms control and non-proliferation agreements and commitments',[24] relating to activities from 1 December 2000 to 31 December 2001, China came under scrutiny in areas covered by the Biological and Toxin Weapons Convention, the Chemical Weapons Convention, the Nuclear Non-Proliferation Treaty, and the Missile Technology Control Regime. The first three treaties cover the area of weapons of mass destruction (WMD) and the Regime covers the area of delivery systems of WMD. An examination of these four areas helps to reveal China's non-proliferation record, US accusations, and China's response.

THE BIOLOGICAL AND TOXIN WEAPONS CONVENTION

The 1972 Biological and Toxin Weapons Convention (BWC) prohibits the development, production, stockpiling, acquisition or retention of biological and toxin weapons, equipment or means of delivery of

---

[23] Paula A. DeSutter became the first Assistant Secretary in August 2002. The Bureau consists of about 70 employees, most of whom are technical experts. The Bureau took over some of the duties previously performed by the US Arms Control and Disarmament Agency when the Agency was merged into the Department of State in 1999.

[24] Bureau of Verification and Compliance, US Department of State, 'Adherence to and compliance with arms control and non-proliferation agreements and commitments,' [2002] http://www.state.gov/t/vc/rls/rpt/22322pf.htm (accessed 27 July 2004).

such weapons for hostile purposes or armed conflict. As of December 2004, 153 countries, including China and the United States, were state parties to the Convention.[25]

At a BWC Review Conference held in 1986, the state parties adopted a set of non-binding confidence-building measures (CBMs), which were subsequently expanded at the 1991 Review Conference. Among other things, these measures include the exchange of information and data about biological and toxin research and development, and the encouragement of contacts among scientists working in the field. The purpose is to increase transparency and to nurture mutual trust and confidence. Since 1987, over half of the states parties have made one or more CBM declarations. For its part, since 1988 China has reported to the United Nations annually on Convention-related information and data concerning CBMs, in accordance with the decisions of the Review Conferences of the BWC.[26]

A US State Department report says that the US "believes that China had an offensive BW [biological weapons] program prior to 1984 when it became a state party to the BWC, and maintained an offensive BW program throughout most of the 1980s."[27] It further says that China's CBM declarations "are believed to be inaccurate and incomplete."[28] It finds that "China continues to maintain some elements of an offensive biological warfare program."[29] The report therefore concludes that China was not in compliance with BWC obligations. This line of accusation has been made at least since 1993,[30] and repeated in annual reports made by the US Arms Control and Disarmament Agency on China's compliance in this

---

[25] The Biological and Toxin Weapons Convention website, http://www.opbw.org/ (accessed 29 January 2005).

[26] According to 'China's national defence', White Paper, 1998, http://www.china. org.cn/e-white/index.htm.

[27] Bureau of Verification and Compliance, 'Adherence to and compliance with arms control and non-proliferation agreements and commitments'.

[28] *Ibid.*

[29] *Ibid.*

[30] Frieman, *China, arms control, and nonproliferation*, p. 67.

area to Congress.[31] Despite these accusations, they do not seem to have led the US to take any official punitive actions against China in this biological weapons area. One plausible explanation is that the US has its own reservations, as it opposes international inspections of its own biological and chemical facilities,[32] whether they are for military or industrial use. The US, together with Russia, own more than 95 per cent of the world's known chemical weapons tonnage.[33] Any US request for an inspection of Chinese facilities is likely to trigger off similar requests by China or other countries like Russia to inspect US facilities through the Convention.

On the other side, since 1984 when China acceded to the Convention, it has consistently said that it never researched, produced, or possessed any biological weapons and would never do so. So far, no concrete evidence seems to have come to light in the open to support the US "beliefs". This does not mean, however, that the US allegations, which are based on its own classified information, are false, only that they cannot be either verified or refuted by open sources. Apart from the US, there is no other country which publicly accuses China of non-compliance, and because of the absence of a verification system under the Convention, bilateral differences over the issue are often reduced to US accusations and Chinese denials.

THE CHEMICAL WEAPONS CONVENTION

The Convention on the Prohibition of Development, Production, Stockpiling, and Use of Chemical Weapons and on Their Destruction

---

[31] US Arms Control and Disarmament Agency (ACDA), 'Adherence to and compliance with arms control agreements' (1998), at the Nuclear Threat Initiative website, http://www.nti.org/db/china/cbwpos.htm (accessed 27 July 2004). ACDA was reorganised and this reporting work has been taken up by the Bureau of Verification and Compliance under the newly-established office of the Under Secretary for Arms Control and International Security in 2000. No ACDA annual reports were published in 1999, 2000, or 2001.

[32] Terence O'Brien in *Dominion Post*, New Zealand, 28 September 2002, p. A 15.

[33] Glen Browder, 'Toxin politics: alarm bells on chemical arms,' *International Herald Tribune*, 5 July 2004, p. 8.

(Chemical Weapons Convention or CWC) was adopted by the UN Conference on Disarmament (formerly the Conference of the Committee on Disarmament) in Geneva on 3 September 1992, and was opened for signature in January 1993. The Convention is an important disarmament agreement negotiated within a multilateral framework that provides for the elimination of an entire category of weapons of mass destruction under universally-applied international control. It is unprecedented in scope and in the stringency of its verification regime. Its adoption was preceded by negotiations on a chemical weapons ban treaty which went on for 12 years, from 1980 to 1992.[34] In order to prepare for the CWC's entry into force, a Preparatory Commission was established with the responsibility to prepare detailed operation procedures and to put into place the necessary infrastructure for a permanent implementing agency. Known as the Organisation for the Prohibition of Chemical Weapons (OPCW), the commission has its headquarters in The Hague. For four years it laid the groundwork for implementing the Convention: working towards agreement on unresolved issues, establishing procedures for state parties to make declarations, and most importantly the training of more than 200 inspectors (including some Chinese nationals) who, by inspecting both military and industrial sites, would make up the heart of the CWC verification regime.[35] The CWC entered into force on 29 April 1997, with 87 countries having ratified the CWC and hence becoming original state parties to the Convention. With entry into force, the OPCW was formally established.

---

[34] This introduction to the establishment of the CWC is sourced from the CWC website, http://www.opcw.org/html/intro/chemdisarm_frameset.html (accessed 27 July 2004).

[35] In 1993, OPCW had 470 staff members, including 211 inspectors, with a budget of US$90 million. A total of 16,000 facilities and sites were expected to be declared, so the task of inspection was obviously enormous. See F.R. Cleminson, 'Multilateral on-going monitoring and verification (OMV) of compliance: nurturing cost-effectiveness,' the Sixth ISODARCO Beijing Seminar on Arms Control, Shanghai, 29 October–1 November 1998, p. 4.

The PRC is an original state party to the CWC, signing the Convention in 1993 and ratifying it in 1997. It has submitted its initial declaration on time and subsequently all annual declarations. It has also subjected its declared chemical facilities to OPCW inspections. Despite these, the US harbours strong reservations about China's compliance with CWC: it "believes that China has an advanced chemical warfare program, including research and development, production, and weaponization capabilities.... While China claims it possesses no CW [chemical weapons] agent inventory, it is believed to possess a moderate inventory of traditional CW agents."[36] The US therefore "assesses that China maintains an active offensive R&D CW program, a possible undeclared CW stockpile, and CW-related facilities that were not declared."[37] Like the case in the BWC, so far the US has not taken any official punitive action against China. (Under the provisions of the CWC, allegations of active chemical weapons programme can be brought before the OPCW and a challenge inspection can be called.)[38]

China affirms that it has made a positive contribution to the negotiation and conclusion of the CWC, signing the Convention in 1993 and depositing its instrument of ratification in 1997. It says it has earnestly fulfilled its obligations under the Convention. In March 1997, the Chinese government established, under the leadership of a Vice-Premier of the State Council, a National Leading Group on the Implementation of the CWC,[39] as well as its implementation office (National Authority), which was mandated to implement the

---

[36] Bureau of Verification and Compliance, 'Adherence to and compliance with arms control and non-proliferation agreements and commitments'.

[37] *Ibid.*

[38] 'China and chemical and biological weapons (CBW) non-proliferation,' http://www.nti.org/db/china/cbwpos.htm (accessed 27 July 2004).

[39] Little is known about this national leading group or in fact other leading groups in the State Council of the PRC, although a government document has listed the following groups: the National Leading Groups for Rectification and Regulation of Market Economy Order; the National Leading Group for Poverty Alleviation and Development; the National Leading Group for the Work of Reform in Administrative Examination and Approval System; the National Leading Group for Implementation of the CWC; the National Leading Group for Science, Technology

Convention nationwide. The country has also set up various organs at the provincial level to implement the Convention covering the whole country. Since 1995, the government has promulgated several pieces of legislation to provide the legal framework for dealing with the production, trading, use, stockpiling, and the importing and exporting of scheduled chemicals. These include the Regulations of the People's Republic of China on Controlled Chemicals (1995), the List of Controlled Chemicals by Category (1996), the Rules of Implementation for the Regulations of the People's Republic of China on Controlled Chemicals (1997), the List of Items Newly Included in Category Three of Controlled Chemicals (1998), and the Measures on Export Control of Certain Chemicals and Related Equipment and Technologies and Attached Export Control List (2002).[40] The country maintains that it has submitted initial and annual declarations of all

---

and Education; the National Leading Group for Western Region Development; the National Leading Group for the National Medium-to-Long Term Planning for Development of Science and Technology; the National Leading Group for the Reform to the Electric Supply, Telecommunications and Civil Aviation Systems; the National Leading Group for the Work on Amalgamation and Bankruptcy of Enterprises and Reemployment of Laid-Off Workers; the National Leading Group for Supporting the Army and Favouring Their Dependents, Supporting the Government and Cherishing the People. See the 'Gazette of the State Council of the People's Republic of China,' General Office of the State Council, 30 December 2003, Issue No. 36, Serial No. 1107: Institution Building and Personnel Administration, http://www.china.org.cn/e-gongbao/gazette/2003e/gb2003-36e-7.htm (accessed 7 February 2005). Apart from these leading groups under the State Council, there are of course other more powerful leading groups under the Party's Politburo. For some discussions of those groups in the Politburo, see Kenneth Lieberthal, *Governing China: from revolution through reform* (New York and London: W.W. Norton, 1995), pp. 192–208; and Lu Ning, 'The central leadership, supraministry coordinating bodies, State Council ministries, and Party departments,' in David M. Lampton (ed), *The making of Chinese foreign and security policy in the era of reform* (Stanford: Stanford University Press, 2001), pp. 45–48. For some discussions on those groups at the provincial level, see Peter T.Y. Cheung and James T.H. Tang, 'The external relations of China's provinces,' in Lampton (ed), *The making of Chinese foreign and security policy in the era of reform*, pp. 98–104.
[40] See the PRC's Ministry of Foreign Affairs website, http://www.fmprc.gov.cn, Disarmament and Arms Control (assessed 29 July 2004).

kinds on time and in their entirety. Up till May 2004, China has received 74 on-site verifications by the OPCW.[41] In addition, the country has jointly organised two workshops for inspectors and two regional seminars on the implementation of the CWC in Beijing.[42] The latest one was held in September 2004, which brought together 130 delegates from 32 countries.[43]

THE NUCLEAR NON-PROLIFERATION TREATY

The Nuclear Non-proliferation Treaty (NPT) is a landmark international treaty whose objective is to prevent the spread of nuclear weapons and their technology, to promote cooperation in the peaceful use of nuclear energy, and to further the goal of achieving nuclear disarmament and general and complete disarmament. The treaty represents the only binding commitment in a multilateral treaty to the goal of disarmament by the nuclear-weapon states. Opened for signature in 1968, the treaty entered into force in 1970. As of March 2002, a total of 187 parties had joined the treaty,[44] including the five major nuclear-weapon states (the US, Russia, the UK, France and China), making the number of countries ratifying the NPT more than those ratifying any other arms limitation and disarmament agreement. Two declared nuclear states (India and Pakistan) and one suspected nuclear state (Israel) are, however, outside the NPT framework. North Korea was a member of the treaty but announced its withdrawal in January 2003.

To further the goal of non-proliferation and as a confidence-building measure between state parties, the treaty establishes a

---

[41] By the end of October 2003, China had received 68 on-site verifications by the OPCW. China's White Paper on China's non-proliferation policy, http://www.nti.org/db/china/engdocs/nprolwp_03.htm (accessed 23 July 2003).

[42] *Ibid.*

[43] http://www.fmprc.gov.cn/chn/njb/zzjg/jks/jksxwlb/t159088.htm (accessed 15 January 2005).

[44] Treaty on the Non-proliferation of Nuclear Weapons, http://www.un.org/Depts/dda/WMD/treaty/ (accessed 1 August 2004).

safeguard system under the responsibility of the International Atomic Energy Agency (IAEA). The Agency was founded in 1957 and China joined it in 1984. Safeguards are used to verify compliance with the treaty through inspections conducted by the IAEA. In 1988, China entered into such a safeguard agreement, under which nine nuclear facilities in the country were open to IAEA inspections as of April 2002.[45] While the treaty promotes cooperation in the field of peaceful nuclear technology and equal access to this technology for all state parties, safeguards prevent the diversion of fissile material for weapons use.

The treaty obligates the five major nuclear-weapons states not to transfer nuclear weapons, other nuclear explosive devices, or their technology to any non-nuclear-weapon state. For their part, non-nuclear-weapon state parties undertake not to acquire or produce nuclear weapons or nuclear explosive devices. They are further required to accept safeguards to detect diversions of nuclear materials from peaceful activities, such as power generation, to the production of nuclear weapons or other nuclear explosive devices. This must be done in accordance with an individual safeguards agreement, concluded between each non-nuclear-weapon state party and the IAEA. Under these agreements, all nuclear materials in peaceful civil facilities under the jurisdiction of the state must be declared to the IAEA, whose inspectors have routine access to the facilities for periodic monitoring and inspections. If information from routine inspections is not sufficient to fulfil its responsibilities, the IAEA may consult with the state regarding special inspections within or outside declared facilities. There is no confirmed instance of state party governmental transfers of nuclear weapon technology or unsafeguarded nuclear materials to any non-nuclear-weapon

---

[45] Statement by Ambassador Hu Xiaodi, Head of the Chinese delegation, at the 1st session of the Preparatory Committee for the 2005 NPT Review Conference, New York, 8 April 2002, http://www.nti.org/db/china/engdocs/hu0402.htm (accessed 23 July 2004). Two reactors in China under IAEA safeguards are: the Qinshan nuclear power plant near Hangzhou and a heavy-water research reactor in Beijing. See Frieman, *China, arms control, and nonproliferation*, p. 11.

state. However, some non-nuclear-weapon states, such as Iraq, were able to obtain sensitive technology and/or equipment from private sources in states that are party to the NPT.[46]

China signed the NPT in 1992, joined the Zangger Committee in 1997, and implemented dual-use nuclear export controls based on the Nuclear Suppliers Group (NSG) control list in 1998. Established in 1975 under a US proposal with seven member states in response to India's nuclear test a year earlier, the NSG is an unofficial organisation of countries with nuclear capability that exercise control on nuclear exports. China's membership application made in January 2004 was accepted in the following May. Its accession brought the number of members to 41, including the United States, Britain, France and Russia.[47] In January 1999 China signed an additional protocol with the IAEA, and in March 2002 it completed the domestic legal procedures for the entry into force of the protocol, making it the first among the five nuclear-weapon states to do so.[48] The additional protocol allows more intrusive inspections from the IAEA into China's civilian nuclear programme.

Despite China's efforts to comply with the universal principle of nuclear non-proliferation, the US "remains concerned about China's compliance with its nuclear non-proliferation commitments."[49] The US concern dates as far back as in the 1980s, when China was suspected of selling nuclear materials and technologies to Iran and Pakistan. Part of the concern could have arisen out of different interpretations of what the Chinese regard as peaceful use of

---

[46] 'Nuclear Non-Proliferation Treaty,' maintained by Robert Sherman, at http://www.fas.org/nuke/control/ntp/ (accessed 1 August 2004).

[47] 'China joins Nuclear Suppliers Group (28/05/04),' http://www.china-embassy.org/eng/gyzg/t122871.htm (accessed 2 August 2004).

[48] Statement by Ambassador Hu Xiaodi, Head of the Chinese delegation, at the 2nd session of the Preparatory Committee for the 2005 NPT Review Conference, Geneva, 28 April 2003, http://www.nti.org/db/china/engdocs/huxdnpt0403.htm (accessed 22 July 2004). See also 'International Atomic Energy Agency,' http://www.nti.org/db/china/iaeaorg.htm (accessed 23 July 2004).

[49] Bureau of Verification and Compliance, 'Adherence to and compliance with arms control and non-proliferation agreements and commitments'.

nuclear energy, which has been seen by the US as breaching non-proliferation rules. As part of its effort to promote its own peaceful nuclear energy programme and to obtain hard currency and technology, China has nuclear cooperation and trade with a number of countries. It has governmental nuclear cooperation agreements with more than 15 countries, including Argentina, Belgium, Brazil, Canada, Germany, Iran, Japan, Pakistan, Republic of Korea, Romania, Russia, Switzerland, the UK, the US, and the former Yugoslavia.[50] As of April 2003, China has joined 12 international conventions in the field of peaceful uses of nuclear energy.[51]

China pledges to adhere to three principles of nuclear exports, initially pronounced in 1986:[52]

1. All exports should be used exclusively for peaceful purposes;
2. All exports should be subject to IAEA safeguards; and
3. No exports should be re-transferred to a third country without prior Chinese consent.

Despite its declared adherence to these principles, the US has found China's behaviour in this area unacceptable, as cases have been found in which nuclear materials and technologies shipped by Chinese entities, many of which were state-owned enterprises, were destined for states that are fouling the NPT.

THE MISSILE TECHNOLOGY CONTROL REGIME

The Missile Technology Control Regime is an informal and voluntary association of countries which share the goals of non-proliferation of unmanned delivery systems capable of delivering WMD. It is not a treaty but an agreement whereby participating countries undertake to take steps, on a voluntary basis, to control missile proliferation. It has

---

[50] 'Research overview on China and arms control/non-proliferation issues,' http://www.nti.org/db/china/resover.htm (accessed 23 July 2004).
[51] Statement by Ambassador Hu Xiaodi, at the 2nd session of the Preparatory Committee for the 2005 NPT Review Conference, Geneva, 28 April 2003.
[52] Frieman, *China, arms control, and nonproliferation*, p. 27.

become the centerpiece of international efforts to curb the spread of missiles capable of delivering WMD, and is the only multilateral non-proliferation forum on missiles. Originally established in 1987 by the Group of Seven industrialised countries, its membership has grown to include 34 countries as MTCR partners as of August 2004,[53] all of which have (supposedly) equal standing in the regime.

The MTCR was initiated partly in response to the increasing proliferation of WMD, the risk of which is widely recognised as a threat to international peace and security. Traditionally, concern has been focused on state proliferators. After the terrorist attacks on the US in September 2001, it became evident that more also has to be done to decrease the risk of WMD delivery systems falling into the hands of terrorist groups or individuals.[54] One way to counter this threat is to maintain vigilance over the transfer of missile equipment, material, and related technologies usable for systems capable of delivering WMD.

The MTCR rests on adherence to common export policy guidelines (the MTCR Guidelines) applied to an integral common list of controlled items (the MTCR Equipment, Software and Technology Annex). All MTCR decisions are taken by consensus, and MTCR partners regularly exchange information about relevant national export-licensing issues. Many countries recognise that national export-licensing measures on these technologies make the task of countries seeking to achieve capability to acquire and produce unmanned means of WMD delivery much more difficult. As a result, a lot of countries, including all MTCR partners, have chosen voluntarily to introduce export-licensing measures on rocket and other unmanned air-vehicle delivery systems or related equipment, material and technology. However, the regime itself has no verification or enforcement mechanism, and the US chooses to adopt measures under its control to address its concerns over proliferation.

---

[53] Missile Technology Control Regime website, http://www.mtcr.info/english/partners.html (accessed 1 August 2004).

[54] Mohamed El Baradai, Director-General of IAEA, speaking in Sydney, 8 November 2004. See Australian Broadcasting Corporation, http://www.abc.net.au/lateline/content/2004/s1240725.htm (accessed 20 February 2005).

Originally, the regime was formed with a view to curb China's missile proliferation. Now the US would like to include China in the regime, and China has expressed interest in joining, as late as in July 2004, during the Fifth Sino-US Conference on Arms Control, Disarmament and Non-proliferation held in Beijing.[55] Some existing members in the West are, however, worried that China's membership might enable it to gain access to sensitive information about missile design.[56] For its part, China has taken steps to gradually catch up with international standards in non-proliferation. For example, in October 1994 it reiterated its commitment made two years earlier to abide by the guidelines and parameters of the MTCR. In November 2000 it committed not to assist any country in any way in the development of MTCR-class ballistic missiles. On 25 August 2002 it enacted legislation setting out a comprehensive missile-related export control list. China's Ambassador in Disarmament Affairs, Sha Zukang, said in December 2002 that China's Nuclear Export Control List and Export Control List of Nuclear Dual-Use Items and Related Technologies covered all the items and technologies contained in the "Zangger Committee" list and the control list of Nuclear Suppliers Group.[57]

However, in a review made in mid-2003, US Assistant Secretary of State for Verification and Compliance Paula DeSutter said that China's control list was not as comprehensive as the MTCR Annex and that some of the regulations in the Chinese legislation were less than clear-cut.[58] Also, China did not commit itself to requiring

[55] 'Nations team up on arms control,' at *China View*, http://www.chinaview.cn, 21 July 2004.

[56] http://www.nti.org/db/china/intexcom.htm (accessed 23 July 2004).

[57] 'Reinforcing efforts to prevent nuclear proliferation: China's perspective,' Speech by Ambassador Sha Zukang at the Wilton Park conference, Brighton, UK, 17 December 2002, http://www.nti.org/db/china/engdocs/shazukan1201.htm (accessed 23 July 2004).

[58] Remarks made by Assistant Secretary of State for Verification and Compliance Paula DeSutter before the US-China Economic and Security Review Commission, 24 July 2003, http://www.nti.org/db/china/engdocs/desutter_0724.htm (accessed 22 July 2004).

full-scope safeguards in countries receiving its nuclear-related exports, as such a commitment would jeopardise its nuclear trade with Pakistan.[59] According to US official sources, Chinese entities, including Chinese state-owned enterprises, have provided Pakistan with missile-related technical assistance; and firms in China have provided missile-related items or assistance to several other countries of proliferation such as Iran, North Korea and Libya. The US finds such activities contrary to Chinese commitments made,[60] and has started to impose trade sanctions on China since the early 1990s.

China has consistently denied any wrongdoing, arguing that trade sanction is not the way to resolve disputes arising out of these issues. Neither is the use of pre-emptive strikes, referring to the war in Iraq to topple Saddam Hussein, nor the use of maritime interception, referring to the US-instituted Proliferation Security Initiative, which allows Western powers led by the US widespread powers to interdict suspected trade in materials for WMD by land, air, or sea.[61] The Chinese

---

[59] 'China's nuclear exports and assistance,' http://www.nti.org/db/china/nexport. htm (accessed 23 July 2004).

[60] Bureau of Verification and Compliance, 'Adherence to and compliance with arms control and non-proliferation agreements and commitments'.

[61] The Proliferation Security Initiative (PSI), which brings together 11 countries (Australia, Japan, France, Germany, Italy, the Netherlands, Portugal, Poland, Spain, the UK, and the US), was announced by President George W. Bush on 31 May 2003. The grouping has expanded to include 16 countries (*The Asian Wall Street Journal*, 28–30 January 2005, p. M8), including Singapore, Norway, Canada, and others. The initiative seeks to improve the sharing of intelligence regarding the spread of WMD, to shut down illicit laboratories, and to freeze the finance of arms dealers. It also aims to conduct naval exercises to interdict shipments of WMD and their delivery systems, as well as on land and in the air. Official information on this initiative can be found in 'The Proliferation Security Initiative,' Bureau of Nonproliferation, Washington DC, 28 July 2004, http://www.state.gov/t/np/rls/other/34726.htm (accessed 14 February 2005). The group's first success happened in late 2003, when the US worked with the Germans and Italians to block a shipment of centrifuge parts bound for Libya. Apart from an exercise held in the Coral Sea hosted by Australia in 2004, the first PSI exercise in Asia, codenamed "Team Samurai 2004", was held in October 2004 in the sea near Tokyo Bay, involving 900 military personnel from the US, France, Australia and Japan, and observers from

government holds that these actions do not always aim to promote international peace, neither do they conform to international law.[62] Instead, China insists that dialogues and international cooperation should be used to clear any misunderstandings and to diffuse any tensions arising out of these issues.

US SANCTIONS AGAINST CHINA'S "NON-COMPLIANCE"

The US approach to China's compliance behaviour consists of both sticks and carrots, aimed at changing the latter's cost-benefit calculus. It makes clear that proliferation is not cost-free by sending a clear message to China: either trade with proliferators or with the United States. The US has asked China to look at specific entities which the US refers to as "serial proliferators". (It is not known how long the term has come to be in use.) Under US economic sanctions, for example, NORINCO (China North Industries Corporation, a state-owned defence industrial firm under the Commission of Science and Technology of the State Council) was banned from exporting goods to the US worth a total of about US$160 million.[63]

The US has used trade sanctions on many occasions since the early 1990s to punish China for its proliferation behaviour. On 1 April 2004, the US imposed sanctions on five Chinese entities for exporting to Iran items that have the potential to contribute towards the making of WMD. These entities include NORINCO and China Precision Machinery Import/Export Corporation. Both

---

15 other countries (http://www.takungpao.com, 27 October 2004). The next Asian PSI is scheduled to be held in the summer of 2005 near the Malacca Strait, to be sponsored in part by Singapore.

[62] 'China enacts laws to control missile technology exports,' Asia & Pacific Rim, http://www.defensenews.com (accessed 21 July 2004).

[63] Paula DeSutter, Assistant Secretary of State for Verification and Compliance, US Department of State, in 'Compliance diplomacy takes on greater emphasis in arms control,' http://usinfo.state.gov/topical/pol/arms/desuttersp.htm (accessed 22 July 2004).

entities have been referred to by the US government as "serial proliferators". (A comprehensive list of US sanctions against the PRC in this connection can be found in the 2004 Report to Congress of the US-China Economic and Security Review Commission.)[64] The US government admits openly that it has been difficult to establish the exact linkage between the Chinese government and these entities and the extent to which the Chinese government is involved.[65] According to the US, the persistent non-compliance behaviour of these entities may have links with Chinese foreign-policy goals, such as "China's strategic relationship with Pakistan, its desire to avoid instability or regime change in North Korea, or its desire to demonstrate its opposition to a unipolar world."[66] As recently as in January 2005, six Chinese firms, including NORINCO and the China Great Wall Industry Corporation, both of which have strong links with the People's Liberation Army and both have been sanctioned before, were banned by the US from trading with it because of their assistance to Iran to acquire WMD.[67] From January 2001 to April 2005, the State Department had sanctioned foreign companies 115 times over controlled export

---

[64] '2004 Report to Congress of the US-China Economic and Security Review Commission' (Washington: US Government Printing Office, 2004), http://www.uscc.gov, Appendix A.

[65] It may well be that the US government uses sensitive, classified information about the linkage between the Chinese government and these entities as a basis for negotiating with China on other diplomatic issues in a bilateral way. Another interesting point is the alleged weakness of US law which prevents US authorities from sanctioning the parent company whose subsidiaries sell WMD or dual-use materials, without clear-cut proofs that the actions of these subsidiaries are directed by the parent company. Sinopec, China's state-owned oil and gas giant, has escaped US punishment in this way. See Matthew Godsey and Gary Milhollin, 'Curbing arms sales begins at home,' *International Herald Tribune*, 26–27 February 2005, p. 8.

[66] Robert Einhorn, 'China and non-proliferation,' *In the National Interest*, Vol. 2, Issue 13 (2 April 2003), quoted in '2004 Report to Congress of the US-China Economic and Security Review Commission,' p. 134.

[67] *The Standard*, Hong Kong, 19 January 2005, p. A3; *South China Morning Post*, 19 January 2005, p. A5.

shipments and 80 of these sanctions were aimed at Chinese companies.[68]

It is difficult to gauge the effectiveness of trade sanction as a foreign-policy tool, but some observers believe that it has borne some fruits, as the alternative application, lifting, and re-application of trade sanctions have helped to change Chinese behaviour. It has been suggested that China's issuance of a control list of missile sales was made in response to US trade sanctions.[69] Also, China has successively taken actions to come close to curbing some alleged proliferation activities. According to a US analyst, China apparently has taken disciplinary action against the Chinese entity that was sanctioned for engaging in missile assistance to Pakistan.[70] Hu Xiaodi, China's Ambassador for Disarmament Affairs, said in February 2004 that the Chinese government had "investigated and dealt with a number of law-breaking cases and administered corresponding punishments to the units and individuals involved according to law."[71] Vice-Foreign Minister Zhang Yesui also confirmed in a conference speech in July 2004 that the Chinese government had recently "made public penalties on two such companies," without naming them.[72] According to Zhang, the Chinese government has recently set up an "inter-agency contingency mechanism on non-proliferation" to deal with the emergence of isolated proliferation cases expeditiously and effectively. Furthermore, the government has put in place a dialogue

---

[68] Bruce Odessay, 'Chinese weapons proliferation threat a major US concern,' The Washington File, Bureau of International Information Program, US Department of State, http://usinfo.state.gov (accessed 9 May 2005).

[69] Frieman, p. 103.

[70] Einhorn, 'China and non-proliferation,' *In the National Interest.*

[71] Statement by Hu Xiaodi, Ambassador for Disarmament Affairs of China, at the plenary of the 2004 session of the Conference on Disarmament, Geneva, 12 February 2004, http://www.china-un.ch/eng/61979.html (accessed 3 August 2004).

[72] Speech by Vice-Foreign Minister Zhang Yesui at the 5th China-US conference on arms control, disarmament and non-proliferation, 21 July 2004, http://www.china-un.ch/eng/66486.html (accessed 3 August 2004).

mechanism with the "Wassenaar Agreement", and has remained in contact with the "Australia Group". (The Australia Group is a voluntary, informal, export-control arrangement, established in 1985, which brings together some 33 countries as well as the European Commission, to coordinate their national export controls in order to limit the supply of chemicals and biological agents — as well as related equipment, technologies, and knowledge — to countries and non-state entities suspected of pursuing chemical or biological weapons capabilities. All participants are members of the 1997 CWC and the 1972 BWC. The Wassenaar Agreement, entered into by 33 countries in 1996, on the other hand, controls exports of conventional arms and dual-use goods and technologies.)

Apart from defending its non-proliferation record, China also mounts counter attacks on the US and criticises its performance in arms proliferation. Without naming the country, Hu Xiaodi left no doubt which country he was referring to when he said in a disarmament conference in Geneva in February 2002 that the world had witnessed a series of setbacks in arms control in recent times, including:[73]

- The abrogation of the Anti-Ballistic Missile Treaty;
- The adoption of egoistic attitude and double standards on issues of non-proliferation;[74]
- The practice of applying stringent measures on others and lenient ones on oneself with respect to treaty compliance;
- The adoption of certain domestic legislation, which is tantamount to distorting the obligations explicitly provided for in international treaty; and

---

[73] Statement by Hu Xiaodi, Ambassador for Disarmament Affairs of China, at the plenary of the 2002 session of the Conference on Disarmament, Geneva, 7 February 2002, http://www.nti.org/db/china/engdocs/hu0207_02.htm (accessed 23 July 2004).

[74] The Chinese government argued that if the US could sell advanced weapons to Israel and Taiwan counter to China's interests, why China could not sell advanced weapons to Pakistan and Iran counter to US interests.

- The push for speedy conclusion of a treaty with an extremely strict verification regime during negotiations, but making a U-turn when the deal is done to reject out of hand the ratification of such a treaty.[75]

Indeed, in a book analysing Sino-US relations, Radha Sinha, a seasoned political observer, points out that there is a discrepancy between American domestic behaviour and its foreign-policy behaviour: While the US believes in and behaves in accordance with the rule of law domestically, "it operates in the world as if it was beyond the law."[76]

During the Fifth US-China consultation on non-proliferation held in July 2004 in Beijing, a Chinese participant raised the issue of Taiwan and pointed out that the sale of American arms to Taiwan constituted a case of arms proliferation and should therefore be included in the agenda for consultation. This suggestion appears to be Beijing's latest policy initiative to link the issue of Taiwan with the issue of non-proliferation, employing whatever leverage it can harness to trade one issue for another.

Apart from hitting China with a stick, the US also offers some carrots: the US Nonproliferation Bureau has engaged in dialogue with China, offering technical assistance to help China to enhance its compliance observance. This bureau, however, is also responsible for singling out Chinese firms for non-proliferation violations and for organising the Proliferation Security Initiative, targeting partially at Beijing.

Many US suspicions about China's weapons programme arise out of mistrust. The lack of mutual understanding is often blamed on China's lack of transparency in its military strategy and practice. However, no nuclear-weapon state can achieve absolute transparency, and China is no exception. In an essay on China's nuclear

---

[75] This refers most probably to the decision made by the US Senate in 2000 not to ratify the Comprehensive Test Ban Treaty.

[76] Radha Sinha, *Sino-American relations: mutual paranoia* (Basingstoke and New York: Palgrave Macmillan, 2003), p. 193.

transparency, Li Bin, a professor at Tsinghua University in Beijing and an expert on non-proliferation issues, points out that China has to strike a right balance between transparency and its security concerns.[77] In principle, China favours greater transparency as it can clear up misperceptions, enhance mutual understanding, and alleviate suspicions. The reason why China is seemingly less than forthcoming in making its policy and practice totally transparent, according to Lin, is due to a need to protect "its nuclear deterrence until it has built a survivable nuclear retaliatory force." For this reason, China will maintain some ambiguity in some areas while allowing greater transparency in others. Lin puts forward five kinds of nuclear weapon transparency: transparency in nuclear strategy, qualitative transparency, quantitative transparency, clarification of nuclear activities, and acceptance of site visits. Of these, China is more open in strategy and qualitative transparency than in the other three. He points out that China has never declared officially the number of its nuclear weapons, the amount of its stockpiled fissile materials, or the production rate of new nuclear warheads. China is ambivalent about clarifying its nuclear activities, for fear of jeopardising sensitive information to foreign military intelligence agencies or commercial organisations. Also, for fear of exposure to espionage, China sets strict rules to regularise site visits. However, as a result of China's entry into the WTO, the increasing intensity of globalisation, advancements made in technology such as the Internet and commercial satellite imaging, and China's move to deploy a mobile nuclear force, Lin is optimistic that China will become more confident of itself and will take greater measures to increase its nuclear transparency.

CONCLUSION

Although in broad terms the Chinese and American arms control and non-proliferation agendas have converged over the last decade

---

[77] This paragraph is a paraphrase and interpretation of Lin Bin, 'China and nuclear transparency,' http://learn.tsinghua.edu.cn/homepage/2000990313/archive.htm (accessed 24 July 2004).

or so,[78] their differing views on what constitutes proliferation will no doubt remain, and the severity of their differences will depend on fluctuations in bilateral relations. There are inherent problems lurking in the background, such as divergent national interests, mutual mistrust of each other's military intentions, different perceptions of compliance, and different legal interpretations. China's own legal enforcement will remain a big hurdle, not only in non-proliferation commitments, but also in a wide range of other commitments in the areas of trade, human rights, and the protection of the environment.

It has been suggested that China's increasing compliance with the MTCR was the result of a successful application of a combination of political pressures and economic sanctions by the US and, to a certain extent, of coordinated efforts taken by the US and its allies. On the other hand, it is also the result of China's rational calculation of its national interests based on an increasing engagement with the outside world,[79] and on its increasing awareness of the dangers posed by the proliferation of nuclear weapons in neighbouring countries such as India, Pakistan, possibly North Korea, and potentially Japan and South Korea.

It was only in the 1990s that China began to take concrete steps to adopt international non-proliferation norms, join international agreements, and control exports of sensitive nuclear goods and technologies. However, its non-proliferation record in the past decade or so has been described as "uneven", its pattern as "two steps forward and one step back",[80] and the results

---

[78] Evan S. Medeiros, Report on the 3rd US-China conference on arms control, disarmament and non-proliferation, East Asia Nonproliferation Program, Center for Nonproliferation Studies, Monterey Institute of International Studies, October 2000, p. 1.

[79] Tammy Halevy, 'Chinese compliance with the Missile Technology Control Regime: a case study,' The Jewish Institute for National Security Affairs, 31 August 1993, http://www.jinsa.org/ (accessed 1 August 2004).

[80] Bates Gill, 'Two steps forward, one step back: the dynamics of Chinese non-proliferation and arms control policy-making in an era of reform,' in Lampton (eds), *The making of Chinese foreign and security policy in the era of reform*, pp. 257–288.

"a mixed bag".[81] One plausible explanation for this mixed record is the fact that China is still in the throes of transition from isolation to openness and from socialism to market economy, started some 25 years ago. This fact seems to have been ignored by the US authorities, partly because the American style of diplomacy gives relatively little attention to the difficulties faced by transitional societies, and partly because, by giving such sympathetic considerations, the effort to closely monitor China's compliance behaviour and the rationale for applying economic sanctions and political pressure might be compromised.

In July 2004, Vice-Foreign Minister Zhang Yesui said that China was in favour of "resolutely maintaining", "continuously pushing forward", and "constantly improving" the international non-proliferation regime.[82] This represents the latest indication yet that China is in favour of the present status quo in international security, a clear departure from its position some 15 years ago, when it basically detached itself from the international-security-norm system. It is interesting to point out, however, that while China takes steps, sometimes gingerly, sometimes rather boldly, to maintain the status quo, the US apparently moves in the opposite direction, leaving behind step by step the present status quo in pursuit of its absolute national security. The abrogation of the Anti-Ballistic Missile Treaty is seen by some observers as paving the way for the development of the National Missile Defense system and the Theatre Missile Defense system. Billed as defensive systems, both are capable of becoming offensive. This development of a weapon system in space is in addition to the development of more advanced conventional armament. Chinese non-proliferation expert Lin Bin has pointed out that the US government, under the Bush administration, has been pulling out of multilateral non-proliferation regimes.[83] The US Senate's refusal to

---

[81] Einhorn, 'China and non-proliferation'.

[82] Speech by Vice-Minister Zhang Yesui at the fifth China-US conference on arms control, disarmament and non-proliferation, 21 July 2004.

[83] Lin Bin, '*Junbei kongji de xianzhuang yu qianjing* [The current status and future prospects of arms control],' http://learn.tsinghua.edu.cn/homepage/2000990313/archive.htm (accessed 24 July 2004).

accept the Comprehensive Test Ban Treaty is another case in point, making the treaty's global effectiveness very slim. Although the US has rectified the CWC, it has put some obstacles to its practice. The negotiation on verification with regard to the BWC shows little progress. So does the Geneva multilateral disarmament conference, which has not produced any concrete results for a number of years. All these events indicate that the American enthusiasm in forging a multilateral approach to non-proliferation regime seems to have been waning. How this situation would affect China compliance with non-proliferation is intriguing and worth continuous attention.

Chapter

6

China's Compliance in Environmental Protection

As China explodes economically, it is imploding ecologically.

The Economist, 2004[1]

It is the common desire of all peoples and the urgent task of all countries to protect the global environment, to achieve sustainability, and to create a better home.

President Jiang Zemin, 2002[2]

As the most populous country on earth with ten per cent of its rare species of flora and fauna, China's environmental practice is of great importance to us all. Unfortunately, the country is one of the most polluted in the world. Its environmental problems have reached massive proportions. Consider the following:[3]

---

[1] *The Economist*, 10 July 2004, p. 74.

[2] President Jiang Zemin, Opening address at the 2nd Global Environment Facility Assembly held in Beijing on 16–18 October 2002, http://www.fon.org.cn/index.php?id=2767 (accessed 22 July 2003).

[3] Vaclac Smil has published a key reference on the precarious state of China's environment, brought about by a combination of a huge and growing population,

- At least seven of the world's ten most polluted cities are located in China;[4]
- Two-thirds of its 660 cities are surrounded by rubbish dumps;[5]
- A third of the country suffers from severe soil erosion;[6]
- 75 per cent of its lakes and about half of its rivers have been polluted;[7]
- 75 per cent of its wastewater is discharged untreated;[8]
- 93 per cent of the water flow of the Yellow River, whose basin is known as the cradle of Chinese civilisation, fails to meet China's own quality standards;[9]
- 60 per cent of its people drink water that does not meet the World Health Organisation's minimum acceptable standard;[10] and

---

ambitious economic modernisation plans, and expectations of a better standard of living. See his *China's environmental crisis: an inquiry into the limits of national development* (Armonk, New York; London: M.E. Sharpe, 1993). For a more recent book-length exposition of China's environmental woes, see Elizabeth Economy, *The river runs black: the environmental challenge to China's future* (Ithaca: Cornell University Press, 2004). For an article treatment, see Jonathan Fenby, 'China's industrial revolution a great leap into polluted water,' *The Observer*, London, 18 August 2004, p. 9.

[4] *International Herald Tribune*, 19 March 2003, p. B3; Pei Minxin, 'China's governance crisis,' *Foreign Affairs*, September/October 2002, pp. 96–109.

[5] Zhao Bo, *Fansi: Zhongguo liji wenti* [Reflection on the rubbish problem in China], *Zhilang* [*Wisdom*] (1), 2003, http://www.usc.cuhk.edu.hk/wk_wzdetails.asp?ed=2007 (accessed 24 April 2003).

[6] http://www.chinadaily.com.cn/star/2002/0207/fe19-1.html (accessed 27 March 2003). 'Chinese NGOs — carving a niche within constraints,' a January 2003 report from the US Embassy in Beijing, http://www.usembassy-china.org.cn/sandt/ptr/ngos-prt.htm (accessed 6 November 2003).

[7] Pei, 'China's governance crisis,' pp. 96–109. More than 60 per cent of the Yellow River flow is seriously polluted (*South China Morning Post*, 24 April 2003, p. A6) and 70 per cent of the river system in Shenzhen (a city just north of Hong Kong) is heavily polluted (*Mingbao*, Hong Kong, 8 May 2003, p. A24).

[8] Pei, 'China's governance crisis.'

[9] *South China Morning Post*, 24 April 2003, p. A6.

[10] Todd Lappin, 'Can Green mix with Red?' *The Nation*, 14 February 1994.

- One in four people die of respiratory diseases.[11] (The SARS outbreak in the first half of 2003 was but one of many such deadly viruses.)[12]

China is also one of the world's largest contributors to global climate change (although a distant second to the US) and ozone depletion.[13] Indeed, an international survey on the environmental sustainability of 24 selected countries in 2001 puts China near the bottom of a ranking of environmentally-clean countries, only above the Philippines, Saudi Arabia and Haiti, but well below a host of others, with Finland and Norway at the top.[14] It is therefore not an exaggeration to say that environmental time-bombs are ticking in China. Why is this "good earth"[15] in such a terrible state? Two

---

[11] Vaughan Yarwood, 'Growth masks costs of environmental damage,' *New Zealand Herald*, 1 May 2002, p. E6.

[12] SARS stands for Severe Acute Respiratory Syndrome, or atypical pneumonia. It started to break out in southern China's Guangdong province, then spread quickly to Hong Kong and neighbouring countries and to some other parts of the world, including Toronto.

[13] Elizabeth Economy, 'Painting China green: the next Sino-American tussle,' *Foreign Affairs*, March/April 1999, p. 14–18. John Vogler, 'Environment and natural resources,' in Brian White, Richard Little, and Michael Smith (eds), *Issues in world politics*, 2nd ed, (London: Palgrave, 2001) pp. 191–211. In 2002, the US share of carbon dioxide emission of the world's total was 23.5 per cent while China was 13.6 per cent. In per capita terms, the US emitted 19.66 tons of carbon dioxide gas while China emitted 2.55 tons. *Asian Wall Street Journal*, 16 February 2005, p. A8, quoting International Energy Agency sources. The US is home to less than 5 per cent of the world population, but produces nearly a quarter of all the greenhouse emissions, which account for more than 10 per cent of all western Europe combined. See *The Guardian*, 23 August 2003, p. 1.

[14] This measurement of environmental sustainability takes into account an assessment of dozens of variables that influence the environmental health of economies. One of the strongest determinants, besides wealth, is good governance, including a broad commitment to the rule of law. See *The Economist*, 16 March 2002, p. 110.

[15] The term is borrowed from Pearl S. Buck, *The good earth* (Shanghai: Far Eastern Book, 1931), to refer to China, a country that she loved.

Chinese environmental scientists have offered five contributing factors:[16]

- A huge population;
- A rapid process and spread of urbanisation;
- A fast economic growth;
- Inadequate investment in environmental protection; and
- A low level of civic awareness.

Of these five factors, perhaps the last one — a relative lack of a general understanding among the public about the environment and the need for its protection — is the main culprit. This dire situation arises partly out of abject poverty and a low level of development in many rural areas,[17] especially in such faraway provinces as Qinghai, where poor peasants struggle with day-to-day living and where the most convenient and cheap source of fuel comes from the burning of hay, wood, and coal.[18] Also, poor farmers in some of the western provinces cleared native forests to turn hill slopes into cultivated fields in order to make a living, resulting in severe soil erosions.

What has the government done to deal with the situation? China's Great Helmsman Mao Zedong (1893–1976) once suggested

---

[16] Zhang Kunmin and Wang Cao, 'China's sustainable development strategy and international cooperation on environment,' in Tao Zhenghua and Rüdiger Wolfrum (eds), *Implementing international environmental law in Germany and China* (The Hague; London; Boston: Kluwer Law, 2001), p. 1. Different observers offer slightly different factors. For example, Wu Guangfei cites, among others, the low "quality" of its people, a feeble environmental base, a weak legal system, and backward manufacturing technology (See Wu Guangfei in *Juece tansuo* [*Policy-making Research*], Chengzhou, No. 12 (2002), p. 19–20). Xu Dongqing cites as factors lax legal enforcement and the transfer of heavy pollution-causing industries from developed countries to China (see Xu Dongqing in *Qunyan* [*Mass Voices*], Beijing, No. 10 (2002), pp. 12–15).

[17] The World Bank estimates that 100 to 250 million people lived in absolute poverty in China. Cited in Committee on Economic, Social and Cultural Rights' initial report of China, 29 April 2005.

[18] Zhu Hua, 'To stop the Qinghai ecology from worsening: alternative sources of energy,' a seminar presented at the Universities Services Centre for China Studies, Chinese University of Hong Kong, 22 April 2003.

that environmental problems were problems of the rich and therefore they had nothing to do with China's proletariat society. In a frantic move to speed up China's modernisation in order to catch up with the West during the Great Leap Forward from 1959 to 1961, trees were cut down across the country at an alarming rate to provide fuel to fire backyard furnaces in order to produce crude iron and steel. Songs and poems were publicised to promote the spirit that Maoism could "make the mountains bow their heads, the rivers flow uphill" in a great war on nature. Land was reclaimed from lakes without the use of concrete dykes; dams were built without regard to "bourgeois" standards and specifications.[19] The severe erosion of soil and the blatant neglect of agriculture led to large-scale famines and deaths from starvation of 35 million to 50 million people.[20]

China now has come a "long" way since the Maoist days. However, its still dismal environmental record not only inflicts heavy, long-term casualties on its own public health and economic well-being, but also on those of its close neighbours in the Asia-Pacific region. Countries like South Korea and Japan have voiced publicly their concerns over the effect of air pollution from China for more than a decade.[21] In 1988, flooding in Yangzi River washed rubbish all the way up to the west coast of Japan.[22] It has also been reported that desertification in the north of China produced

---

[19] Judith Shapiro, 'The rocky road to a green economy,' *South China Morning Post*, 22 April 2003, p. A11.

[20] Judith Shapiro, *Mao's war against nature: politics and the environment in revolutionary China* (Cambridge: Cambridge University Press, 2001), p. 86. Jasper Becker, *Hungry ghosts: China's secret famine* (London: John Murray, 1996). Chang Jung's latest book on Mao quotes a death toll of 38 million (Reported in ITN Channel 4, London, 4 June 2005). See Chang Jung and Jon Halliday, *Mao: the unknown story* (London: Jonathan Cape, 2005).

[21] For example, it is estimated that up to 40 per cent of air pollution in South Korea originated from China. See Fenby, 'China's industrial revolution a great leap into polluted water.'

[22] Zhang Yulin and Gu Jingtu, *Shui shi huanjing wuyan di juida shouhaizhe?* [Who are the biggest sufferers of environmental pollution?] (2003?), articles collected by the Universities Service Centre for China Studies at the Chinese University of Hong Kong, http://www.usc.cuhk.edu.hk/wk.asp

sandstorms that reached eastwards across the Pacific Ocean to Los Angeles.[23] For China itself, how to strike a right balance between fast economic growth on the one hand and proper environmental protection on the other will have an important bearing on its modernisation outcome and international standing. The country has by now entered into many international environmental agreements. But how compliant is it with the commitments it has made under those agreements? How willing and capable is it in complying with global environmental norms and rules? What does sustainable development mean to China? How do red tape, fear, inexperience, and ignorance affect its efforts to protect its environment? And how do government in-fighting and the growth of green non-governmental organisations within China affect its compliance? This chapter tries to address some of these and other related questions. It starts by looking at the beginning of environmental thinking and practice in contemporary China so as to provide a backdrop to inform later analysis.

THE DEVELOPMENT OF ENVIRONMENTAL PROTECTION

China started to tackle its environmental problems with some earnest only after adopting a reform and opening-up policy in the late 1970s and subsequent to its accession to a number of international environmental treaties. Before 1979 China had only entered into about six of these treaties. Thereafter the number had increased steadily, reaching over 40 by 1993.[24] During the 1990s China signed 25 international environmental treaties and entered into a large number of bilateral and multilateral projects dealing with

---

[23] http://www.blacksmithinstitute.org

[24] Alastair I. Johnston, 'China and international environmental institutions: a decision rule analysis,' in Michael B. McElroy et al (eds), *Energizing China: reconciling environmental protection and economic growth* (Harvard University Committee on Environment, 1998), p. 570. A complete list of environmental treaties that China has signed can be found on the website of the State Environmental Protection Administration of China, http://www.zhb.gov.en/enclish/treaty.php3 (accessed 28 March 2003). A more detailed list can be found in the Chinese version of the same website.

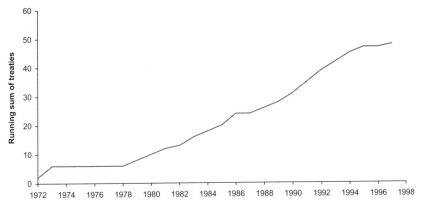

Figure 6.1 China's Accession to Environmental Treaties, 1972–1997 (Cumulative Sum)

Sources: Cai and Voigts 1993, quoted in Alastair I. Johnston, 'China and international environmental institutions: a decision rule analysis,' in Michael B. McElroy et al (eds), *Energizing China: reconciling environmental protection and economic growth* (Harvard University Committee on Environment, 1998); China Environmental Protection – Environmental Treaties, http://www.zhb.gov.cn (accessed 27 March 2003).

environmental issues (see Figure 6.1 for a cumulative sum of China's accession to environmental treaties). From 1993 to 1996, the number of these projects reached a total of 405, involving some US$3.2 billion.[25] In terms of bilateral cooperation, between 1980 and February 1999, the Chinese government signed 28 protocols, conventions, memos, or joint declarations with 24 governments on environmental cooperation.[26]

In 1983 the State Council (the Chinese government cabinet) declared that environmental protection was one of China's basic policy goals. From then on, agencies and policies of environmental management were gradually being set up. Since 1989 the Chinese government has actively taken part in the comprehensive preparations of the UN Conference on Environment and Development. Its State Planning Commission, State Science and Technology Commission,

---

[25] *Ecological Environment and Protection*, Beijing, No. 4 (2002), p. 13.

[26] Zhang and Wang, 'China's sustainable development strategy and international cooperation on environment,' p. 14.

National Environment Protection Agency and other units have introduced new ideas and ways to deal with environmental protection and the issue of development in China, including such concepts as sustainable development and integrative decision-making.

The principle of sustainable development, as understood in the West and in the global text as embodied in the discussions and documents of the United Nations system, has been transplanted to and accepted by Chinese officials and academics without much hesitation. The principle that the current use of natural resources by humankind should not jeopardise their use by future generations is generally accepted by China's elites. How to assess sustainability of particular resources and how to distribute their use fairly, however, may be open to some debates between China and the outside world. The Chinese have often argued that a fairer distribution of global wealth is required and that the rich countries in the world should do more to protect the global environment than the poor countries, because the rich countries have exploited more of the world's resources in their early industrialisation. What is more interesting, though, is the integrative decision-making approach that the Chinese adopt to deal with decision-making in environmental matters. This approach takes to task the vertical authoritative decision-making style that Chinese leaders are used to. The wordings *zonghe juece* or integrative decision-making (some literature in China uses the term "synthetic decision-making" as an English translation) first appeared in a central government document dealing with economic reform, and the phrase became widely used in the 1990s in documents dealing with environmental issues.[27] According to Shi Yan,[28] an official of the Jiangsu Environmental Protection Bureau, this integrative approach embraces five basic principles: sustainable development; an emphasis on economic development as well as environmental protection; preventive measures; pragmatism; and science and democracy. (The inclusion

[27] *Huanjing daobao* [*Environmental Herald*], Nanjing, No. 3 (2001), p. 9.
[28] Shi Yan, 'On the environment-development synthetic decision-making system,' in *Huanjing daobao*, No. 1 (2000), p. 3.

of science and democracy has an historical ring to it, as "Mr Science" and "Mr Democracy" were branded as models to be followed in order to modernise China during the early Republican era in the 1910s and the 1920s, especially during the May Fourth Movement of 1917–1921.) The approach aims to achieve an optimal outcome from a balanced approach to economic development and environmental protection. It involves a macro-strategic view to organise economic and social development and it requires a scientific approach based on the development of legal and institutional support so that proper assessments of the state of the environment can be made.[29]

The National Environmental Protection Agency (NEPA) is the principal organ dealing with environmental issues in China, but until the late 1980s it did not exist as an independent government department. From 1984 to 1988, NEPA's predecessor, the National Environmental Protection Bureau, operated under the auspices of the Ministry of Construction. Before that, a small environmental Protection Office served as China's only watchdog group. It was established in 1973 under the State Council subsequent to China's participation in the 1972 United Nations Conference on the Human Environment in Stockholm, the first international environmental gathering that China participated after its entry into the United Nations in October 1971, unseating Taiwan in the process. It has participated in other major international environmental meetings since then.

In 1998 NEPA was upgraded to the ministry-level State Environment Protection Administration (SEPA),[30] with 300 full-time staff, compared with some 6,000 in the US Environmental Protection Agency.[31] Although there are around 40,000 environmental officials

---

[29] Zhang Xiangming, 'The effect of environmental awareness to synthetic decision-making of environ-development,' in *Huanjing daobao*, No. 3 (2000), p. 23–25.

[30] Zhang and Wang, pp. 3–7.

[31] Elizabeth Economy, 'Heading off an environmental catastrophe,' *South China Morning Post*, 29 January 2003. p. 14. According to the 17 January 2005 issue of *Nanfang zhoumo* [*Southern Weekend*], SEPA has 200 staff members, while the US Environmental Protection Agency has 10,000 in Washington DC alone.

and more than 110,000 lawyers in China,[32] only a handful of them are specialists in environmental law.[33] In carrying out its work, SEPA often clashes with other ministries responsible for economic development, and sometimes, in the name of economic development, the Communist Party overrules recommendations made by SEPA. Occasionally SEPA has turned to the public to put pressure on the government to get its way, a strategy that has proved to be quite effective. With the tacit support of Premier Wen Jiabao,[34] SEPA has been asserting its authority recently in various ways. In January 2005 it ordered the halt of 30 huge dam projects across 13 provinces,[35] for failing to file the necessary environment impact assessments demanded by the Environmental Impact Assessment Law which came into effect in September 2003. In the same month it published a list of 46 power plants that had failed to make provisions for desulfurisation.[36] In April 2005 it declared illegal a project to line the lake bed of Yuanmingyuan or Beijing's Old Summer Palace with plastic sheets to prevent water seepage. SEPA organised the first-ever public forum to discuss what many environmentalists

---

[32] As of 1996, there were nationwide more than 2,500 environmental protection administration departments above the county level with a total staff of 88,000 engaged in various environmental control activities. And the total number of environmental protection workers employed by various departments and enterprises exceeds 200,000. See White Paper, *Environmental protection in China* (Information Office, State Council, 1996), http://english.peopledaily.com.cn/whitepaper/14(2).html (accessed 21 July 2003).

[33] *South China Morning Post*, 7 February 2003, p. 8.

[34] Wen highlighted the government's resolve to promote harmony between man and nature — economic growth and environmental protection — in his Government Work Report presented at the National People's Congress in March 2005.

[35] *The Standard*, Hong Kong, 2 February 2005, p. A1. Some two months later, by early May 2005, all 30 projects were back in operation, apparently after filing their assessment reports (*South China Morning Post*, 6 May 2005, p. A8). Some observers say that SEPA was under powerful political pressure to lift the ban. However, the incident has shown at least that environmental law has to be followed and that the publicity surrounding the case may have raised the profile and importance of environmental issues.

[36] *South China Morning Post*, 12 March 2005, p. A6.

described (the palace project) as an ecological disaster. Pan Yue,[37] the active, new vice-director of SEPA, plans to hold more public hearings in future to solicit the opinions of experts, company executives and environmentalists on environmentally-sensitive projects.

In terms of organisational structure (see Figure 6.2), SEPA sits on top of local Environmental Protection Bureaus in various provinces, but in practice, since the heads of local bureaus are appointed by provincial governors,[38] the enforcement of environmental laws is subject to the sway of bureaucratic rivalries and vested interests at local levels. As a result, environmental projects can be forced to give way to commercial projects. For example, the construction of the Three Gorges Dam has attracted many worldwide concerns over its environmental impact on human habitat and ecological balance. Also, in the name of economic development, many historical sites and avenues in the capital city Beijing have to give way to infrastructural projects such as massive road works and high-rise buildings.

In brief, China started to pay attention to the state of health of its environment in the 1970s, in the aftermath of the height of the Cultural Revolution. At least five nationwide environmental protection conferences had been held in 1973, 1983, 1989, 1992 and 1996. The first two, convened during China's state-planning system, set out the necessary though preliminary principles, goals and norms of environmental protection. The other three conferences were held in the transition period from plan to market-orientated economy. The 1989 conference adopted a legal framework, known as the

---

[37] Pan Yue, a 45-year-old outspoken critic, assumed his vice-directorship in March 2003. He runs against powerful vested business and political interests, but seemingly he is not afraid to exercise his powers. He is noted for proposing the idea of green GDP, an index that deducts the cost of resource consumption and environmental damage from conventional gross domestic product. He is reportedly to have cast his eye on a place among the fifth generation of leaders to take the helm at the 18th National People's Congress in 2012, when the present leadership retires (*Ibid.*). Pan is the son-in-law of Liu Huaqing, former vice-chairman of the Central Military Commission.

[38] *Ibid.*

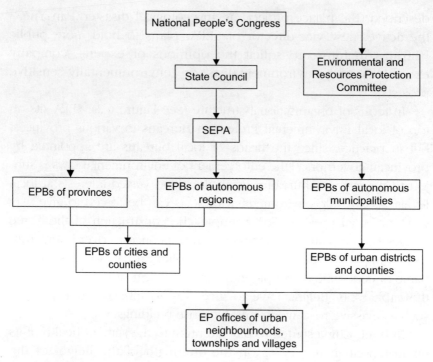

Figure 6.2 Administrative Structure of China's Environmental Protection

Source: Slightly modified from Wang Yan, Richard K. Morgan, and Mat Cashmore, 'Environmental impact assessment of projects in the People's Republic of China: new law, old problems,' in *Environmental Impact Assessment Review*, Vol. 23, Issue 5 (2003), p. 552, citing an adaptation from SEPA, 2001.
Notes: SEPA — State Environmental Protection Administration.
      EPBs — Environmental Protection Bureaus.

Environment Protection Law, promulgated by the legislature. In fact, the National People's Congress passed a provisional set of laws relating to environmental protection back in 1979. At the 1992 conference, the ideas of sustainable development and other related concepts, as expounded in the United Nations Environmental and Development Conference, found their way to the Chinese environmental discourse.[39] China was the first country to adopt and turn the

---

[39] Xu Gangxi and Shan Yang, 'On the frame [sic] of environmental protection policy,' *Huanjing daobao*, No. 1 (2001), pp. 1–2.

1992 UN Agenda 21 into its own version of China Agenda 21, to deal with its environmental management.[40] In drafting its own Agenda 21 and in designing its many environmental programmes, China received a lot of help and advice from the United Nations Development Programme. Also, in 1992, the Chinese government set up the China Council for International Cooperation on Environment and Development, a high-level "non-governmental"[41] advisory body with the purpose "of further strengthening cooperation and exchange between China and the international community in the field of environment and development."[42] Consisting of more than 40 leading specialists and well-known public figures from China and other countries, the Council advises the government on environmental matters.[43] The 1996 conference reinforced the idea and strategy of sustaining development in environmental protection work.[44] From then on, many other conferences and discussions have been held at various levels of government and it can be said that the issue of environmental protection has taken root in China.

DOMESTIC ENVIRONMENTAL LEGISLATION

Among the many ways to show the extent of international compliance such as the submission of compliance reports on a regular basis and cooperation with international monitoring and verification, the extent to which a country passes domestic legislation to match its international obligations is of fundamental importance. Towards the end of 2002, China had completed six pieces of legislation relating to environmental protection, 13 sets of resource

---

[40] *Zhongguo dai baike quanshu: huanjing kexue* [*China encyclopaedia: environmental science*] (Beijing: China Encyclopaedia Press, 2002), p. 5.

[41] Or, more correctly, GONGO — government-organised NGO.

[42] http://svr1-pek.unep.net/cciced/english/index.htm

[43] White Paper, *Environmental protection in China.*

[44] The conference proceedings were published in a book entitled *Dixiqi quanguo huanjing baohu huiyi wenjian huibian* [*A collection of documents of the 4th national conference on environmental protection*] (Beijing: China Environment Science Press, 1996).

management laws, and 395 items of environmental protection standards.[45] Another record shows that there are at present 140 central government regulations and 1,020 provincial and municipal rules relating to environmental protection.[46] In 1996 the Information Office of the State Council published a White Paper entitled *Environment protection in China*, giving details of China's environmental policy and work.[47] During the Ninth Five-Year Plan (1996–2000), 60,000 heavy pollution-causing small enterprises were closed down.[48] Also, for the first time, environmental protection targets have been written into China's Tenth Five-Year Plan (2001–2005), including comprehensive policies for improving the environment, mainly through pollution control, biological/ ecological protection, and the development of an environmental industry. Despite the existence of a rather comprehensive body of law, the problem remains that they are rarely followed, due to competing interests (between economic development and environmental protection), a low level of legal understanding, inconsistencies in some areas of law and widespread practice of corruption at many levels of government. Also, some big state-owned enterprises managing the construction of huge projects worth billions of dollars tend to ignore legal regulations by just absorbing the maximum fine of US$24,000 into their operational costs.[49] It would be much cheaper to pay the fine than to refit plants with cleaning equipment.[50]

---

[45] *Ecological Environment and Protection*, in *Fuyin baokan jiliao* [*Reprints of Materials from Books and Journals*], N2, China Renda Social Science Information Center, Beijing, No. 4 (2002), p. 54.

[46] *South China Morning Post*, 7 February 2003, p. 8.

[47] A soft copy is available at http://english.peopledaily.com.cn/whitepaper/14(6).html

[48] *Huanjing gongzuo tongxun* [*Bulletin of Environmental Work*], No. 1, 10 January 2002, p. 3.

[49] Susan Jakes, 'Power play: China's underdog environmental agency scores a big victory,' *Times* magazine, Internet ed., 14 February 2005. SEPA can fine the developer of any illegal projects 50,000 to 200,000 yuan and seek a court ruling to enforce its ban. See *The Standard*, 2 February 2005, p. A1.

[50] Fenby, 'China's industrial revolution a great leap into polluted water.'

Of the many international environmental treaties that China has entered into in recent years, its ratification of the 1997 Kyoto Protocol in September 2002, agreeing to limit its greenhouse gas emission, is of great significance because of its impact on local industries. China is the second largest emitter of greenhouse gases after the United States, due largely to the widespread burning of coal to produce energy. On a per capita basis, however, the energy use and emissions of these gases in China remain far below levels found in richer countries. These emissions are, for example, roughly one-eighth of those in the US on a per capita basis.[51] As a developing country, China is in fact exempt from setting emission quotas.[52] As a way to control such emissions, China has ordered the closure of tens of thousands of small mines producing low-grade coal, inefficient factories and state-owned enterprises, partly as a way to cut economic costs and partly to reduce greenhouse gas emission. The effect has not been very profound, as local governments are sometimes reluctant to close these mines and factories down for fear of rising unemployment and social riots. The task of controlling gas emission has been complicated by China's booming economy. Coal consumption has been rising at a rate of about eight to ten per cent and more cars are being sold and used. General Motors predicts that China will account for 18 per cent of the world's growth in new car sales from 2002 through to 2012, compared with 11 per cent in the US and nine per cent in India.[53] The overall result of China's effort to control gas emission and its increasing use of energy threatens international effort to curb global warming. Although the production of coal in China has been cut, its imports of coal from the outside, especially from Australia, have been on the rise. The International Energy Agency in Paris predicts that the increase in greenhouse gas emissions from 2000 to 2030 in China alone could nearly equal the increase from the entire industrialised world.[54]

---

[51] Keith Bradsher, 'China's boom adds to global warming problem,' *New York Times*, 22 October, 2003.

[52] So is India.

[53] Bradsher, 'China's boom adds to global warming problem'.

[54] *Ibid.*

China's ratification of the Kyoto Protocol stands in stark contrast to the stance taken by the US and Australia, which refuse to accept the Protocol in order to protect their domestic industries, to the dismay of many European countries and Japan, the latter being one of the main architects of the Protocol. When President George W. Bush rejected the Kyoto Protocol in 2001, he portrayed China's exemption as a serious flaw.

THE EMERGENCE OF ENVIRONMENTAL NGOS

The national conference on environmental protection in 1992 discussed, among other things, integrative decision-making and public participation. While the idea of integrative decision-making has been briefly discussed earlier, the idea of public participation is interesting because of its implications for China's democratic development. There may be different understandings as to what the public is supposed to mean in China, but over time there seems to be a general understanding that it refers to the general public, including individuals and private groups and organisations. In recent publications on public participation in environmental protection in China,[55] it has been suggested that public participation should be mutual and directed in reciprocal ways, that is, public input into government processes as well as government consultation with private citizens and groups. Also, the input and consultation processes should be open and transparent and should be conducted in a "scientific way". Furthermore, decisions made must be acceptable to those who are directly and indirectly affected.

An indirect indicator of China's compliance behaviour is the government's policy towards the growth of environmental non-governmental organisations (NGOs).[56] In 1997, only a handful of

---

[55] For example, Han Sha-sha, 'On public participation of environmental planning,' *Huanjing daobao*, No. 3 (2001), pp. 13–14; and Wang Zhigang, Chen Bingdu, and Chen Xingeng, 'Mechanism and efficiency of public administration in environmental impact assessment,' *Huanjing daobao*, No. 3 (2000), pp. 1–3.

[56] For a graphical presentation of the growth of these NGOs, see Yang Guobin, 'Environmental NGOs and institutional dynamics in China,' *The China Quarterly*, No. 181 (March 2005), p. 51, Figures 2 and 3.

NGOs of various kinds existed in China, most of which were based in Beijing. By August 2002 there were more than 250 NGOs across the country, in every province.[57] Since the 1990s concerned Chinese scholars have started to organise NGOs to promote environmental awareness. The first one,[58] called Friends of Nature, was formally registered in March 1994 with the Ministry of Civil Affairs.[59] This was followed by another well-known NGO, Global Village of Beijing, founded in 1996.[60] Others include Green Volunteer League formed in 1995 in Chongqing, Green Earth Volunteers formed in 1996 in Beijing, Yunnan Pesticides Eco-Alternatives Centre, the Han Hai Sha Desert Volunteers Network, and the Sichuan Green-River Environmental Protection Foster Association. As of May 2005, the website of Friends of Nature lists 48 such environmental NGOs.[61] Their programmes and activities are mostly funded by overseas

---

[57] *South China Morning Post*, 21 August 2002. This number seems small, probably due to a stricter definition of NGO used by the source, and therefore a large number of government-sponsored NGOs have been excluded. *The Law yearbook of China* indicates that there were 142,121 *shehui tuanti* (or social organisations) and 124,491 *minban feiqiye danwei* (private non-enterprise units, such as research and educational institutes and foundations). See *Zhongguo falue nianjian* [*Law yearbook of China*] (Beijing: Press of Law Yearbook of China, 2004), p. 1,073. Zhuang Ailing, founder of Shanghai-based Non-Profit Organisation Development Centre, estimates that China at present has approximately 700,000 to 800,000 NGOs. See *Shanghai Daily*, 23 August 2004, p. 12.

[58] Although the China Environment and Development International Cooperation Committee, formed in April 1992, was billed as an NGO, it is largely a government-sponsored organisation.

[59] Under China's Social Organisations Law, all NGOs in China are required to register with the Ministry of Civil Affairs and to have a sponsor. This legal requirement ensures that NGOs will come under the control of the government. Some NGOs choose not to register while others try to register as business corporations, since the latter is easier to do so, but there are taxation implications. As of 2003 China is in the process of revising these laws, making it easier for NGOs to function in China. See 'Chinese NGOs — carving a niche within constraints,' A January 2003 report from the US Embassy in Beijing, http://www.usembassy-china.org.cn/sandt/ptr/ngos-prt.htm (assessed 11 June 2003).

[60] For some of their work, see the websites of Friends of Nature (http://www.fon.org.cn) and Global Village of Beijing (http://www.gvbchina.org).

[61] http://www.fon.org.cn/index.php?id=2684

sources, with foundations like Ford, Rockefeller Brothers Fund and Winrock International annually contributing millions of dollars.[62] Chinese environmentalists made their debut on the international stage when they attended the World Summit on Sustainable Development, held in Johannesburg, South Africa, in late August 2002. The 20 delegates from mainland China's environmental NGOs were sponsored by the British Embassy, the US-based Ford Foundation, and Canada's Civil Society Project.[63] Although the voice of Chinese environmentalists was said to be feeble at international forums,[64] they have started to link up with international NGOs and to lobby or work with the government and the industrial sector at home to help alleviate environmental problems,[65] especially working with SEPA. After the Johannesburg Summit, returning Chinese delegates held a conference in Nanjing in September 2002 to brief their colleagues in China and, as a result, they drew up an action plan to outline their future work in the country, stressing the importance of the contributions made by NGOs and promoting the ideas of sustainability and public participation, among others.[66]

Unlike other kinds of NGOs, green groups in China are seen in a peculiar light by the authorities.[67] On the one hand, they are perceived as less threatening, as they tend to work with the government to lessen environmental damages which the government

---

[62] *Far Eastern Economic Review,* 10 April 2003, p. 30.

[63] *South China Morning Post,* 16 August 2002, p. 9.

[64] See the article entitled 'NGO to voice their views louder,' http://www.gvbchina.org/English/englishintro.html

[65] Many international environmental NGOs, such as WWF, Ecologia, Pacific Environment, Friends of the Earth, and Greenpeace have set up projects or opened offices in China. See Yang Guobin, 'Global environmentalism hits China,' YaleGlobal online, http://yaleglobal.yale.edu/acticle.print?id=3250 (accessed 6 February 2004).

[66] http://www.fon.org.cn/index.php?id=2770

[67] For useful analyses of green NGOs in China, see Yang, 'Environmental NGOs and institutional dynamics in China,' pp. 46–66; Jonathan Schwartz, 'Environmental NGOs in China: roles and limits,' *Pacific Affairs,* Vol. 77, No. 1 (Spring 2004), pp. 28–49.

sometimes finds difficult to tackle on its own. These NGOs work more efficiently to motivate individuals to take steps to protect their environmental interests. On the other hand, the fact that they can raise the level of public awareness over some rather volatile social and environmental issues poses a potential threat and challenge to the authorities. Furthermore, the government is worried that such groups may eventually lead to the establishment of some kind of political party, like what had happened before in many countries in the West. Somehow in China, the government and the emerging NGO sector have to learn to live and work with each other. During the campaign to compete for the hosting of the 2008 Olympics, the Beijing Olympic Organising Committee, a semi-governmental body, for the first time invited environmental NGOs to attend proceedings as advisors, in order to promote the green image of the forthcoming Beijing games.

An adventurous NGO initiative is the setting up of the Centre for Legal Assistance to Pollution Victims in Beijing in 1999, with substantial financial support from Ford Foundation. The director of the centre is an environmental lawyer and a professor at the China University of Politics and Law named Wang Canfa. The centre provides a channel for citizens to voice their discontent with actions taken by the government. Through legal proceedings, ordinary folks can seek compensation from the government and business corporations. Up till 2002, the centre had fielded thousands of telephone calls and taken 22 cases it deemed most worthy to the courts. In a landmark case raised by the centre on behalf of 100 peasant families against a paper factory for dumping toxic chemicals into Shiliang River in eastern Jiangsu Province that affected their livelihood, a local court ruled against the factory and awarded compensation of 5.6 million yuan to the families affected.[68] According to influential green activist Liang Congjie,[69] this was a landmark case because

---

[68] http://www.planetark.org

[69] Liang was the founder of Friends of Nature. He is the grandson of Liang Qichao, an influential turn-of-the-century scholar who hoped to reform China's moribund imperial system along democratic lines. This relationship helps, as he commands

before 1992 almost nobody in China ever used environmental law to protect himself or herself.

CHINA'S ENVIRONMENTAL DIPLOMACY

China's domestic environmental awakening bears a close relationship with its international environmental diplomacy, which in turn has a close tie with its UN diplomacy. The United Nations Conference on the Human Environment, held in Stockholm in 1972, set off an unprecedented development of new international environmental treaties. Before that, only a dozen or so international treaties with relevance to the environment were in force; 25 years later, more than 1,000 such instruments existed.[70.] Having entered the world body a year earlier, China sent a delegation to the UN Human Environmental Conference. The bulk of China's environmental diplomacy, however, was conducted after it had adopted its reform and opening-up policy in the late 1970s. According to its State Environmental Protection Administration, China upholds five basic principles in its environmental diplomacy:[71]

1. A balance between economic development and environmental protection;
2. In international environmental cooperation, the international community should give due consideration to the special conditions and needs of developing countries, particularly in two

---

considerable respect as the heir to his family's formidable intellectual legacy. Liang is also a member of the Chinese People's Political Consultative Committee. An historian by training, Liang spent most of his time during the 1980s doing cross-cultural analyses of ancient encyclopedias in China and the West. See Lappin, 'Can Green mix with Red?'

[70] Michael Faure and Jürgen Lefevere, 'Compliance with international environmental agreements,' in Norman J. Vig and Regina S. Axelrod (eds), *The global environment: institutions, law, and policy* (Washington, DC: Congressional Quarterly, 1999), p. 138.

[71] SEPA (ed), *Zhongguo huanjing baohu ershiyi shiji yizhang* [*China's environmental protect Agenda 21*] (Beijing: SEPA Press, 1995), pp. 260–261.

aspects. One is the area of poverty and underdevelopment, which constitutes the root cause of environmental degradation in these countries. To solve this problem, developing countries must maintain a certain level of economic growth in order to tackle the problem of poverty, to increase their ability to protect their environment, and to take part in international environmental protection. It is imperative, therefore, that the North should treat the South fairly. A new international economic order should be created so that developing countries can maintain sustainable economic growth. The other aspect relates to such long-standing environmental problems as desertification, soil erosion, drought, and polluted water in developing countries, as these problems hamper economic growth and affect the environment domestically, regionally, and internationally;

3. International environmental protection must follow the principle of "common but differentiated responsibility". In their relentless drive for economic growth, developed countries have contributed and still contribute to global environmental problems. They should therefore devote a greater share of their international effort to combat environmental problems by extending aid and transferring environmental technology to the developing world;

4. In international environmental cooperation, mutual respect of the integrity of state sovereignty and the principle of non-interference should be upheld; and

5. Environmental protection and development should not be detached from the development of peace and stability.

These principles show China's concern that countries should not use environmental issues as a pretext to interfere in the domestic affairs of others and that rich countries should contribute more resources to help poor countries to deal with environmental problems. In short, these principles spell out China's desire for equality and justice in world affairs. How to achieve a right balance between economic growth and environmental protection in practice, however, remains controversial and difficult to determine precisely.

INTERNATIONAL COMPLIANCE: HOW EFFECTIVE?

There seems to be little publicly-visible international pressure on China to keep its environment clean, compared with other issues such as trade and human rights. In the area of human rights, pressure has been put on China quite regularly, either bilaterally by individual countries, especially those in the West, or multilaterally through the United Nations system or human rights organisations, to improve its human rights practice. Similarly, in the area of trade under the purview of the World Trade Organisation, bilateral and multilateral pressures can be brought to bear on China to goad it to abide by WTO rules. In addition, WTO membership requires China to meet certain environmental trade standards. Perhaps international pressure will mount when diseases arising out of poor environmental hygiene spread from China to other countries, like the case of SARS. From a realist or mercantilist perspective, most foreign governments apparently could not care less if poor environmental standards in China weaken its economic health or reduce its international economic competitiveness, given the anarchical and self-help nature of international politics. (This kind of attitude, however, cannot be said of international environmental NGOs, which usually have objectives different from governments and nation-states.) Also, advanced countries can set up trade barriers to bar China's environmentally sub-standard products from entering their countries, a system permissible under the current WTO rules. China's trade ministry estimated that some US$4 billion worth of Chinese exports had been adversely affected in this way.[72] Various estimates of the cost to China's loss of production due to health problems of its workforce and other environmental damages range from 3.5 to 15 per cent per annum.[73] The greatest cost is in the health and productivity

---

[72] Carlos Lo Wing-hung and Chung Shan-shan 'China's green challenges in the twenty-first century,' in Joseph Y.S. Cheng (ed), *China's challenges in the twenty-first century* (Hong Kong: City University of Hong Kong Press, 2003) p. 735.
[73] For example, *The Economist* (11 May 2002, p. 77) puts the figures at 3.5 to 7.7 per cent. Vaughan Yarwood, however, suggests a figure ranging from

losses associated with urban air pollution, which the World Bank estimates at more than US$20 billion per year. Water scarcity in cities costs another US$14 billion in lost industrial output. In rural areas, water scarcity and pollution contribute to crop loss of about US$24 billion annually.[74] China's economy has been growing at around 9 to 10 per cent per year in the past decade or so. If all its environmental problems were kept under control, then it could have been growing at a hypothetical rate of 12.5 to 25 per cent per annum! From the opposite perspective, environmental damage has eroded its economic growth and may, in some provinces like Shanxi,[75] Guangdong, Shandong, Jiangsu and Zhejiang,[76] reduce the economic growth to zero or even below.

One major difficulty in enforcing international environmental compliance globally lies with the United States. As the most powerful country on earth, it can play a leading role in international environmental protection if it chooses to do so, as in many other political and economic issues. However, it lacks the credibility and moral high ground to demand other countries to comply with international environmental standard when it fails to do so. The Bush administration casts doubts on the scientific basis of some of the environmental problems such as global warming and ozone depletion. The real reason, however, as has been pointed out by ardent environmentalists, is that the US wants to protect its own industries and its interests, giving low priorities to environmental protection measures that affect adversely its economic output or employment situation.

3.5 to 8 per cent (Yarwood, 'Growth masks costs of environmental damage'). Elizabeth Economy suggests a figure of 8 to 12 per cent (Economy, 'Heading off an environmental catastrophe'). And the Chinese Academy of Sciences puts the figure at 15 per cent (*Ershiyi shiji jingji baodao* [*21st Century Business Herald*], 3 March 2005, p. 8).

[74] Economy, 'Heading off an environmental catastrophe.'

[75] *Shanghai Daily*, 23 August 2004, p. 12.

[76] Florence Chan, 'The state of pollution,' *Asian Times*, Internet ed., 16 March 2005.

FACING THE GREEN CHALLENGE

Although the Chinese government now gives high priority to environmental protection, there still exist formidable obstacles. As Elizabeth Economy has pointed out, the protection of the environment "remains far below priorities such as economic development, maintaining social stability and enhancing military capabilities."[77] During the Ninth Five-Year Plan (1996–2000), China spent 360 billion yuan on measures to protect the environment, representing 0.93 per cent of its gross domestic product and reaching a historical high in such spending.[78] This spending was a significant increase over a similar expenditure during the Eighth Five-Year Plan, which amounted to 130 billion yuan, representing 0.73 per cent of the GDP.[79] Although the government announced in August 2000 that 9 billion yuan (about US$1 billion) would be spent on environmental improvement that year and a total of 100 billion yuan was set aside to protect the environment surrounding Beijing from 1998 to 2008, when the Beijing Olympic Games are scheduled to be held,[80] China's national budget for environmental protection is still limited to about 1.5 per cent of annual GDP.[81] In comparison, developed countries already spent about 1 to 2 per cent of their GDP on environmental protection even in the 1970s, with the US spending 2 per cent and Japan, 2 to 3 per cent.[82] According to one

---

[77] *Ibid.*

[78] *Huanjing gongzuo tongxun*, No. 1 (10 January 2002), pp. 4 and 6.

[79] Lo and Chung, 'China's green challenges in the twenty-first century,' p. 720. In his opening address at the second Global Environmental Facility Assembly, Jiang Zemin said that from 1998 to 2002, China had invested 580 billion yuan in environmental protection and ecological development (Jiang's address in 2002), so apparently China has been increasing quite rapidly its investment in this area since the mid-1990s.

[80] Jane Sayers, 'China's environmental crisis enters the public arena,' *Asiaview*, Murdoch University, Perth, Australia, November 2000; *Beijing wanbao* [*Beijing Evening Post*], 19 February 2003, p. 4.

[81] Economy, 'Heading off an environmental catastrophe'.

[82] *Ecological Environment and Protection*, No. 3 (2003), p. 25.

estimate,[83] about 80 per cent of China's environmental protection budget comes from abroad.

To change the mindset of the general public and their habits (of eating and working) on a massive scale is by no means easy. According to two Chinese analysts, China's engine of growth at the expense of proper environmental protection can be likened to a locomotive without a proper brake: The urban areas "export" its pollution to the rural areas; local officials do whatever they can to attract investment, relegating the work of environmental bureaus from a supervisory role to that of an observer or bystander.[84] The age-old practice of corruption worsens the situation and makes resolution of environmental problems more difficult. For example, it has been reported that, in the Three Gorges Dam project, rampant occurrences of corruption happened. In September 2002, governmental officials said 234 cases of corruption had been uncovered in connection with the project, involving US$5 million in funds that would have been allocated for compensation to relocated families.[85]

A discussion of these challenges that China faces does not mean that China has done little to address its environmental problems. On the contrary, in the past two decades or so, the country has strengthened its environmental law and policy, raised the profile of its environmental administration and given it more power to act, increased its spending on practical measures, and relaxed its policy towards the growth and the work of green NGOs. Specifically, things that have been done include, among others, tree-planting, environmental clean-up, and improved urban sanitation. In Beijing, 20,000 diesel buses have been replaced by LPG or electric vehicles.[86] Legislation relating to environmental Impact Assessments

---

[83] Miranda Scherer, talk given at the Woodrow Wilson Center, Washington DC, 4 June 1997.

[84] Zhang and Gu, *Shui shi huanjing wuyan di juida shouhaizhe?*

[85] *The Globe and Mail*, 4 June 2003, http://www.threegorgesprobe.org (accessed 11 November 2003).

[86] http://www.blacksmithinstitute.org

started to be debated in the National People's Congress (China's Parliament) in 1998, and was approved by its Standing Committee in October 2002 to provide the groundwork for evaluating the environmental impact of factory operations and construction projects.[87] Legal channels are made available to those who have been disenfranchised by pollution. Two newsletters with wide readership are in circulation: one published by the Ministry of Agriculture; the other, entitled *China Environmental News*, by SEPA. Many periodicals have also appeared. Titles include *Environmental Education, Advances in Environmental Science, Shandong Environment, Sichuan Environment, Environmental Protection in Xinjiang, Resources and Environment in Yangtze Basin, Fujian Soil and Water Conservation, Fujian Environment, Land Greening, Henan Water Resources, Environment Herald,* and so on.[88] According to China's White Paper on 'Environmental protection in China', there are more than 30 local environmental newspapers and several hundred professional periodicals. China Environmental Science Press was established in 1980, and by 1995 it had published over five million copies of books of 860 titles on the environment. In 1995 a philosophy teacher at Sichuan University named Liao Xiaoyi began to develop television programmes on environmental protection for China Central Television. Together, two such programmes — "Environment and China" and "Environmental Time" — attracted more than 150 million Chinese viewers.[89] In 1996 she helped to found the Global Village of Beijing, which has become one of the leading environmental NGOs in China, and she has since attended many international meetings on environmental protection.

Given China's huge geographic and population sizes, its regional diversities, and its late attention to environmental matters, it

---

[87] *Zhongguo huanjing bao* [*China Environmental News*], Beijing, 31 December 2002. p. 3.
[88] My research in the Universities Service Centre for China Studies at the Chinese University of Hong Kong, July 2003 and March 2005.
[89] http://www.gvbchina.org/English/englishintro.html (accessed 30 September 2002).

is difficult to make an accurate assessment of the efficacy of its environmental work. It would be fair to say that some progress has been made in the 25 years or so since the adoption of the reform and opening-up policy. However, much more work remains to be done if the country is to avert a drastic deterioration in its environment. In the long run, China's hope lies with education:[90] how to introduce the idea of the common good and to raise the level of civic awareness. From 1985 to 1995, China's institutions of higher education had trained some 88,000 professionals in environmental areas. As of 2001, 30,000 students received environmental training in tertiary institutions, run by some 140 colleges and universities.[91] Two Chinese commentators point out that, apart from focusing on university students, attention should be paid to students of all ages, the general public, government and Party leaders, and people in villages and rural areas.[92] The nurturing of NGOs and their collaboration with overseas groups is another way. NGOs in China serve as a partner with the government and as a bridge between the government and the public. As far as the government is able to control them and to make them work for its advantage while minimising their potential threat to its authority, then there is hope for a good workable relationship, given China's current political system and culture. On the other hand, these NGOs, while responding to political conditions and taking opportunities offered by the media, the Internet, and international NGOs, challenge the state and the market by expanding political possibilities. They serve as both sites and agents of democratic social change.[93] The media play an important role in exposing ineptitude and corruption. A survey on media

---

[90] China's illiteracy rate in 2004 was 6.72 per cent, which means that 85 million people were illiterate. See *Mingbao*, Hong Kong, 5 October 2004, p. A26. The country spends one-third less than India on education, although its per capita GDP is 50 per cent higher. See Pei Minxin, 'With Jiang gone, China can rebalance,' *International Herald Tribune*, 21 September 2004, p. 8.

[91] White Paper, *Environmental protection in China*.

[92] Yao Jun and Zhao Ye in *Huanjing daobao*, No. 1 (2002), pp. 39–40.

[93] Yang, 'Environmental NGOs and institutional dynamics in China,' pp. 46–66.

coverage of environmental matters, conducted by Friends of Nature, shows that between 1995 and 1999 such reporting had tripled.[94] Ultimately, much depends of political change towards a more democratic system with increasing transparency of operation and a greater degree of accountability, in environmental as well as other matters.

CONCLUSION

China has taken three perspectives to look at the issue of environmental protection: first, a traditional perspective in which the responsibility to protect the environment lies with rich countries in the developed world; second, a developmental perspective in which China sees a need for it to take some responsibilities as well, as a member of the international community and as it has been adversely affected by the worsening state of its own environment; third, a global perspective in which China has a responsibility to participate actively and positively in global environmental protection. China's current approach bears largely the hallmark of the first perspective, but it moves steadily towards adopting an approach that combines the second and the third.

In a cross-country analysis of the international environmental commitments of democracies, Eric Neumayer finds that a stronger positive link exists between democracies with environmental commitments than with environmental outcomes.[95] In other words, there is a gap between commitments and compliance even in liberal democracies. This observation seems to apply to China too, although China is not a liberal democracy. At present, the country shows a strong commitment to abide by the rules of international environmental regimes, but the outcomes may not fully satisfy domestic and international demands. This is due mainly to its

---

[94] Sayers, 'China's environmental crisis enter the public arena.'

[95] Eric Neumayer, 'Do democracies exhibit stronger international environmental commitment? A cross-country analysis,' *Journal of Peace Research*, Vol. 39, No. 2 (2002), pp. 139–164.

inability, rather than its unwillingness, to improve its environmental record. There is therefore a need for the outside world to offer China expertise and resources in order to help it overcome some of its difficulties. Hence capacity building should ideally be the focus of attention of China's environmental diplomacy as well as the environmental policies of other countries towards China.

The greatest domestic challenge of China's increasing environmental interest lies in the public awareness of the rights and wrongs of environmental protection, and hence the duties and obligations of citizenship and of the government. The idea of public good emerges slowly and the demand for public participation in environmental policy-making suggests a move towards democratisation and greater demand for political change. This trend of development augers well for China as a whole in the long run, but may run counter to vested interests, resulting in conflicts between ordinary people and the Party/government in the short to medium term.

Chapter

7

China's Compliance in Human Rights

What are human rights? Are they the human rights of the majority? Are they the human rights of a minority? Or are they the human rights of the entire citizenry? The meaning of human rights as spoken of by the Western world and as spoken of by us are two different things. There is no common language.

China's paramount leader Deng Xiaoping, 1979[1]

Chinese society is becoming more open and pluralistic, if not with the speed or scope that I would wish for.

German Chancellor Gerhard Schroeder, 2005[2]

The question of Beijing's human rights theory and practice — whether the PRC will become more compliant with universal human rights norms — is crucial to any assessment of the future of Chinese democratisation.

Professor Samuel S. Kim, 2000[3]

---

[1] Yu Haocheng in *Apple Daily News*, Hong Kong, 23 March 1998, p. G3, cited in *Inside China Mainland*, Taipei, June 1998, p. 4.

[2] The German Chancellor speaking to lawmakers in Berlin as he sought support for lifting the EU arms embargo on China. Cited in *The Standard*, Hong Kong, 15 April 2005, p. A2.

[3] Samuel S. Kim, 'Human rights in China's international relations,' in Edward Friedman and Barrett L. McCormick (eds), *What if China doesn't democratize? Implications for war and peace* (Armonk, NY and London: M.E. Sharpe, 2000), p. 130.

The concept of human rights, as is generally understood, grew out of European experiences and then spread to other parts of the world.[4] China, as an old civilisation, has its long tradition of handling relationships among individuals and between individuals and society. Liberal-democratic principles that individuals are equal to one another and that each individual has inalienable rights are on the whole foreign to the traditional Chinese mind.

This chapter starts by giving a brief introduction to the growth of human rights awareness in the contemporary world and in China. It then gives a background to the divergent views on human rights between China and the West, followed by China's engagement with international human rights regimes, focusing on China's compliance or otherwise with the rules and norms of those regimes. Subsequently, the chapter analyses China' bilateral human rights diplomacy with the outside world, especially with the US and the EU. Finally, it examines what China has done to further its human rights discourse, with the publication of White Papers giving some details of China's policy in this field and its initiation of human rights dialogues with other countries and international organisations.

HUMAN RIGHTS REGIMES IN THE CONTEMPORARY WORLD

The Universal Declaration of Human Rights, adopted by the UN General Assembly in 1948, is the source of international law on human rights. To put this declaration into legally-binding treaties, the General Assembly in 1966 adopted the International Covenant on Economic, Social and Cultural Rights and the International Covenant on Civil and Political Rights. Both covenants entered into force in 1976. In addition, nations have negotiated 25 major and

---

[4] For a recent article which traces the origins of human rights tradition to its anthropology in Christian ideas, see Anthony J. Langlois, 'The elusive ontology of human rights,' *Global Society: Journal of Interdisciplinary International Relations*, Vol. 18, No. 3 (July 2004), pp. 244–261.

many lesser human rights conventions, protocols, and other instruments.[5] Before its entry into the United Nations in 1971, China had been largely acting outside the international community, calling for independence, liberation, revolution, and the solidarity of the Third World against imperialism, revisionism, and hegemonism. After a period of cautious observation as a member state of the UN, in 1979 China began to attend meetings of the UN Human Rights Commission as an observer, and in 1982 it became a member of that commission. Thereafter, it began to increase its participation in various sub-commissions promoting the rights of minorities, indigenous populations, children, migrant workers, and the like. With other Third World countries, it promoted the idea of a "right to development", which the UN General Assembly enacted by resolution in 1986.[6]

The Helsinki accords of 1975 gave new impetus to the international human rights movement and led to the founding of many non-governmental organisations in the human rights field, including Amnesty International, Human Rights Watch, and others. China has remained distant from them because of their critical views of its human rights record.

DEVELOPMENT OF HUMAN RIGHTS IN CHINA

Samuel Kim of Columbia University divides the post-Cultural Revolution development of human rights discourse in China into three time periods:[7]

- In the initial period (1976–1981), there was no change to speak of as Beijing stood firm on Maoist collective rights and non-participation in international human rights regimes;

---

[5] Andrew Nathan and Robert Ross, *The Great Wall and the empty fortress* (New York and London: W.W. Norton & Co., 1997), p. 178.

[6] *Ibid.*, p. 181.

[7] Samuel S. Kim, 'Human rights in China's international relations,' in Edward Friedman and Barrett L. McCormick (eds), *What if China doesn't democratize? Implications for war and peace* (Armonk, NY; and London: M.E. Sharpe, 2000), p. 152.

- The second period (1982–1988) witnessed China's participation in the international human rights regime, accession to eight of the 25 major UN human rights conventions, and a subtle but significant shift towards the interdependence and indivisibility of the first generation (civil and political) and second generation (economic and cultural) of human rights; and
- The third post-Tiananmen period (June 1989 to the present) proved to be most confusing and turbulent. (See Appendix III for a timeline of some major human rights developments in China since 1989.)

Before China's adoption of a policy of reform and opening up to the outside world under Deng Xiaoping in 1979, the issue of human rights was regarded as capitalist or bourgeois, and it was politically sensitive and highly dangerous to talk about it.[8] Two political campaigns launched by the government in 1984 and 1987 branded human rights as "spiritual pollution" and "bourgeois liberalisation".[9] As a result of the Tiananmen Incident in June 1989, China has been severely criticised for its abuse of human rights. Either as a way to fend off Western attacks or as a result of China's gradual process of opening up, or both, the country published for the first time its White Paper on human rights in 1991 and followed up with a progress report in 1996. Apart from the Chinese Constitution, which gives a long list of individual rights guaranteed by the state, the 1996 progress report refers to two sets of laws as significant steps in improving the rights of Chinese citizens. The Administrative Procedural Law, passed in 1990, allows citizens to sue "administrative organs and their staff when their legal rights and interest are infringed upon by specific administrative actions of these organs and persons." The new State Compensation Law, on the other hand, stipulates that if the legal rights and interests of citizens are infringed upon by state organs and their staff, "the aggrieved persons have the

---

[8] Zhou Wei, 'The study of human rights in the People's Republic of China,' in James T.H. Tang (ed), *Human rights and international relations in the Asia-Pacific region* (London and New York: Pinter, 1995), p. 83.

[9] Xin Chunying in *Human Rights Dialogue*, New York, Vol. 3 (December 1995), p. 5.

right to get state compensation."[10] China reported that, in 1996, 4,864 major cases relating to dereliction of duty and infringement of citizen's personal and democratic rights were investigated and those responsible prosecuted.[11] In 2004 the number of government functionaries investigated and prosecuted for human rights abuses totalled 1,595.[12] In early 2004 the Constitution was amended to include a specific reference to respect and protect human rights. In January 2005 the China Society for Human Rights Studies launched in the *People's Daily* a column entitled "100 Q & A on Human Rights", which would discuss two questions each week and would run for a year. The column provided a systematic introduction to all the international human rights instruments. In the following April, the UN Association of China and *China Youth Daily* co-sponsored a competition to test readers on their knowledge of human rights.[13]

Under China's political structure and culture, human rights are granted by the state and can easily be taken away by the state. If individual human rights run against state interests, the latter will usually prevail. The Chinese government's defence of its human rights record rests on the doctrine of exclusivity and cultural relativism based on concepts which promote subsistence, development, and collective rights over individual rights.[14] The official line argues that the protection of the people against starvation and

---

[10] *Beijing Review*, special issue on 'Human rights: progress in China,' January 1996, p. 10. Many of China's existing laws relating to human rights issues can be found in *Zhongguo renquan nianjian* [*China human rights yearbook*] (Beijing: Contemporary World Press, 2000).

[11] *Beijing Review*, 16–22 June 1997, p. 15; 21–27 April 1997, p. 14.

[12] As reported in China's White Paper entitled *China's progress in human rights in 2004*, cited in *People's Daily*, Internet ed., 13 April 2005.

[13] Introductory statement by the Head of the Chinese delegation, H.E. Ambassador Sha Zukang, at the UN Committee on Economic, Social and Cultural Rights hearing on China's initial report, 27 April 2005.

[14] Michael C. Davis (ed), *Human rights and Chinese values: legal, philosophical, and political perspectives* (Hong Kong: Oxford University Press, 1995), pp. vii and 21. See also *Beijing Review*, 4–10 March 1996, pp. 18–21.

exploitation and the promotion of economic growth can ensure the right to life and development. *Beijing Review* said that in 1986 the United Nations adopted a declaration on the right to development, affirming that the right to development is an inalienable human right, and in 1996 the world body adopted a Vienna Declaration and Platform for Action, acknowledging the right to development as a "universal" and "inalienable" right and a component of basic human rights.[15] In this area, China has achieved remarkable results by feeding its population, 22 per cent of the world's total, with only 7 per cent of the world's arable land.[16] It aims to attain the goal of *xiao-kang* (a moderately well-off society)[17] by the 21st century. In general, the Chinese government regards human rights issues as domestic affairs, citing Western criticisms of its human rights record as infringements of its sovereignty and interference in its domestic affairs. It goes so far as to accuse Western countries, in particular the United States, as practising hegemonism by using human rights as a foreign policy weapon against China.[18] Likewise, it has condemned Western countries for using international forums, such as the United Nations Commission on Human Rights meetings, as tools for political confrontation with developing countries, including China.[19]

Zhu Feng, a politics professor at Peking University, suggests that due consideration should be given to cultural relativism in assessing the human rights record of any country. He says that cultural relativism does not reject cultural universalism, but is against

---

[15] *Beijing Review*, 14–20 April 1997, p. 7.

[16] *Ibid.*, 16–22 December 1996, p. 4; 16–22 June 1997, p. 14.

[17] For an incisive analysis, see John Wong, 'Xiao-kang: Deng Xiaoping's socio-economic development target for China,' *Journal of Contemporary China*, Vol. 7, No. 17 (March 1998), pp. 141–152.

[18] Liang Lihua, '*Renquan waijiao* [Human rights diplomacy],' *Dangdai shijie yu shehui zhuyi* [*Contemporary World and Socialism*], Beijing, No. 1 (1995), p. 65. Professor Wang Huning of Fudan University, Shanghai, calls this kind of hegemonism "cultural hegemonism". He also uses the term "cultural sovereignty". See Wang Huning, 'Cultural expansion and cultural sovereignty,' in Wang Jisi (ed), *Wenming yu guoji zhengzhi* [*Civilisations and international politics*] (Shanghai: Shanghai People's Press, 19950), p. 342.

[19] *China Daily*, 21 March 1996, p. 4.

the absolute universalisation of human rights.[20] His reading of international human rights law is one that allows relativism to play a role in human rights practice in different countries. Also, cultural relativism does not negate the raising of universal standards, but that should be done gradually, because of other national priorities such as the stopping of external interference.[21] Zhu's arguments appear convincing, but he does not seem to have cautioned against the possibility that those in power may abuse human rights and how that sort of possibility can be avoided in the process of gradual change. Also, he does not specify a time frame in which cultural relativism may move towards a commonly-accepted universal standard. Surely, it is hard to pin-point specific details in such kind of analysis, since human rights observance is very much linked to a host of factors, including the legal, social, economic, and political systems of the countries under consideration, and the changes in the common understanding (if there is one) of what constitutes the universal standard over time.

Zhu explains that traditional Chinese culture stresses the importance of such concepts as "collectivism", "the harmony between people and the universe", and "order", and that the concept of human rights is not only a legal, but also a moral, concept.[22] In defending China's preference for cultural relativism, he says that cultural relativism is not against some fundamental moral principles. Rather, it acknowledges the progressiveness of world culture without neglecting the tradition and history of ethnic cultures and the importance of having a free choice of economic and developmental models.[23] Here Zhu has made an important

---

[20] Apparently, this argument is in line with the remarks made by Andrew Nathan that "universality does not mean uniformity." See Andrew J. Nathan, 'Foreword,' in Marina Svensson, *Debating human rights in China: a conceptual and political history* (Lanham: Rowman & Littlefield, 2002), p. viii.

[21] Chu Feng, ' *Wenhua xiangdui zhuyi yu guoji renquan* [Cultural relativism and international human rights],' in Liang Shoude et al (eds), *Guoji shehui yu wenhua [International society and culture]* (Beijing: Peking University Press, 1997), pp. 175–176.

[22] *Ibid.*, pp. 163–164.

[23] *Ibid.*, p. 162.

point on the freedom of choice that is so cherished in Western, especially American, societies, but has been applied differently sometimes by Western countries with respect to international relations.

The divergent understanding of human rights between China and the West can be seen in a wider context of the understanding between the developing and the developed world. The focus of contention is the importance placed on development relative to human rights. To the developing world, development rights are more important than human rights.[24] The former is part and parcel of the latter, and the protection of the former is necessary for the safeguarding of the latter. Only when "equality in development" is achieved can a reasonable international order be maintained. As such, development rights are universal and inseparable from the rights of developing countries. Economic development is a prerequisite to the full realisation of human rights. Poverty and economic underdevelopment are the major obstacles to efforts made to realise human rights goals. Because of different stages of development in the developing world, different countries have different understandings of what exactly constitutes human rights and what emphasis should be stressed. Of all the constituent elements of human rights, the most important ones to the Chinese are the rights to survive and the satisfaction of basic human needs such as food and shelter, followed by education.

The West has a different view, regarding development and human rights as two separate issues, the former being an "economic goal" rather than a human rights issue. In December 1986, when the 41st United Nations General Assembly passed a declaration recognising development rights as an inseparable part of human rights, the United States was the only country that voted against the

---

[24] The rest of this paragraph consists of my summary of Luo Yanhua, '*Ruhe kandai renquan yu fazhan di guanxi* [How to view the relationship between human rights and development],' in Liang Shoude et al (eds), *Mianxiang ershiyi shiji de Zhongguo guoji zhanlue* [*Facing China's international strategy in the 21st century*] (Beijing: Chinese Academy of Social Sciences Press, 1998), pp. 353–362.

adoption of the declaration.[25] This is understandable given America's view on human rights and on individualism, and its champion role in these and other global issues. Also, given the fact that the US is already one of the most developed countries in the world, it can afford to pay relatively little attention to developmental issues.

Although the official Chinese discourse on human rights is still largely reactive, the increasing willingness on the part of the Chinese government to enter into dialogues on such issues can be seen as a way to resist foreign interference and to preserve the Chinese way of life.[26] The setting up of the China Society for Human Rights Studies and China's official defence of its human rights record do reflect the country's concern over its international image.[27] The human rights issue in China is closely related to China's conceptual-isation of sovereignty. In a news briefing on 10 March 1995, Vice-Premier and Foreign Ministry Qian Qichen stressed that China was developing its high degree of socialist democracy according to its social and economic conditions. It was a socialist democracy with Chinese characteristics, deriving its identity from its own culture and tradition, unlike the situation in Western countries.[28]

In recent times, the Chinese have adopted a strategy of attack in addition to defence when US human rights groups criticise its human rights record. For example, in response to the *1997 human rights report*, published by the US State Department to review the human rights situation around the world (other than the US), an official Chinese report says that "violent crimes are so serious [in the US] that 65 persons die each day of violence and that more than 6,000 people are seriously maimed as a result of violence. The mortality rate from violence in the United States is ten times that in China."[29] The same sort of criticism was made in early 2005 in

---

[25] *Ibid.*, p. 354.

[26] Xin in *Human Rights Dialogue*, p. 5.

[27] Interestingly, the Party School of the CCP Central Committee has a Research Centre on Human Rights. See *China Daily*, 6 February 1997, p. 4.

[28] Note the use of the term "socialist democracy" instead of "socialism". TV news, Beijing, 10 March 1995.

[29] *Beijing Review*, 9–15 March 1998, p. 6.

retaliation to US annual review of China's human rights record when China said that "about 31,000 Americans are killed and 75,000 wounded by firearms [in the US] each year, which means more than 80 people are shot dead each day."[30]

A common Chinese government defence against outside accusation of its violation of human rights is the assertion that the individuals involved are criminals or that China takes the necessary actions in order to maintain the country's stability. Interestingly, to this defence, there seems to be little refutation from Western accusers to the effect that those victims of human rights abuse are not criminals according to the Chinese criminal code or legal practice, or that the committed acts of those victims of human rights abuses do not contribute instability to Chinese society. The way out for most Western accusers is that the legal standard in China is not up to their desirable standard. The instability argument, on the other hand, is open to debates, although President Bill Clinton did acknowledge in his speech in Beijing in mid-1998 that "the Chinese...understand better than I the price paid over time at various moments in history for disruption and upheaval in China, so there is an understandable desire to have stability in the country. Every country wants stability."[31]

Columbia University professor Andrew Nathan sums up well the Chinese perspectives on human rights:[32]

- The Chinese official jurisprudence views rights not as "natural" but as given by the state.[33]
- Human rights are to be limited and defined by law.

---

[30] *Human rights record of the United States in 2004* (Beijing: State Council Information Office, March 2005), http://www.chinaview.cn, 3 March 2005. According to Yu Quanyu, vice-president of the China Society for Human Rights Studies, China's first reports on human rights in the United States were issued by the society before the National People's Congress's Foreign Affairs Committee took over the role. Only in recent years have the reports on the US been issued by the State Council Information Office. See *South China Morning Post*, 7 March 2005, p. A4.

[31] *The Sunday Times*, London, 5 July 1998, p. 43.

[32] Andrew J. Nathan, 'Human rights in Chinese foreign policy,' *The China Quarterly*, No. 139 (September 1994), p. 623.

[33] Or, to be precise, the Chinese Communist Party since the Party controls the state.

- Constitutional rights are not seen as limitations on the law but as goals of national rights of self-determination and development over the rights of individual citizen.
- Human rights affairs are domestic rather than international issues.
- The Chinese government regards states, not individuals, as subjects in international law, so human rights cannot be used as a justification to interfere in the sovereignty of a state.[34]

According to Nathan, "Beijing's response to international human rights pressures demonstrated strategic consistency, central co-ordination, realism and tactical flexibility. Chinese policy consisted of ideological and substantive measures combining resistance and compromise."[35]

In sum, the tactics used by the Chinese government include counter-attacks on human rights violations in the West and the double standards that they use in criticising China and other countries. The government's argument stresses cultural difference, the non-interference in domestic affairs and sovereignty, and the criminal activities of offenders. On the positive side, the Chinese government publishes White Papers on human rights, and enters into dialogues and exchanges with the West on human rights issues.

China's efforts to promote human rights have gained some recognition, as well as the sympathy and support of many developing countries. For example, at the preparatory meeting of the UN-sponsored World Conference on Human Rights held in Bangkok in 1993, China gained the cooperation of 38 of the 39 countries to establish the concepts that UN human rights work should be guided by the principles of non-interference in the domestic affairs of states; non-selectivity (not to single out specific countries for criticism); the priority of collective and development rights; and cultural relativism.[36] To a certain extent, it has also been able to

---

[34] Nathan, 'Human rights in Chinese foreign policy,' p. 629.
[35] *Ibid.*, p. 639.
[36] The only country to opt out was Japan. See *ibid.*, p. 640.

convince realists in the West that confronting China head-on on these issues may not be in the overall interests of their countries.

CHINA'S PARTICIPATION IN HUMAN RIGHTS REGIMES

According to China's White Paper on human rights published in 2005, China is a member of 21 international human rights conventions.[37] The Office of the United Nations High Commissioner for Human Rights singles out eight major human rights instruments, with which China is associated (see Table 7.1).

Table 7.1 Status of China's Ratification of the Major Human Rights Instruments

Instrument	In Force as of
International Covenant on Economic, Social and Cultural Rights	27 June 2001
International Covenant on Civil and Political Rights	Signed 5 October 1999; Not yet ratified as of Sept 2005
International Covenant on the Elimination of All Forms of Racial Discrimination	28 January 1982
Convention against Torture and Other Cruel, Inhuman or Degrading Treatment or Punishment	3 November 1988
Convention on the Elimination of All Forms of Discrimination Against Women	3 September 1981
Committee on the Rights of the Child (CRC)	1 April 1992
CRC Optional Protocol 1 (child soldiers)	Signed 15 March 2001
CRC Optional Protocol 2 (sale of children)	3 January 2003

Source: Adapted from 'The People's Republic of China and the international human rights system,' Office of the United Nations High Commissioner for Human Rights, January 2005.

---

[37] *China's progress in human rights in 2004* (Beijing: State Council Information Office, 2005), cited in *People's Daily*, Internet ed., 13 April 2005.

As of early 2005, China has set up a task force to pave the way for the rapid ratification of the International Covenant on Civil and Political Rights, which is generally regarded as a fundamental international human rights treaty.[38]

How compliant is China with the terms of these treaties? Australian researcher Ann Kent has put forward five measures to gauge a state's compliance in human rights affairs:[39]

1. Accession to human rights treaties, the acceptance of the norms that this entails, and acceptance of the right of UN bodies to monitor conditions and of its obligation to respond;
2. Procedure compliance with reporting and other requirements;
3. Substantive compliance with the requests of the UN body, exhibited in international or domestic behaviour;
4. *De jure* compliance, or the implementation of international norms in domestic legislative provisions; and
5. *De facto* compliance, or compliance at the level of domestic practice.

Stephanie T. Kleine-Ahlbrandt, Programme Manager of the Asia-Pacific Unit of the United Nations Office of the High Commissioner for Human Rights, points out two major ways to monitor China's compliance with international human rights regimes within the UN.[40] One is through UN human rights mechanisms,

---

[38] German Foreign Minister Joschka Fischer, speaking on Tibet at the Commission on Human Rights, Item No. 9, 22 March 2005. On 28 February 2001, the Standing Committee of the National People's Congress of the PRC ratified the International Covenant on Economic, Social and Cultural Rights, with some reservations on issues relating to labour rights, such as the freedom to form and to join unions. A spokesman of the Standing Committee said that it took China three years and four months to ratify the Covenant, compared with Britain's eight years, Italy's 11 years and Belgium's 15 years. The spokesmen also said that Taiwan's signing of those Covenants in the name of China in 1966 was "illegal". See Xinhua News in http://www.china.org.cn/ (accessed on 4 July 2001).

[39] Ann Kent, *China, the United Nations, and human rights: the limits of compliance* (Philadelphia: University of Pennsylvania Press, 1999), p. 7.

[40] I am grateful to Stephanie T. Kleine-Ahlbrandt, for her e-mail correspondence and advice in early 2005.

including the treaty bodies which monitor China's compliance with the international instruments that it has ratified. The main body dealing with human rights issues in the United Nations is the Commission on Human Rights,[41] established by the Economic and Social Council in 1946. As part of its response to violations of human rights, the Commission set up subsidiary bodies such as the Sub-Commission for the Promotion and Protection of Human Rights, and bodies to investigate human rights problems in specific countries, as well as thematic working groups and special rapporteurs that reported back to it. These working groups and special rapporteurs form a second way to monitor China's compliance. The Sub-Commission consists of 26 experts, including one Chinese national.[42] They are elected on a regional basis to ensure adequate representation of different regions, legal systems and cultures. The annual three-week session of the Sub-Commission is attended by a large number of observers, representing NGOs, intergovernmental organisations, the UN Secretariat, and an increasing number of governments. The Sub-Commission is said to offer "the best hope" for dealing with human rights issues at the international level,[43] as it consists of experts who apply norms and procedures according to consistent, rigorous, and non-selective rules. For the most part, they operate away from the glare of publicity and on a regular basis.[44]

---

[41] The 53-state Commission on Human Rights completed its six-week 61st session in Geneva in April 2005. It is scheduled to be restructured into a slimmer and more credible Human Rights Council in 2006. UN Secretary-General Kofi Annan wants future members to have a "solid record of commitment" to human rights and for them to be directly elected by a two-third majority of the UN General Assembly. But both ideas have met opposition. See *South China Morning Post*, 23 April 2005, p. A11.

[42] The Chinese member is Chen Shiqiu (alternative Liu Xinsheng), whose term of office runs until 2006. http://www.unhchr.ch/html/menu2/2/subcmem.htm (accessed 22 April 2005).

[43] Kent, *China, the United Nations, and human rights*, pp. 53–54. Undated with information drawn from the website of the Sub-Commission http://www.unhchr.ch/html/menu2/2/sc.htm (accessed 22 April 2005).

[44] Kent, p. 239.

UN Special Rapporteurs of the Commission on Human Rights monitor China's compliance with international standards by a certain theme. The treaty bodies are committees of independent experts nominated by state parties. They monitor seven main international human rights treaties, including:

1. the International Covenant on Civil and Political Rights;
2. the International Covenant on Economic, Social and Cultural Rights;
3. the International Convention on the Elimination of All Forms of Racial Discrimination;
4. the Convention on the Elimination of All Forms of Discrimination Against Women;
5. the Convention against Torture and Other Cruel, Inhuman or Degrading Treatment or Punishment;
6. the Convention on the Rights of the Child; and
7. the International Convention on the Protection of the Rights of All Migrant Workers and Members of Their Families.

Each treaty body reviews reports submitted by state parties on a periodic basis. During the report review, treaty bodies discuss steps taken to implement the treaties and to adopt a set of concluding observations and recommendations, which identify specific human rights problems and provide recommendations for corrective action. These observations and recommendations are widely disseminated and to which the government concerned is expected to respond.

China is a party to five of the seven major international human rights instruments (it has not ratified the International Covenant on Civil and Political Rights yet and has not signed the International Convention on the Protection of the Rights of All Migrant Workers and Members of Their Families, as of early 2005). China has submitted reports under various conventions, with some overdue reports with regard to a few conventions. China ratified one of the more important conventions — the International Covenant on Economic, Social and Cultural Rights — in June 2001 and submitted its first report on time in June 2003. The report was considered by a supervisory Committee of the Covenant, consisting of 18 members, in May 2005. As a result, the committee recommended Beijing to abolish forced labour, allow workers to form independent trade unions outside the structure of the All China Federation of Trade Unions, and end discrimination against women, the disabled and migrants. It said Beijing should also enforce a minimum wage, ban child labour, ensure abortions were voluntary, and inspect safety and health conditions in all sectors. In addition, the committee of experts asked Beijing to ratify more of the International Labour Organisation's conventions, of which it had only ratified three of the 18.[45]

Up to January 2005 three of the special procedures set up under the UN Commission on Human Rights have conducted missions to China: the Special Rapporteur on Freedom of Religion and Belief, the Working Group on Arbitrary Detention, and the Special Rapporteur on the Right to Education.[46] As of May 2005 the Special Rapporteur on Torture was scheduled to make a visit, the US Commission on International Religious Freedom would also visit soon, and the International Committee of the Red Cross would set up an office in Beijing shortly.[47]

Since 1998 the Office of the United Nations High Commissioner for Human Rights (OHCHR) has been engaged in a dialogue with the Chinese government. The dialogue resulted in the signature of a Memorandum of Intent (MOI) between OHCHR and the Chinese Ministry of Foreign Affairs on 7 September 1998. A needs assessment mission to China, which took place in March 1999, established the willingness and potential of the Chinese government to cooperate with OHCHR on a long-term technical cooperation

---

[45] *Sunday Morning Post*, Hong Kong, 15 May 2005, p. 6. For a full report, see concluding observations of the Committee on Economic, Social and Cultural Rights, UN document reference: UNESC E/C.12/1/Add. 107, 13 May 2005.
[46] 'The People's Republic of China and the international human rights system,' Office of the United Nations Office of the High Commissioner for Human Rights, January 2005, p. 4.
[47] Frank Ching, 'On the right track,' *South China Morning Post*, 11 May 2005, p. A15.

programme on a wide range of human rights issues. Based on the mission's findings, a draft Memorandum of Understanding (MOU) on mutual agreement to cooperate in the development and implementation of technical cooperation programmes was submitted to the government. The MOU text was finalised and agreed upon during an OHCHR mission to Beijing in September 2000, and was signed by the High Commissioner for Human Rights and the Chinese Foreign Minister on 20 November 2000. The MOU covers the areas of administration of justice, human rights education, "legal development" including legal and legislative reform, the right to development and economic, social and cultural rights. Joint activities which have been carried out under the MOU include human rights and the police, human rights education, human rights and prison administration, human rights for judges and lawyers, human rights and disability, and human rights in the punishment of minor crimes. The former High Commissioner Mary Robinson (whose tenure spanned from September 1997 to September 2002) engaged in human rights dialogues with key Chinese officials both in Geneva and during her six visits to China.[48]

While Chinese government delegates have presented many reports to various committees of the UN body dealing with human rights issues, expounding China's viewpoints and defending its human rights record, these various committees have also presented concluding observations or reports making suggestions to the Chinese government to improve its human rights standard. Concluding observations have been made by:[49]

- the Committee on the Elimination of Racial Discrimination;
- the Committee on the Elimination of Discrimination Against Women;
- the Committee on Economic, Social and Cultural Rights;
- the Committee on the Rights of the Child;

---

[48] 'The People's Republic of China and the international human rights system,' p. 5.
[49] *Ibid.*, pp. 17 ff.

- the Committee against Torture; and
- the Human Rights Committee.

And the reports include those of:[50]

- the Special Rapporteur on violence against women, its causes and consequences;
- the Special Rapporteur on the right to education;
- the Special Rapporteur on contemporary forms of racism, racial discrimination and xenophobia;
- the Special Rapporteur on adequate housing as a component of the right to an adequate standard of living, and on the right to non-discrimination;
- the Special Rapporteur on freedom of religion or belief; and
- the Working Group on arbitrary detention.

Ann Kent has conducted an extensive research on China's compliance with UN treaty bodies on human rights. She found that in general China was long in reporting its domestic legal administrative procedures but short on practical implementation. This style of reporting occurred in areas covered by the Committee Against Torture, the Committee on the Elimination of All Forms of Racial Discrimination, and the Committee on the Rights of the Child. The experiences of thematic special rapporteurs and working groups monitoring aspects of China's civil rights varied. On the whole, China had done a lot to obligate with procedural compliance, such as the submission of reports, although its invitations to special rapporteurs to visit the country were selective. Also, its substantive compliance raised doubts. China therefore is at its best in procedural matters, to a certain degree it has done well in *de jure* compliance, but remains rather poor in *de facto* compliance in substantive terms.[51] The gap between *de jure* and *de facto* compliance varies across different sectors of human rights and across different interpreters of each of the two types of compliance.

---

[50] *Ibid.*
[51] Kent, pp. 110–111.

China's human rights record will certainly remain an issue in the UN human rights institutions. However, as long as developing countries account for a majority of the membership of the UN and as long as China retains its influence in the world body, especially in the Security Council where it holds the power to veto, UN human rights institutions are unlikely to censure Beijing too heavily.[52]

CHINA'S BILATERAL HUMAN RIGHTS DIPLOMACY

The issue of human rights received relatively little attention in China's media or academic circles until the late 1970s,[53] and it was during the 1990s that the issue became a major stumbling block in China's diplomatic relations with the West, especially as a result of the 1989 Tiananmen Incident. So far, heated exchanges have occurred largely between China and the US and, to a lesser extent, between China and some western European countries.

Western concerns over China's human rights include, among others things, political persecutions and unfair trials, the treatment of dissidents in Tibet and elsewhere in the country, religious persecutions, the Falungong movement, and the one-child policy. These concerns reached a climax in 1989. During the early 1990s, the Clinton Administration, because of its moral stand, put human rights issues high on the agenda of its diplomatic relations with other countries. The US only decoupled the link between human rights and trade with respect to China in 1994, following rapid expansion in bilateral trade. Until China's entry into the WTO in late 2001, China's trading status was subjected to an annual scrutiny and a difficult passage through Congress, during which the issue of human rights came to the fore for deliberation. Also, since 1979, the United States Department of State has included China in its annual report on the situation of human rights around the world.[54]

---

[52] Wan Ming, *Human rights in Chinese foreign relations: defining and defending national interests* (Philadelphia: University of Pennsylvania Press, 2001), pp. 127–128.
[53] *Ibid.*, p. 3.
[54] A report on human rights practices in China (including Hong Kong and Macau) in 2002 was released by the Bureau of Democracy, Human Rights, and Labor of the

In a book published in 2001, Wan Ming, a professor at George Mason University in the US, examines in detail China's human rights relations with the United States,[55] Europe, Japan and the United Nations. Wan says that the issue will continue to figure prominently in the bilateral relationship between China and the US. Despite the small influence wielded by human rights groups in the US, they can still set a certain limit to the development of US policy towards China. Even advocates for deeper engagement and the setting up of strategic dialogues with China insist that human rights should not be sidelined. Chinese dissident groups operating in the United States, supported by sympathetic media and scholars there, still influence public and congressional opinion in the US. In addition, social forces such as the Falungong movement, unleashed by economic reform, are likely to continue to attract attention in the US.[56]

On 28 February 2005 the US government published annual country reports reviewing human rights situations around the world, including a lengthy report covering China, Tibet, Hong Kong and Macau.[57] The report says that the Chinese "government's human rights record remained poor, and the government continued to commit numerous and serious abuses." Also, it accuses the Chinese government of using "the international war on terror as a pretext for cracking down harshly on suspected Uighur separatists...." Furthermore, the government maintained tight restrictions on

---

State Department on 31 March 2003. See http://www.state.gov/g/drl/rls/hrrpt/ 2002/18239.htm for the full report. In response, China issued immediately an annual tit-for-tat report accusing US unilateralism as the root of human rights violations around the world, especially the wars in Afghanistan and Iraq. The report also blasted a loss in civil rights and a rise in racism in the US in the aftermath of the September 11, 2001 terrorist attacks in New York and Washington DC. See *South China Morning Post*, 4 April 2003, p. A7; *The Standard*, 4 April 2003, p. A-10.
[55] For an up-to-date analysis of the differing views of China and the US on human rights, see Zhou Qi, 'Conflicts over human rights between China and the US,' *Human Rights Quarterly*, Vol. 27, No. 1 (February 2005), pp. 105–124.
[56] Wan, *Human rights in Chinese foreign relations*, p. 65.
[57] The report can be downloaded at http://www.state.gov/g/drl/rls/hrrpt/ 2004/41640.htm (accessed 3 April 2005).

various kinds of freedom, including that of speech and of the press, assembly and association, privacy and religion.

As was customary in the past few years, the Chinese government immediately released its own report on the human rights situation in the US, dismissing US claims and blaming it for intruding into China's domestic affairs. In its 'Human rights record of the US in 2004' published on 3 March 2005, the Chinese government accuses the US of maltreating detainees in the latter's campaign against terrorism and draws attention to violent crimes in connection with gun use in the US.

The US approach to China's human rights is rather unique, borne out of US national interests and its political status and system. Rosemary Foot describes the US as "a leading norm entrepreneur",[58] and Andrew Nathan and Robert Ross allude to the dynamics of American politics that give special impetus to human rights issues.[59] Sophia Woodman, on the other hand, says that the US has forsaken a "dialogue and cooperation" approach, which is the typical approach adopted by many European countries.[60]

Subsequent to the Tiananmen Incident, from 1990 to 2004 (inclusive, apart from 1991, 1998, 2002 and 2003),[61] the United States and the West sponsored 11 proposals to pass a resolution to condemn China's human rights situation before the UN Commission on Human Rights, but all of them failed to harness enough support to carry the vote.[62] Because of the US proposal to condemn China in

---

[58] Rosemary Foot, *Rights beyond borders: the global community and the struggle over human rights in China* (Oxford: Oxford University Press, 2000), p. 46.

[59] Nathan and Ross, *The Great Wall and the empty fortress*, p. 185.

[60] Sophia Woodman, 'Bilateral aid to improve human rights,' *China Perspectives*, No. 51 (January–February 2004), p. 28.

[61] The US decided not to bring a UN resolution on China in 2003 because it said it saw improvements in China. There was no resolution in 2002 when the US was not a member of the UN Commission on Human Rights.

[62] For details of the votes (of proposed countries, those in favour of no action, those opposed, and those in abstention) from 1990 to 1999, see *Zhongguo renquan nianjian*, pp. 1,735–1,738. See also 'China foils US bid at UN human rights session,' *People's Daily*, Internet ed., 19 April 2001.

March 2004, the Chinese government has since suspended human rights dialogues with the US. The US government decided not to introduce a United Nations resolution critical of China's human rights policy in 2005, citing improvements made in human rights in the country in the past year.

While there are debates as to whether containment or engagement would provide a better policy guide to deal with China on human rights issues, a recent study which investigates the case of the US threat to remove China's most favoured nation status following the Tiananmen Incident in 1989, suggests that engagement offers a better, more effective solution.[63] According to John Kamm, executive director of the Dui Ha Foundation, a human rights NGO based in San Francisco, Beijing is proud that it has signed more international human rights treaties than the US, and that it sometimes files reports called for under the treaties' obligations in a more timely fashion than the US.[64]

According to Wan Ming, the issue of human rights in Sino-European relations is likely to be managed within a framework of a distant and non-confrontational manner, as strategic and economic interests between the two parties will ensure the maintenance of a stable relationship. In the long run, because of differences in values and belief systems between the two, the issue of human rights will not disappear altogether.[65] To be sure, international human rights groups will not cease to lobby the US and European governments to put pressure on China to improve its human rights record, on a bilateral or multilateral basis. With respect to Sino-Japanese relations, human rights will not be a major issue in the official relationship between the two countries. However, since Japan is allied solidly with the United States, its view towards

---

[63] Li Yitan and A. Cooper Drury, 'Threatening sanctions when engagement would be more effective: attaining better human rights in China,' *International Studies Perspectives*, Vol. 5, Issue 4 (November 2004), pp. 378–394.

[64] John Kamm, 'Engaging China on human rights,' a speech made at The Brookings Institution, Washington DC, 14 October 2004.

[65] Wan, *Human rights in Chinese foreign relations*, p. 84.

China's human rights record will be influenced by US interests.[66] The significance of this influence, however, depends on Japan's assessment of the overall importance of its relations with China at any given point in time.

In the midst of criticisms made by the West based on moral or political grounds, China's human rights record is expected to improve over time as it continues to reform and open up. The constitutional amendment made in March 2004 to respect and protect human rights, although interpreted by some observers as largely symbolic,[67] is a step forward in this direction. It represents a strong indication that the government pays increasing attention to the issue of human rights. Much depends, however, on China's strengthening of its legal system and the promotion of human rights awareness. The rising prominence of trade between China and the outside world, the global campaign against terrorism, and China's effort to ease the nuclear tension between North Korea and its neighbours have put the issue of China's human rights to a back seat, at least for the time being. The signing of trade deals in Beijing in October 2003 during a visit made by a high-level EU delegation has been cited as an example of the West's sidelining of China's human rights issue. The deals include China's sizeable investments in the EU's satellite navigational project called Galileo and the easing of visa restrictions on Chinese tourists visiting the EU.[68]

---

[66] Wan, p. 105.

[67] Freda Wan, 'Changes could be just symbolic, observers fear,' *South China Morning Post*, Internet ed., 15 March 2004.

[68] China's investment in the Galileo project amounts to £160 million (US$276.3 million). See *The Guardian*, London, quoted in *Taipei Times*, 9 December 2003, p. 6. The total project costs Euro3.2 billion or US$4.15 billion. The project is scheduled to enter into service in 2008. Consisting of 30 satellites and ground stations, the project carries both civilian and military applications, and there are suspicions that China's participation would enable it to bypass the arms embargo imposed by EU and the US. The Galileo project has the potential to rival the US Navstar global positioning system in providing both military and civilian use. See David Lague, 'Guiding China's missiles: EU satellite project would improve accuracy,' *International Herald Tribune*, 19 April 2005, pp. 1 and 4.

As a result of the Tiananmen Incident, the EU and the US have since imposed an arms embargo on China. At present the EU considers whether it should lift the embargo. Opinions are divided among member states. France and Germany favour the lifting. Their leaders argue that time has changed and the original rationale for imposing the embargo is no longer valid. China has become an increasingly important trade partner. In addition, France is also of the opinion that developing a stronger link with China will help to balance US unilateral actions and influence around the world. Other countries in the EU, especially some in Northern Europe, still think that China's human rights issue is a major concern and that China needs to further improve its human rights record before the lifting can be carried out. The US and Japan are against the lifting. They fear that the acquisition of advanced weapons and high technologies by China might increase its aggressiveness, thereby upsetting the balance of power in East Asia and putting American troops in the Asia-Pacific at risk. The US threatens to impose trade sanctions on Europe if the EU does lift the embargo. The passing of the anti-secession law in March 2005 by Beijing authorising the use of force against Taiwan should the latter declare formal independence and the rising tensions between China and Japan over Japan's war past, its history textbooks, and the disputed Diaoyutai/Senkaku islands add to the concerns of those who are already worried about the effects of the lifting. EU foreign ministers meeting in Brussels in April 2005 decided to postpone the lifting, originally planned for in mid-2005, to a later date. They encouraged China to ratify swiftly the International Covenant on Civil and Political Rights as one way to improve China's determination to improve and protect human rights. The EU also urged Beijing to release Tiananmen prisoners, reform China's re-education-through-labour penal system, and ease media censorship.[69] To allay the fears of the US, the EU said it would adopt an export control over the sale of arms to China should the ban be lifted.

---

[69] *The Guardian*, 13 May 2005, p. 1.

On the other hand, China has said that even if the ban is lifted, the country cannot afford to buy expensive weapons. Foreign Minister Li Zhaoxing said in March 2005 that China did not need "expensive" and "useless" weapons from the EU, but emphasised that the arms embargo was a "political discrimination" against Beijing, which was not compatible with the spirit of comprehensive strategic partnership between China and the EU.[70] The sentiment that the 16-year-old arms embargo was "anachronistic" and "discriminatory" was also echoed by French Prime Minister Jean-Pierre Raffarin, when he visited Beijing in late April 2005 to witness the contract-signing ceremony for a deal under which China agreed to buy 30 Airbus airplanes worth US$3.2 billion. In 2004 trade between France and China grew by 19 per cent to US$22.2 billion.[71]

As far as international NGOs working in the area of human rights are concerned, Amnesty International, Human Rights Watch, and Human Rights in China adopt a more confrontational, containment style of approach towards China. Others such as Sweden's Raoul Wallenberg Institute of Human Rights,[72] the Norwegian Institute of Human Rights, and the Danish Institute for Human Rights adopt a more "softly-softly" engagement approach. Obviously, China works with the latter group of NGOs in carrying out human rights projects in China while ignoring or refuting the criticisms of the former.

China's largely defensive response to outside criticisms comes in many forms. Apart from signing and ratifying international human rights treaties, it has started to talk with the West on human rights,[73]

---

[70] *South China Morning Post*, 7 March 2005, p. A4.

[71] *International Herald Tribune*, 22 April 2005, p. 3.

[72] Jonas Grimheden, a senior researcher working for Raoul Wallenberg Institute of Human Rights, speaking at a seminar on human rights development cooperation with China, at the Universities Service Centre for China Studies, Chinese University of Hong Kong, 22 November 2004.

[73] According to executive director John Kamm of the Dui Hua Foundation, since the early 1990s the Chinese government has initiated bilateral human rights exchanges with about a dozen countries and about 100 rounds of human rights talks have taken place. See Kamm's speech entitled 'Engaging China on human rights'.

publish White Papers giving its official views on the issue, and marshal a human rights discourse from the perspective of the developing world in international forums.

WHITE PAPERS ON HUMAN RIGHTS

In the past decade or so, the Information Office of the State Council of China has published at least five White Papers relating to human rights, giving a positive gloss over its achievements in the area.[74] At the same time, these papers help to explain China's situation and increase the transparency of its policy. For example, the paper on *The situation of Chinese women*, published shortly before the United Nations' Fourth World Conference on Women held in Beijing in 1995, says in its foreword that Chinese women today enjoy equal rights as men and that "women hold up half the sky." *The progress of human rights in China*, published in December 1995, points out that for four years since the publication of the first White Paper on human rights in 1991, China has raised its standard of living and improved its human rights record. For instance, the plan to quadruple the 1980 GNP by the year 2000 was realised ahead of schedule in 1995.[75] Also, China had promulgated and put into effect the Police Law, the Public Procurators Law, the Judges Law, the Prison Law and a series of other laws.[76] Furthermore, China has set up various organisations to study the issue of human rights at various levels of government. The most notable one is the Chinese Society for the Study of Human Rights, which has been actively involved in

---

[74] The publication in April 2005 of *China's progress in human rights in 2004* is said to be 8th of its kind. See, for example, *People's Daily*, Internet ed., 13 April 2005. China's White Papers can be downloaded at http://english.people.com.cn/ whitepaper/home.html

[75] According to the US report on human rights in China for 2004, a widening wealth gap exists: "The [Chinese] Government reported that urban per capita disposable income in 2003 was $1,028 and grew by 9 per cent over the previous year, while rural per capita cash income was $317 and grew by 4 per cent."

[76] *The progress of human rights in China* (Beijing: Information Office, State Council, December 1995), p. 16.

expounding China's views on the issue, especially to overseas audiences. The country has also sent delegates to participate in many international forums to exchange ideas, including the World Human Rights Conferences held in Bangkok and Vienna in 1993. In a similar way, *Progress in China's human rights cause in 1996*, published in March 1997, updates the improvements made in China's economic development as well as in human rights areas. It reiterates China's determination to further improve on various fronts. With little exception, *New progress in human rights in the Tibet Autonomous Region*, published in February 1998, states that "the Region's economic and social development has been remarkably speeded up, thus further promoting the development of the cause of human rights there."[77] A recent White Paper entitled *China's progress in human rights 2004*,[78] published in April 2005, says that China's human rights record has improved, citing its booming economy and efforts to reduce taxes on farmers as proof. The report also highlights better employment opportunities, progress in poverty reduction and even the rising number of cars on the country's roads. However, hardcore critics say that there is little or no progress made in freedom of assembly, freedom of expression, and freedom of religion. Nicolas Becquelin, research director of Human Rights in China, says that the report was more a "diplomatic exercise" to counter-balance the repeated criticisms of the mainland's human rights record by the West — with little relation to reality.[79]

HUMAN RIGHTS DIALOGUES

In global diplomacy, dialogues play an important part in enhancing mutual understanding, although it is difficult to assess accurately their effectiveness in enhancing one's national interests. Much

---

[77] *New progress in human rights in the Tibet Autonomous Region*, p. 2.

[78] Full text can be found at http://english.people.com.cn/whitepaper/hr2005/hr2005(7).html (accessed 15 April 2005).

[79] *South China Morning Post*, 14 April 2005, p. A6.

depends on the level of expectation. It is easy to discard dialogues when expectations are set very high and the returns are seen to be low. However, dialogues remain a diplomatic instrument to break political deadlock and to maintain a channel of communication, which is necessary if not sufficient for resolving conflicts. Without dialogues, misperceptions can brew and can lead to inappropriate decisions and destructive behaviour.

From the early 1990s to late 2004, the Chinese government had initiated bilateral human rights exchanges with about a dozen countries. There had been 19 rounds of human rights dialogues between China and the EU. The United Kingdom had held 12 rounds of human rights dialogues with China, the Swiss had held seven, and the Australians eight.[80] After some 13 rounds of talks, Beijing suspended its official dialogue with Washington in March 2004 in response to the introduction by the US of a country resolution condemning China's record at the annual meeting of the UN Human Rights Commission in Geneva. In all, there had been about 100 rounds of human rights talks between the Chinese government and foreign governments.[81]

China had hosted three visits by the UN Working Group on Arbitrary Detention. Apart from the Special Rapporteur on Torture, the UN religious intolerance rapporteur and representatives of other treaty bodies and thematic mechanisms had visited the country. In its mission report to the UN Commission on Human Rights following its visit to Beijing, Sichuan and Tibet in September 2004, the UN Working Group on Arbitrary Detention expressed concern that none of the recommendations, including, for example, a clear definition of "endangering state security", made in its earlier reports had been implemented by the Chinese.[82] A special Rapporteur on Religious Intolerance once remarked that the gap between China's *de jure*

---

[80] 'China invites human rights delegation,' Australian Associated Press, 21 October 2004.
[81] Information in this paragraph is largely taken from Kamm, 'Engaging China on human rights.'
[82] Oral statement by Tenzin Samphel on Item 11 on civil and political rights at the 61st Session of the UN Commission on Human Rights, 14 March to 22 April 2005.

compliance and *de facto* compliance was a manifestation of a deep-rooted political and legal culture that required time, political will and education to eradicate.[83] Apart from governmental organisations, China has been reluctant to allow independent international or domestic NGOs to monitor human rights conditions within its borders.

To manage the growing number of dialogues with foreign countries and with the UN, China's Ministry of Foreign Affairs has established a Human Rights Division in the Department of International Organisations and Conferences. It has appointed a Special Representative on Human Rights to specifically manage the dialogues. However, China does not have a national human rights office or an ombudsperson to deal with human rights complaints brought by ordinary citizens against the government.

CONCLUSION

In the past two decades or so, China has made some progress in promoting and protecting human rights at home. It has approved or joined 21 international human rights conventions and has participated in various global forums to discuss human rights issues.

China's strategy in dealing with Western criticisms of its human rights record has changed from a reactive to a proactive stance, from a purely defensive mode to a combination of defence and counter-attacks, from a flat denial to some moderation in its responses and even admissions of shortcomings, from closely guarding its sovereignty to partially opening up to outside inspections and scrutiny, from a strictly domestic, unilateral interpretation to some acknowledgements of universal features, and from a tight seclusion to active engagements with others in open dialogues.

China, however, is most likely to continue to resist overt, explicit pressure on it to change. Within the United States, some quarters suggest that it would be useful to continue to put pressure on China to force it to improve its human rights record, while others recognise the

---

[83] Kent, p. 116.

futility of exerting excessive pressure and confronting China head-on in these issues. China has gradually shifted part of its attention from economic rights to development or solidarity rights,[84] while still paying scant attention to political rights, as a way to deflect the emphasis placed on political rights by the West, especially by the US.

Samuel Kim sums up well the differences between Asian understanding and Western understanding of human rights by suggesting that those differences evolve around three major issues: (1) the theory of universality versus the theory of cultural or developmental relativism; (2) the right to intervene versus the principle of state sovereignty; and (3) the prioritisation or the interdependence and indivisibility of different categories of human rights, namely, political rights, economic rights, and solidarity rights.[85] For China, it is clear that although the country now acknowledges some degree of universality in human rights, it still places more emphasis on cultural and developmental relativism. Although it has joined United Nations peacekeeping activities in a number of conflict zones around the world and thus contributing to some sort of intervention, it still places overwhelming importance on the principles of state sovereignty and non-interference in domestic affairs. And it stresses time and again the relative importance of economic, cultural, and solidarity rights over civil and political rights in the developing world.

The measurement of China's compliance with global human rights norms remain elusive as far as China is able to command a Third World majority in human rights views and behaviour, and as far as China grows and remains strong so that it is able to resist Western pressure on it to make drastic improvements over a short period of time. However, the issue of human rights, especially the Tiananmen Incident, will remain a stigma in China's diplomacy: it has to cope with a bad global image for some time to come.[86]

---

[84] Statement by La Yifan, Alternative Representative of the Chinese delegation, at the 61st Commission on Human Rights, Item 7: right to development, March 2005.

[85] Kim, 'Human rights in China's international relations,' p. 131.

[86] I borrow this last sentence from John F. Copper and Lee Ta-ling, *Coping with a bad global image: human rights in the People's Republic of China, 1993–1994* (Lanham: University Press of America, 1997).

Chapter

8

Conclusion

China changes the world by changing itself.

Professor Yuan Ming, 2004[1]

The rise of China has highlighted, among other things, the issue of its responsibility in world affairs. Whether or not China is a responsible member of the international community can best be judged not only by the Chinese government alone, but also, and more importantly, by ordinary Chinese and outside observers. This study has focused on China at the state level: How does the outside world perceive China's responsibility and its compliance with international norms and rules? And what is China's own view on such perceptions? From the analyses done in the previous chapters, we can see that the Chinese government would like very much to be seen as a responsible power, and it does care a lot about its international image in the global community.

This book has demonstrated that a good way to begin to look at China's international responsibility is to examine the extent of its

---

[1] A remark made by Professor Yuan Ming, Deputy Dean, School of International Studies, Peking University, in her public lecture on Chinese foreign policy, delivered at the Chinese University of Hong Kong, 18 October 2004.

involvement in world affairs. China's participation in international organisations and its membership of international regimes and treaties serve as useful measures to gauge its global responsibility. Membership of international organisations and regimes is a rather simple but a basic measure, while compliance with the international norms and rules that are embodied in these organisations and regimes is a more refined measure. In this regard, the book has tried to gauge China's compliance in four crucial areas of international relations: world trade, arms control and non-proliferation, environmental protection, and human rights. China's compliance in human rights regimes and, to a certain extent, in environmental protection regimes, is an additional, direct indicator of its domestic responsibility towards its own citizens, in comparison to its compliance behaviour in world trade and arms control.

China has made substantial progress in the four areas discussed, since its opening up to the outside world in the late 1970s. However, the degree of compliance varies across these areas (summarised in Table 8.1), and much more work remains to be done across the board if China were to improve its compliance image and to meet the expectations of its major trade and strategic partners. While the country is relatively more open in world trade practices, it is less so in the area of arms control and non-proliferation, as military and defence matters are highly sensitive. The issues of human rights and environmental protection are somewhere in between the issue of trade on the one hand and arms control on the other in terms of China's degree of openness and its depth of compliance. China has to strike a right balance between the need to engage openly with the outside world and, at the same time, the need to prevent other countries from exploiting these issues to intrude in its internal affairs, thereby challenging its authority to govern as well as limiting its potential for growth, in economic as well as political terms. Although its compliance record (or score, for that matter) varies, ranging from good to satisfactory in the areas of global trade and arms control, and from fair to poor in the fields of human rights and environmental protection, it can be concluded that China's overall compliance record in global affairs is satisfactory to good,

Table 8.1 Summary Findings of China's Global Compliance, 2005

	Arms Control	Global Trade	Human Rights	Environmental Protection
No. of treaties signed or ratified	29+ NPT CTBT	WTO + a few regional free-trade agreements	21+ ICESCR ICCPR	40+ Kyoto Protocol
Treaty compliance	Controversial	Satisfactory; more to be done	Progress made; more to be done	Fighting an uphill battle
Problem areas	"Illegal" sales of arms; dual-use products	Agriculture; IPR; transparency	Various abuses and violations	Three Gorges; SARS
Nature of non-compliance	Politically sensitive	Transitional problems from socialist to market orientation	Non-interference; assertive engagement	Poor understanding of "public goods"
Compliance response	Slow	Quick	Intermediate	Quick
Sources of capacity-building	IAEA, USA	WTO, USA EU	UNCHR USA, EU	UNEP UNDP
US role	Sole superpower	Economic supremacy	American values	Domestic interests
China's goal	Minimal deterrence	Economic growth	Authority preservation	Slow progress
China's grade*	B Satisfactory	B+ Good	B– Fair to poor	C Poor

* These grades are arbitrary but indicative. At least they serve as a basis for comparison. Most analysts give China a healthy "B plus" for its work under the WTO after two years of membership, according to Andrew K. Collier, 'Mainland settles in with global trade principles,' *South China Morning Post*, Internet ed., 20 September 2003.

Abbreviations:
CTBT   Comprehensive Test Ban Treaty
IAEA   International Atomic Energy Agency
ICCPR   International Covenant on Civil and Political Rights
ICESCR   International Covenant on Economic, Social and Cultural Rights
IPR   Intellectual Property Rights
NPT   Nuclear Nonproliferation Treaty
SARS   Severe Acute Respiratory Syndrome (atypical pneumonia)
UNCHR   United Nations Commission on Human Rights
UNDP   United Nations Development Programme
UNEP   United Nations Environment Programme

given the difficulties that it faces in its economic, social and political transitions, and given the fact that compliance measurement is difficult to make. In any case, it seems that China's record is no worse than many developing countries in a comparable stage of development.

The difficulties in making a fair and accurate assessment of the responsibility and compliance of a country in global affairs lie in different national conditions and developmental experiences, resulting in diverse interpretations of rule compliance, in the absence of a universally-accepted standard of measurement. However, by acceding to a large number of international treaties and participating actively in the activities of an increasing number of international organisations, especially in the areas of trade, arms control, environmental protection, and human rights, China has deepened its integration with the rest of the world. It has agreed to comply with the relevant international norms and rules embodied in these treaties and organisations without much stiff resistance or resentment in the past three decades.

This book has studied at some length China's responsibility and compliance in global affairs in general and in the four areas in particular. Further analyses can be made by focusing on some specific issues in the four areas and beyond, such as China's export control of weapons, especially dual-use equipment; its control over certain sectors of trade; its policies towards labour rights; its balancing between economic growth and environmental protection; legal, political, and economic reforms; the linkage between domestic responsibility and global responsibility; and so on. In complying with international rules, China is in a process of redefining its national interests (becoming less self-centred) and renegotiating its state sovereignty (becoming less absolute in its understanding).[2] In

---

[2] The Chinese hold on state sovereignty has undergone some changes in the sense that it is less tenacious now than before, considering the adoption of the "one country, two systems" formula to take back Hong Kong in 1997, the signing of the Treaty of Amity and Cooperation with the ASEAN countries in October 2003, and the calling on the United States, Australia and some Asian countries to help to settle its conflict with Taiwan, especially in preventing Taiwan from declaring formal independence.

comparative terms, China is still very defensive of its sovereignty. In contrast, liberal democratic states feel relatively more secure and comfortable in the existing world order, because of their enormous power and strength, and because their vested interests are well protected and promoted. At least, the US as the sole superpower vows openly to protect and promote those interests, against any unwelcome encroachment from non-liberal democracies. While accepting the costs involved in participating in a wide range of international activities, China has also reaped handsome benefits.[3]

Although China's compliance record looks satisfactory, disagreements between China and the West, especially between China and the United States,[4] over Chinese compliance will persist, driven by competing national interests and different perceptions and values. Apparently, China needs outside help to build up its capacity to comply, especially in strengthening its legal system and in streamlining its management practices. The outside world should welcome China's compliance, as its compliance is beneficial to all parties concerned, because of the resulting global stability and common prosperity. In the process of global interaction, China learns to acquaint itself with the rules of engagement with other states and organisations. Will China internalised the relevant ideas and practices from the outside, or will it adapt tactically just to advance its national interests? Different scholars seem to see things differently. Alastair Iain Johnston of Harvard University suggests that China adapts rather than internalises the values and norms of international society.[5] David Lampton of Johns Hopkins University and some of his colleagues, however, argue that the distinction between adaptation and internalisation is not clear, and therefore some sort of

---

[3] Ann Kent, *China, the United Nations, and human rights: limits of compliance* (Philadelphia: University of Pennsylvania Press, 1999), pp. 350–357.

[4] For a critical review of America's record of international legal compliance, see Nicole Deller et al (eds), *Rule of power or rule of law* (New York: The Apex Press, 2003).

[5] Alastair I. Johnston, 'Learning versus adaptation: explaining change in Chinese arms control policy,' *The China Journal*, No. 35 (1996), pp. 27–61.

combination of adaptation and learning may best describe China's integration with the world.[6] Because the process of transition to a situation of full international compliance is so complex, fluid, and long drawn-out, there will always be room for debates as to whether or not China genuinely harmonises itself with global norms and practices. Interestingly, it is not only countries spearheaded by the US that have to find a right balance between containing China and engaging China, INGO people working in China in the human rights field find that the Chinese people working in a similar field also "want both cooperation and continuing pressure on the [Chinese] government, and the two have an essential synergy".[7] (See Figure 8.1 for a model of China's global learning.)

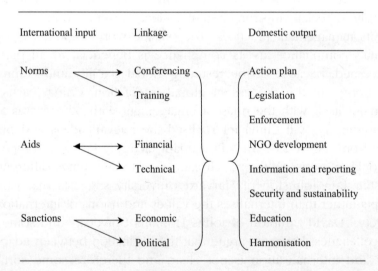

Figure 8.1 A Model of China's Global Learning

Source: Ideas from Dr Yu Hongyuan, Lingnan University, Hong Kong, with modifications.

---

[6] David M. Lampton (ed), *The making of Chinese foreign and security policy in the era of reform* (Stanford: Stanford University Press, 2001), pp. 34–35 and 225–228.
[7] Sophia Woodman, 'Bilateral aid to improve human rights,' *China Perspectives*, No. 51 (January–February 2004), p. 45.

Clearly the US plays a leading role in monitoring China's compliance in the fields of trade, arms control, and human rights. However, whether or not the US would play a similar role in environmental protection is not certain, as it does not seem to comply well with international environmental standards, in the area of climate change for example.[8] Nevertheless, in the newly-instituted ministerial-level bilateral forum between the two countries, the issue of environmental protection is included as an agenda item for discussion. (This forum started in 2005, held in the US and the next 2006 forum is scheduled to be held in China.) Since January 2002, the US government has been stalling the requests and efforts of UN human rights monitors to inspect the conditions of prisoners detained in the US detention centre at Guatanamo Bay, Cuba.[9] The US record in arms control is not inspiring either, as it pulled out of the Anti-Ballistic Missile Treaty with Russia and failed to ratify the Comprehensive Test Ban Treaty. Its attitude and policies towards the International Criminal Court and the UN Security Council are not encouraging. As pointed out by scholars such as Margaret Pearson in the field of international financial institutions and Wendy Frieman in the field of arms control and non-proliferation, there is a difference between China's compliance with global rules and norms on the one hand and with the standard, agenda and national interest of the US on the other. While the US is the only powerhouse able to implement both controls and sanctions, the progress in the control mechanisms are undermined by its own more general attitude of unilateralism.[10] At the very least, US behaviour sometimes does not inspire the confidence of other nations in the multilateral rule system.

---

[8] However, some American states such as California take actions to address the problem of global warming and climate change, citing the validity of scientific evidence. ITN TV Channel 4 news, London, 22 June 2005.

[9] BBC World News, 23 June 2005.

[10] Thanks to Professor Richard Balme of the Department of Government and International Studies at the Hong Kong Baptist University for alerting me to this, in his e-mail correspondence on 5 May 2005.

China's global responsibility will always be challenged as long as its human rights record remains flawed. Also, its worsening environmental situation across the country only exposes the ugly side of uncoordinated development which pays little or no regards to environmental impact.

Trading one issue for another, such as human rights for trade, is not uncommon, although the exact linkage between the two issues is difficult to establish. For example, the US government, under the Clinton administration, decoupled the issue of human rights from trade with respect to China in 1994. Another example is the French and German approaches towards such a linkage. In witnessing the contract signing ceremony in Beijing in April 2005 to sell Airbus passenger jets to China, French Prime Minister Jean-Pierre Rafferin said that the arms ban imposed on China because of the Tiananmen Incident was outdated and discriminatory.[11] Trade between China and France exceeded US$13 billion in 2003, a 61 per cent increase over a year earlier.[12]

Given the fact that nation-states are still the main actors in international affairs, each trying to maximise its national interests in a largely anarchical world, what constitutes compliance in global affairs and what sort of standards should be used to gauge compliance remain contested. It seems to be a truism that throughout human history, victors of conflicts set rules to manage others in a post-war inter-state system and interpret those rules to their advantage. This situation ensures that winners are rewarded and their interests enhanced, while the defeated or vanquished are left with little choice but to adhere to those rules, albeit grudgingly at first in most cases.[13] The international system that we inherit today is one that the West, in particular the United States, dominates, in terms of

---

[11] Sun Shangwu, 'China, France ink deals worth US$4b,' *China Daily*, Internet ed., 22 April 2005.

[12] 'France backs China over Taiwan,' The Associated Press, Internet ed., 2004 (accessed 27 January 2004).

[13] For a vigorous and substantive analysis along this line, see John G. Ikenberry, *After victory: institutions, strategic restraint, and the rebuilding of order after major wars* (Princeton: Princeton University Press, 2001).

rule making and rule adjudication. For instance, in the WTO, all the trade negotiation rounds have been conducted according to the timetable of the US and a small number of advanced industrialised countries, reflecting the interests of the West.[14] In nuclear non-proliferation, the US dominates the game. Its war against Iraq and its policies towards North Korea and Iran are good indicators. In the field of human rights, it is the West, and again the US in particular, that sets the norms and rules for others to follow, and that chastises those who do not. The primacy of states over other entities as actors in international society means that international regimes and organisations are often starved with resources to carry out their chartered mandates.

Although China was not exactly a defeated country in the Second World War, it had been humiliated by Western imperialism for a century before the end of the war and emerged thereafter as an impoverished nation, largely ignorant of international rules and practice. Domestic upheavals like the Great Leap Forward in the 1950s and the Cultural Revolution in the 1960s and early 1970s mean that China entered or re-entered the world stage in their aftermath as a novice, despite the reportedly brilliant performances of individual diplomats such as Zhou Enlai in the Third World in the 1950s and Qiao Guanhua in the UN in the 1970s. International and domestic conditions dictate that it plays the role of a follower of international rules. For example, in the WTO, China has been much more a follower than a leader, as its delegation to the Geneva trade talks has been small and understaffed, and as it is busy trying to catch up with the rules and norms of the organisation as well as its Transition Review Mechanism process.[15] The same can be said of China's participation in many IOs. Certainly, many domestic and international conditions have changed dramatically in the last two to three decades. To Andrew Nathan and Robert Ross, "China is a big

---

[14] *21st-Century Economic Herald*, Internet ed., 15 March 2004.

[15] Written testimony of Margaret M. Pearson in a hearing on 'Is China playing by the rules? Free trade, fair trade, and WTO compliance,' before the Congressional-Executive Commission on China, 24 September 2003, http://www.cecc.gov (accessed 20 October 2004).

enough power that its choice is not merely between obeying the world's rules or flouting them. It may join the international regimes ... as much in order to change them as to obey them...."[16]

What China can do to change the rules that it does not like is speculative at this stage. However, China is expected to exert greater influence over the multilateral trading system: "It will likely press for reform of WTO anti-dumping rules, guard against attempts to use labour and environmental issues as disguises for protectionism, and possibly push for reduction of agricultural subsidies."[17] To what extent will China exert its new-found strength? Most Chinese scholars caution the display of excessive assertiveness. Fan Xiaojun of Shenzhen University near Guangzhou suggests that China should neither act as a challenger nor follower. Instead, it should aim at maximising its national interests by devoting its energy to the setting up of regional security mechanisms and the strengthening of regional economic interdependence.[18] Fan, of course, looks at the situation in a very broad way. In the multitude of engagements with the international system, it would be inevitable that China will follow most of the existing rules, avoid major conflicts with the big powers wherever possible, and try to master the intricacies of the rules as soon as possible in order to protect its interests first before attempting to change or revise those rules to its liking. In this way, China is most likely to be a follower cum small challenger. Much depends on how fast China builds up its capacity to act according to the interest-maximisation principle.[19] It has moved away from

---

[16] Andrew Nathan and Robert Ross, *The Great Wall and the empty fortress* (New York and London: W.W. Norton & Co., 1997), p. xiv.

[17] Ramesh Adhikari and Yang Yongzheng, 'What will WTO membership mean for China and its trading partners?' *Finance & Development*, a quarterly magazine of the IMF, Vol. 39, No. 3 (September 2002).

[18] Fan Xiaojun, '*Canyu he peiyu guoji guanxi de jidu jianshe* [China: to engage and form the international order],' *Guoji Guanxi Xueyuan xuebao* [*Journal of the University of International Relations*], Beijing, No. 2 (2002), pp. 16–20 and 26.

[19] *Guoji guize jidingquan yu Zhongguo de weizhi* [The struggle over international rules and China's position], *Shijie zhishi* [*World Knowledge*], Beijing, No. 6 (2002), p. 40.

fighting against unfair norms and unjust rules to join the status quo of hegemonic governance. Unwittingly, it uses constructivism to further its realism goals. Chinese scholars also recognize the role played by big powers in developing and sustaining a rule-based system: according to a Marxist perspective, rules exist to service the rulers; and from a sociological point of view, rules are also made to protect the weak and the minority so that a stable society can be maintained to work for the benefits of the ruling class.[20]

The US takes on as its responsibility the leadership of the world, China the attainment of modernity. The latter wants to see the development of a fairer, more democratic order of international relations based on sovereign equality. Such an international order would be beneficial to China, as the country, being the largest developing country in the world, still struggles as an underdog in the current system. The US, on the other hand, works hard to promote a free world, although it is often left unsaid what exactly this free world is or should be. A free world can be one in which the poor and the oppressed can aspire to achieve a higher standard of living free of oppression; it can mean a situation in which the rich and the powerful, because of the resources available to them, can exercise its freedom to further "exploit" the poor and lock the developing world firmly in an unequal system of exchange; or it can be both. For their respective ideological reasons, the Chinese government would not say that it will promote a freer world, nor would the US government say that it will promote a fairer and more democratic order of international relations (to be distinguished from the development of individual democracies in accordance with American instructions and allied to the US). Both countries, however, would say that they have a (domestic) democratic system, although one is socialist, and the other liberal.

For the rich and the poor countries of the world to work together cooperatively, there must be some kind of *modus operandi* that is acceptable to both sides. In the WTO, the poor member

---

[20] *Ibid.*, p. 43.

states are accorded with developing country status, called "special and differential treatment", under which they are allowed to have some leeway to bring themselves in line with the rules of the organisation. They are given less stringent terms of membership or a longer time to reach full compliance. China is accorded with such a status, but because of its economic size and its potential for growth, many rich member states of the WTO were worried, and they negotiated with China to lay down stricter conditions for its membership. They are cautious not to give away too much.[21]

In the climate change regime, under the concept of "common but differentiated responsibility", countries such as China and India are exempted from reducing their emission of greenhouse gases because of their development-country status, whereas all members of the industrialised world have to apply various measures to cut down their emission of such gases. The US says that the generous treatment of China and India is unfair and is one of the reasons why the US pulled out of Kyoto Protocol. In the field of human rights, there is the well-known debate between liberal democracies and authoritarian states about universal rights versus relative rights and about the linkage between different stages of development and the observance of human rights standards. In the area of non-proliferation, the US acts as if it is the final arbiter as to who has the right to develop nuclear energy, not to mention the development of nuclear weapons. According to Randall Peerenboom, in international law, "the doctrine of 'margin of appreciation' allows states a certain latitude in determining what restrictions are necessary based

---

[21] For example, under the so-called transitional product-specific safeguard mechanism, which will be effective for 12 years after China's entry into the WTO, China's trade partners may impose restrictions on Chinese imports based on "market disruption or the threat of market disruption". This is much stringent than the normal WTO standard, which allows the imposition of import restrictions only if there is "serious injury" or a "threat of serious injury". A special safeguard mechanism is in place until 2008 to restrict Chinese export of textile products after the phasing out of a global quota on 1 January 2005. See Adhikari and Yang, 'What will WTO membership mean for China and its trading partners?' See footnote 77 of Chapter 4.

on the particular circumstances of that state. The latitude varies according to the area of concern, with states tending to have more leeway regarding determinations of what is necessary to ensure national security and stability...."[22] The precise latitude of this "margin of appreciation" becomes the bone of contention between the world's rich countries and their poor cousins in international regimes. A vivid example is China's copyrights record. In a media interview, Jin Xu, the deputy head of the American affairs division of China's Ministry of Commerce, said that "China's intellectual property protection doesn't have as long a history as the United States, but we've been making the fastest progress in the world."[23] A similar situation can be found in China's participation in many international organisations and its establishment of rule of law in the country. Should the world, especially those countries in economic and political competition with China, give it some leeway? How much should the leeway be? These questions will no doubt persist, as China further integrates with the rest of the world.

Given the fact that China enters the world of international regimes and rules which have been shaped by the West, its participation in these regimes and rules is, by necessity and like most other countries in a similar situation, guided by choice and selection. This is so despite observations made by analysts like Ann Kent that "China's selective adaptation to globalisation, and its unwillingness to accept its concomitant responsibilities of transparency, openness and accountability, had created a heavy burden, not only for the government, but [also] for its people and for its relations with the rest of the world."[24] To Chinese leaders, national interest is paramount. For those regimes and rules which are in the main

---

[22] Randall Peerenboom, *China's Long March toward rule of law* (Cambridge: Cambridge University Press, 2002), p. 97.

[23] Chris Buckley, 'US official gives China a last nudge on piracy,' *International Herald Tribune*, Internet ed., 14 January 2005.

[24] Ann Kent, 'China's growth treadmill: globalization, human rights and international relations,' *The Review of International Affairs*, Vol. 3, No. 4 (Summer 2004), p. 538.

technical in nature, like science and sports, China can make a quick decision to engage with them. For those which are largely institutional in nature, dealing with important issues of politics like the UN and the WTO, China usually takes a longer time to consider carefully the pros and cons of membership, and negotiation for entry can take a long time. For those which are mainly cultural and social in nature, like the issue of human rights, China can resist some of the norms and rules, and take measures to protect its own interests and defend its own views. Learning to play by the rules of the international game is a long process, as China adjusts and adapts wherever possible, taking into consideration its domestic conditions and external pressures. Flexibility and pragmatism is the order of the day, a far cry from the days of Mao more than a quarter of a century ago.[25] China's selective and conditional engagement with the world is not particularly Chinese. Other developing countries as well as developed countries also base their foreign policy behaviour on their respective calculations of national interests.

Ultimately, whether or not China can carry out its duties as a responsible member of the international community, as seen by itself and others, depends very much on how well it can tackle its domestic problems in the foreseeable future. According to the *People's Daily*, a group of 98 Chinese experts, many of whom are drawn from top think tanks such as the Chinese Academy of Sciences and the Chinese Academy of Social Sciences, predicts that China faces huge challenges posed by ten problems before 2010:[26]

1. The problem of unemployment;
2. Problems associated with rural development, agriculture, and the plight of farmers;
3. The problem of finance;
4. The gap between the rich and the poor;

---

[25] The idea of this paragraph comes from Wang Yizhou, *Zhongguo jueqi yu guoji kuize* [The rise of China and international rules],' *Guoji jingji pinglun* [*International Economic Review*], Nos 3–4 (1998).
[26] *People's Daily*, Internet ed., 2 September 2004.

5. The question of ecology and resources;
6. The Taiwan issue;
7. The question of globalisation;
8. Structural problems in its political, economic, and social systems;
9. The problem of confidence and creditability; and
10. The problem of AIDS and public hygiene.

Other scholars also identity problems such as reform of the state-owned enterprises, the development of a social safety net, education investments and reform, the management of NGOs, and so on.[27] Under the rubric of political and social problems, lots of issues deserve attention, including the issue of corruption, the establishment of a legal system, the reform of the political system, relations between the Party and the people, and others.[28] Considering the myriad of factors involved, predicting China's future is a hazardous task, a fact readily acknowledged by many China watchers.

The Chinese government puts its faith on economic growth as a way to consolidate its rule. However, as pointed out in Chapter 6, environmental degradation has already started to eat substantially into this growth. Besides, China's economic structure is potentially unstable. Despite its phenomenal economic growth in the past two decades, many people still live in abject poverty. In the countryside, 800 million people or some 60 per cent of the country's population have an average income of less than one US dollar a day.[29] Worse

---

[27] The view of Ding Yuanzu, a research fellow of the National Development and Reform Commission under the State Council, cited in the Friends of Nature website, http://www.fon.org.cn/forum/showthread.php?threadid=3874 (assessed 22 July 2003).

[28] Charles Wolf, a fellow at Rand and the Hoover Institution in the US cites eight problems that China faces in its development: unemployment, corruption, HIV/AIDS and epidemic disease, water resources and pollution, energy consumption and prices, fragility of the financial system and state-owned enterprises, possible shrinkage of foreign direct investment, and Taiwan and other potential conflicts. See Charles Wolf, 'Eight threats to China's economic miracle,' *South China Morning Post*, Internet ed., 7 August 2003.

[29] *The Economist*, Internet ed., 7 April 2005.

than that, China's rich-poor gap is the worst in the world. A survey conducted by the Chinese Academy of Social Sciences shows that in 2002, half the wealth gap in China was accounted for by urban-rural divide. Moreover, there was a growing gap within urban areas, between the ordinary working class and the new middle and super-rich classes. The top five and ten per cent of earners in China accounted for 19.8 per cent and 31.9 per cent respectively of the country's revenue in that year.[30] Considering the fact that China is ruled by a strong authoritative government, and given the submissive nature of its ordinary folks to authority, a feature nurtured through centuries of culture, China's fragile economic structure may still be kept under control and may move forward without a total collapse.[31]

Although China's increasing compliance with the rules of the existing international treaty system has helped to move the world as a whole towards greater convergence in values and identities, divergences will no doubt continue to exist in the foreseeable future. The "end of history" à la Francis Fukuyama is not yet in sight in any clear-cut way.

China has been described as negatively or passively responsible in world affairs rather than positively or actively responsible.[32] The same can be said of the nature of its compliance. The country has a culture of authoritativeness and submission, and of rule by law rather than rule of law. Because of this cultural background and its generally low level of modernisation, China can hardly be expected to take a lead in changing the global order on its own or on behalf of the Third World. It could join collective Third World efforts initiated by others. The Group of 21, which China supports, is led by Brazil, South Africa, India, Argentina, and others. But the sheer size of its economy makes its presence a major force to be reckoned with.

---

[30] *The Daily Telegraph*, 27 February 2004, p. 18.

[31] I borrow this idea from a conversation with Joseph Chan, an independent researcher in Hong Kong, 15 May 2005.

[32] Harry Harding, book review on Elizabeth Economy and Michael Oksenberg (eds), *China joins the world: progress and prospects* (New York: Council on Foreign Relations, 1999), *The China Quarterly*, No. 161 (March 2000), pp. 304–305.

The call for a united front to conduct world trade negotiations, adopted by the Asia-African Summit in Jakarta in April 2005, was a collective effort rather than a particularly strong Chinese initiative. The only notable exceptions to this phenomenon are the Boao Forum and the Shanghai Cooperation Organisation, where China has been actively involved in a leadership role, in setting up the institutional structures as well as in shepherding their development. China's multilateral diplomacy is constrained by a number of systemic factors, including its domestic developmental problems, its weak legal culture, its low level of general education,[33] its fragile comprehensive national power, its limited resources to train enough qualified diplomats to adequately manage its expanding scope of foreign affairs, and the language difficulties in international diplomacy (English being the lingua franca). China has a long way to go, and a lot more to learn in the process in order to become a world-class, normal power. The growth of a nascent civil society and the increasing use of the Internet may lead to more openness and transparency, and slightly greater degree of freedom and democracy, but the existence of civil society is only a necessary condition, not a sufficient one.[34] NGOs can serve as agents for change, but other factors are needed to help to generate a democratic system. In any case, the influence of NGOs in the country still lags very much behind that of the state and the market, and their activities are checked and controlled by the state, so much so Michael Frolic calls it "state-led civil society" with Chinese characteristics,[35] although NGOs may sow "seeds of democracy".[36]

---

[33] China spends 2.5 per cent of its annual budget on compulsory free education, compared with 4 per cent on the average for developing countries. See Committee on Economic, Social and Cultural Rights Review Initial Report of China, 29 April 2005.

[34] Yang Guobin cautions against an overly optimistic view of the role of the Internet in the development of civil society in China. See his 'The Internet and civil society in China: a preliminary assessment,' *Journal of Contemporary China*, Vol. 12, No. 36 (August 2003), pp. 453–475.

[35] B. Michael Frolic, 'State-led civil society,' in Timothy Brook and B. Michael Frolic (eds), *Civil society in China* (Armonk, NY: M.E. Sharpe, 1997), pp. 46–67.

[36] Merle Goldman, *Sowing the seed of democracy in China: political reform in the Deng Xiaoping era* (Cambridge, MA: Harvard University Press, 1997). Suzanne

In the process of moving itself out of isolation, China faces some fundamental structural problems in the international community, as the core values, institutional designs, behavioural norms, and decision-making processes as well as the style of international regimes are Western-orientated.[37] China may choose to remain in the margin of global development, but if it wants to continue to open up and engage with the outside world, it has to choose either to participate selectively in international regimes, or merge with them completely, or together with other frustrated participants change those values and norms.[38] It is a hard, if not a cruel, choice!

Ogden uses the term "inklings of democracy" in her book entitled *Inking of democracy in China* (Cambridge, MA: Harvard University Asia Center, 2002).

[37] Liu Jie, *Jijihua shengcun: Zhongguo heping jueqi de zhanlue jueze* [*Regimenazation* [sic]: *the strategic choice in the course of China's peaceful rise*] (Beijing: Shishi chubanshe, 2004), p. 6.

[38] *Ibid.*, pp. 296–297.

Four IGOs with Both China and Taiwan as Members, 2000

The Asia-Pacific Association of Agricultural Research Institutions was founded in 1990 to promote the exchange of scientific know-how and information in agriculture. It is based in Bangkok and has an office in New Delhi. Members come from 18 countries and territories. They fall into three categories: full members (fee-paying); associate members (non-fee-paying); and other organisations (non-fee-paying). China is listed as a full member, whereas Taiwan is listed as an associate member. Associate members are mostly research institutions or universities, and Taiwan's membership is represented by the Asian Vegetable Research and Development Center in Taiwan. Apparently China is not an active member, as the Association is currently trying to persuade China to become full-time member.[1]

The International Office of Epizootics is a world organisation for animal health. It was created by an international agreement on 25 January 1924 in Paris, signed by 28 countries. As of March 2001,

---

[1] http://www.apaari.org/ (accessed 25 May 2001). See also the *Yearbook of international organizations* 2000–2001, Vol. 1A, p. 125.

it comprises 157 member countries and territories, including China (under its official name of the People's Republic of China) and Taiwan (under the name of "Taipei China").[2]

The International Organisation of Legal Metrology was established in 1955 in Paris to promote the global harmonisation of legal metrology procedures. These are legislative, administrative and technical procedures to ensure the appropriate quality and credibility of measurements related to official controls, trade, health, safety and the environment. Members come from governments of 57 countries, including China. Taiwan is a corresponding member under the name "Chinese Taipei". There are corresponding members from 48 countries.[3]

The International Seed Testing Association, established in 1921 and now based in Switzerland, aims to develop, adopt and publish standard procedures for sampling and testing seeds and to promote uniform application of these procedures for the evaluation of seeds moving in international trade. It also promotes research in all areas of seed science and technology. Members are individuals or science laboratories from 73 countries and territories. At present China has five member stations and Taiwan six.[4]

---

[2] http://www.oie.int/ (accessed 25 May 2001). See also the *Yearbook*, Vol. 1B, p. 1,484.

[3] http://www.oiml.org/ (accessed 25 May 2001). See also the *Yearbook*, Vol. 1B, p. 1,492.

[4] http://www.seedtest.org/ (accessed 25 May 2001). See also the *Yearbook*, Vol. 1B, p. 1,534.

China's Treaty Accessions in Arms Control, Disarmament, and Non-Proliferation, 1952–2004

Type	Treaty	Date of Signature
Nuclear	Latin America Nuclear Weapons-Free Zone	1973
	South Pacific Nuclear Weapons-Free Zone	1987
	Convention on the Physical Protection of Nuclear Material	1989
	Non-Proliferation Treaty	1992
	Comprehensive Test Ban Treaty	1996
	Protocols I & II to the African Nuclear Weapons-Free Zone Treaty	1996
	Protocol Additional to the Agreement between China and IAEA for the Application of Safeguards	1998
Chemical	Chemical Weapons Convention	1993
Biological	Geneva Protocols	1952
	Biological and Toxin Weapons Convention	1984

(Continued)

(Continued)

Type	Treaty	Date of Signature
Conventional	Convention on Conventional Weapons	1981
	Protocol on Prohibitions or Restrictions on the Use of Mines, Booby-Traps and Other Devices	1981
	Protocol on Blinding Laser Weapons	1998
	Amended Protocol on Prohibitions or Restrictions on the Use of Mines, Booby-Traps and Other Devices	1998
	Protocol Against the Illicit Manufacturing of and Trafficking in Firearms, their Parts and Components and Ammunition	2002
Outer space	Outer Space Treaty	1984

Source: Slightly modified from the website of the Ministry of Foreign Affairs, PRC, http://www.fmprc.gov.cn/chn/wjb/zzjg/jks/jkcjty/t119286.htm (accessed 15 January 2005).

Appendix

III

Chronology of China's Human Rights Issue, 1989–2005

1989	June 4	Tiananmen Incident. The West, led by the US, imposes economic sanctions on China.
1990	since	The US and the West criticise China's record at the annual UN Human Rights Commission.
		The US publishes an annual report on human rights, reviewing human rights violations by various countries, including China.
1993		China attends the World Human Rights Conference in Vienna and its preparatory meeting in Bangkok.
1995	June	Harry Wu arrested in China on charges of illegal entry.
1995	September	At the 4th UN Conference on Women held in Beijing, Hillary Clinton criticises countries (without naming China) of forced abortion and the suppression of religious freedom.

1997	September	EU and the PRC resume human rights dialogue without preconditions.
	October 25–November 2	Jiang Zemin visits the US.
	October 27	China signs the International Covenant on Economic, Social and Cultural Rights (ICESCR).
	November	Dissident Wei Jingsheng released.
1998	January 3	China invites UN High Commissioner for Human Rights to visit.
	April	Dissident Wang Dan released.
	June/July	Bill Clinton visits China. The debate between Clinton and Jiang over human rights is broadcast live on state radio and television.
1999	October 5	China signs the International Covenant on Civil and Political Rights.
2001	June 27	China ratifies the ICESCR.
2004	March	China amends Constitution to respect and protect human rights.
2005	April	EU delays lifting the arms embargo imposed after Tiananmen.
2005	June 4	US calls on China to re-examine the Tiananmen Incident. China rebuffs, accusing the US of interfering in its domestic affairs.

Sources: http://www.hrw.org/hrw/campaigns/china-98/chron298.htm and others.

Selected Bibliography

A. CHINESE SOURCES

21st-Century Economic Herald.

Beijing Review.

Chen Quansheng and Liu Jinghua, '*Quanqiu zhong de Zhongguo yu shijie* [China and the world under globalisation],' *Zhongguo waijiao* [*Chinese Diplomacy*], No. 3 (2000).

China Daily.

Chu Feng, '*Wenhua xiangdui zhuyi yu guoji renquan* [Cultural relativism and international human rights],' in Liang Shoude et al (eds), *Guoji shehui yu wenhua* [*International society and culture*] (Beijing: Peking University Press, 1997).

Ecological Environment and Protection, in *Fuyin baokan jiliao* [*Reprints of materials from books and journals*], N2, China Renda Social Science Information Center, Beijing.

Fan Xiaojun, '*Canyu he peiyu guoji guanxi de jidu jianshe* [China: to engage and form the international order],' *Guoji Guanxi Xueyuan xuebao* [*Journal of the University of International Relations*], Beijing, No. 2 (2002).

Guoji guize jidingquan yu Zhongguo de weizhi [The struggle over international rules and China's position], *Shijie zhishi* [*World Knowledge*], Beijing, No. 6 (2002).

Guoji wenti yanjiu [*International Studies*], Beijing.

Hu Zhongshan, '*Lun guoji zhengzhi zhong de kuize, yuanze he faze* [On rules, principles, and laws in international politics],' 14 October 2004, http://www.polisino.org

Huanjing daobao [*Environmental Herald*], Nanjing.

Huanjing gongzuo tongxun [*Bulletin of Environmental Work*].

Jiang Zemin, Opening address at the second Global Environment Facility Assembly held in Beijing on 16–18 October 2002, http://www.fon.org.cn/index.php?id=2767

Liang Lihua, '*Renquan waijiao* [Human rights diplomacy],' *Dangdai shijie yu shehui zhuyi* [*Contemporary World and Socialism*], Beijing, No. 1 (1995).

Lin Bin, '*Junbei kongji de xianzhuang yu qianjing* [The current status and future prospects of arms control],' http://learn.tsinghua.edu.cn/homepage/2000990313/archive.htm

Liu Jie, *Jijihua shengcun: Zhongguo heping jueqi de zhanlue jueze* [*Regimenazation* [sic]: *the strategic choice in the course of China's peaceful rise*] (Beijing: Shishi chubanshe, 2004).

Liu Jinji, Liang Shoude, Yang Huaisheng et al (eds), *Guoji zhengzhi dacidian* [*A dictionary of international politics*] (Beijing: Chinese Academy of Social Sciences Press, 1994).

Luo Yanhua, '*Ruhe kandai renquan yu fazhan di guanxi* [How to view the relationship between human rights and development],' in Liang Shoude et al (eds), *Mianxiang ershiyi shiji de Zhongguo guoji zhanlue* [*Facing China's international strategy in the 21st century*] (Beijing: Chinese Academy of Social Sciences Press, 1998).

Mingbao, Hong Kong.

Pang Zhongying, '*Zai bianhua de shijieshang zhuiqiu Zhongguo de diwei* [To establish China's status in a changing world], *Zhijie jingji yu zhengzhi* [*World Economics and International Politics*], Beijing, No. 1 (2000).

People's Daily.

Qiao Weibing, '*Nengzhanhou Zhongguo yu guoji jizhi de hudong guanxi* [Interactive relations between China and international regime after the Cold War],' in *Guoji zhengzhi yanjiu* [*Studies of International Politics*], Beijing, No. 1 (2001).

SEPA (ed), *Zhongguo huanjing baohu ershiyi shiji yizhang* [*China's environmental protect Agenda 21*] (Beijing: SEPA Press, 1995).

Su Changhe, '*Zhongguo yu guoji zhidu* [China and international regimes],' *Shijie jingji yu zhengzhi*, No. 10 (2002).

Wang Yizhou, *Zhongguo jueqi yu guoji kuize* [The rise of China and international rules],' *Guoji jingji pinglun* [*International Economic Review*], Nos 3–4 (1998).

White Papers of the Chinese government, http://www.china.org.cn/e-white/

Xiao Huanrong, '*Zhongguo de daguo zeren yu diqu zhuyi zhanlue* [China's duty as a big power and the strategy of regionalism],' *Shijie jingji yu zhengzhi*, No. 1 (2003).

Yang Jingyu, '"*Rushi*" *yu woguo de fazhi jianshe* ["WTO entry" and the building of our country's legal system],' *Qiushi* [*Seeking Truth*], March 2002.

Zhang Xiangming, 'The effect of environmental awareness to synthetic decision-making of environ-development,' in *Huanjing daobao*, No. 3 (2000).

Zhao Bo, *Fansi: Zhongguo liji wenti* [Reflection on the rubbish problem in China], *Zhilang* [*Wisdom*], No. 1 (2003), http://www.usc.cuhk.edu.hk/wk_wzdetails.asp?ed=2007

Zhongguo dai baike quanshu: huanjing kexue [*China encyclopaedia: environmental science*] (Beijing: China Encyclopaedia Press, 2002).

Zhongguo huanjing bao [*China Environmental News*], Beijing.

Zhongguo renquan nianjian [*China human rights yearbook*] (Beijing: Contemporary World Press, 2000).

Zhou Baogen, 'A constructivist analysis of China and international nuclear non-proliferation regime,' *Shijie jingji yu zhengzhi*, No. 2 (2003).

Zhou Xiaoshi and Jin Minli, '*Maoyi zhengduan fengxian wenti de sikao* [Probing into trade dispute risks after China's entry into the WTO],' *International Economics and Trade Research*, Guangzhou, No. 1 (2002).

Zhu Kaibing and Qiu Guo, '*Lun guoji shehui de duili chongtu yu daguo zeren* [Antagonism and conflicts in the international society and the responsibilities of the big powers], *Guoji Guanxi Xueyuan xuebao* [*Journal of the University of International Relations*], Beijing, No. 4 (2002), pp. 15–20.

B. US GOVERNMENT DOCUMENTS

Aldonas, Grant, Testimony at a hearing of Congressional-Executive Commission on China on 6 June 2002 to consider China's WTO compliance, http://www.cecc.gov/pages/hearings/060602/

Baucus, Max, Statement made at a hearing of Congressional-Executive Commission on 'WTO: will China keep its promises? Can it?' 6 June 2002, http://www.cecc.gov/

Bureau of Verification and Compliance, US Department of State, 'Adherence to and compliance with arms control and non-proliferation agreements and commitments,' [2002], http://www.state.gov/t/vc/rls/rpt/22322pf.htm

'Chinese NGOs – carving a niche within constraints,' a January 2003 report from the US Embassy in Beijing, http://www.usembassy-china.org.cn/sandt/ptr/ngos-prt.htm

Clark, Donald, Testimony at a hearing of Congressional-Executive Commission on China on 6 June 2002 to consider China's WTO compliance.

Donnelly, Shaun, Testimony before the US-China Commission's Public Hearing on WTO Compliance and Sectoral Issues, 18 January 2002, http://usinfo.state.gov/regional/ea/uschina/donnelly.htm

Kapp, Robert A., Testimony to the Subcommittee on Trade, Committee on Ways and Means, US House of Representatives, 10 July 2001, http://www.uschina.org/public/testimony/testimony12.html

Kapp, Robert A., Testimony to the Trade Policy Staff Committee of the US Trade Representative on 18 September 2002, http://www.uschina.org/public/testimony/testimony13.html

Lash III, William H., Testimony before the US-China Commission's Public Hearing on WTO Compliance and Sectoral Issues, 18 January 2002.

Murch, Christian, Statement made at a hearing of Congressional-Executive Commission on 'WTO: Will China keep its promises? Can it?' on 6 June 2002.

Pearson, Margaret M., Written testimony at a hearing on 'Is China playing by the rules? Free trade, fair trade, and WTO compliance,' before the Congressional-Executive Commission on China, 24 September 2003, http://www.cecc.gov

Quam, David, Testimony before the US-China Commission, 18 January 2002, http://www.uscc.gov/tesqua.htm

Report on human rights practices in China (including Hong Kong and Macau) in 2002, released by the Bureau of Democracy, Human Rights, and Labor of the State Department on 31 March 2003, http://www.state.gov/g/drl/rls/hrrpt/2002/18239.htm

Report to Congress of the US by the China Security Review Commission, July 2002, chapter 3.

C. JOURNAL ARTICLES

Adhikari, Ramesh and Yang Yongzheng, 'What will WTO membership mean for China and its trading partners?' *Finance & Development*, a quarterly magazine of the IMF, Vol. 39, No. 3 (September 2002).

Alter, Karen J., 'Do international courts enhance compliance with international law?' *Review of Asian and Pacific Studies*, Seikei University Center for Asian and Pacific Studies, Japan, No. 25 (July 2003).

Chen Jie, 'China's Spratly policy,' *Asian Survey*, Vol. 34, No. 10 (October 1994).

Downs, George W., 'Enforcement and the evolution of cooperation,' *Michigan Journal of International Law*, Vol. 19, No. 2 (1998).

Downs, George W., David Rocke, and Peter Barsoom, 'Is the good news about compliance good news about cooperation,' *International Organization*, Vol. 50, No. 3 (1996).

Economy, Elizabeth, 'Painting China green: the next Sino-American tussle,' *Foreign Affairs*, March/April 1999.

Einhorn, Robert, 'China and non-proliferation,' *In the National Interest*, Vol. 2, Issue 13 (2 April 2003).

Gill, Bates, 'Discussion of "China: a responsible great power",' *Journal of Contemporary China*, Vol. 10, No. 26 (February 2001).

Johnston, Alastair Iain, 'Engaging myths: misconceptions about China and its global role,' *Harvard Asia Pacific Review*, Vol. 2, No. 1 (Winter 1997/98).

Kent, Ann, 'China's growth treadmill: globalization, human rights and international relations,' *The Review of International Affairs*, Vol. 3, No. 4 (Summer 2004).

Kim, Samuel, 'China in and out of the changing world order,' Center of International Studies, World Order Studies Program Occasional Paper No. 21, Princeton University, 1991.

Koskenniemi, Martti, 'International law and hegemony: a reconfiguration,' in *Cambridge Review of International Affairs*, Vol. 17, No. 2 (July 2004).

Li Yitan and A. Cooper Drury, 'Threatening sanctions when engagement would be more effective: attaining better human rights in China,' *International Studies Perspectives*, Vol. 5, Issue 4 (November 2004).

Liang Wei, 'China's WTO negotiation process and its implications,' *Journal of Contemporary China*, No. 33 (November 2002).

Moodel, Michael and Amy Sands, 'Introduction: new approaches to compliance with arms control and non-proliferation agreements,' *The Nonproliferation Review*, Vol. 8, No. 1 (Spring 2001).

Nathan, Andrew J., 'Human rights in Chinese foreign policy,' *The China Quarterly*, No. 139 (September 1994).

Pei Minxin, 'China's governance crisis,' *Foreign Affairs*, September/October 2002.

Wang Yan, Richard K. Morgan, and Mat Cashmore, 'Environmental impact assessment of projects in the People's Republic of China: new law, old problems,' in *Environmental Impact Assessment Review*, Vol. 23, Issue 5 (2003).

Weiss, Thomas G., 'Researching humanitarian intervention: some lessons,' *Journal of Peace Research*, Vol. 38, No. 4 (July 2001).

Woodman, Sophia, 'Bilateral aid to improve human rights,' *China Perspectives*, No. 51 (January–February 2004).

Xia Liping, 'China: a responsible great power,' *Journal of Contemporary China*, Vol. 10, No. 26 (February 2001).

Yahuda, Michael, 'China's foreign relations: the Long March, future uncertain,' *The China Quarterly*, No. 159 (September 1999).

Yahuda, Michael, 'China's search for a global role,' *Current History*, Vol. 98, No. 629 (September 1999).

Yamashita Hikaru, 'Fighting terrorism and fighting humanitarian emergencies: two approaches to "elastic" sovereignty and international order,' *Cambridge Review of International Affairs*, Vol. 18, No. 1 (April 2005).

Yang Guobin, 'The Internet and civil society in China: a preliminary assessment,' *Journal of Contemporary China*, Vol. 12, No. 36 (August 2003).

Zhou Qi, 'Conflicts over human rights between China and the US,' *Human Rights Quarterly*, Vol. 27, No. 1 (February 2005).

D. BOOKS AND BOOK CHAPTERS

Bilder, Richard B., 'Beyond compliance: helping nations cooperate,' in Dinah Shelton (ed), *Commitment and compliance: the role of non-binding norms in the international legal system* (Oxford: Oxford University Press, 2000).

Bull, Hedley, *The anarchical society: a study of order in world politics*, 3rd ed (Basingstoke and New York: Palgrave, 2002).

Chan, Gerald, *China and international organisations* (Hong Kong: Oxford University Press, 1989).

Chan, Gerald, *Chinese perspectives on international relations: a framework for analysis* (Basingstoke: Macmillan, 1999).

Chayes, Abraham and Antonia Handler-Chayes, *The new sovereignty: compliance with international regulatory agreements* (Cambridge: Harvard University Press, 1995).

Cheng Sijin, 'Gauging China's capabilities and intentions under Deng and Mao,' in Cathal J. Nolan (ed), *Power and responsibility in world affairs: reformation versus transformation* (Westport, Connecticut; London: Praeger, 2004).

Clemens, Walter C. Jr., 'China,' in Richard Dean Burns (ed), *Encyclopedia of arms control and disarmament* (New York: Charles Scribner's Sons, 1993).

Davis, Michael C. (ed), *Human rights and Chinese values: legal, philosophical, and political perspectives* (Hong Kong: Oxford University Press, 1995).

Deng, Francis M., et al, *Sovereignty as responsibility: conflict management in Africa* (Washington, DC: The Brookings Institution, 1996).

Deng Yong and Wang Fei-Ling (eds), *China rising: power and motivation in Chinese foreign policy* (Lanham: Rowman & Littlefield Publishers, Inc., 2005).

Deng Yong and Wang Fei-Ling (eds), *In the eyes of the dragon: China views the world* (Lanham: Rowman & Littlefield Publishers, Inc., 1999).

Duffy, Gloria 'Arms control treaty compliance,' in Richard Dean Burns (ed), *Encyclopedia of arms control and disarmament* (New York: Charles Scribner's Sons, 1993).

Economy, Elizabeth and Michel Oksenberg (eds), *China joins the world: progress and prospects* (New York: Council on Foreign Relations Press, 1999).

Faure, Michael and Jürgen Lefevere, 'Compliance with international environmental agreements,' in Norman J. Vig and Regina S. Axelrod (eds) *The global environment: institutions, law, and policy* (Washington, D.C.: Congressional Quarterly, 1999).

Foot, Rosemary, *Rights beyond borders: the global community and the struggle over human rights in China* (Oxford: Oxford University Press, 2000).

Frieman, Wendy, *China, arms control, and nonproliferation* (London: RoutledgeCurzon, 2004).

Haas, Peter M., 'Choosing to comply: theorising from international relations and comparative politics,' in Dinah Shelton (ed), *Commitment and compliance: the role of non-binding norms in the international legal system* (Oxford: Oxford University Press, 2000).

Hu Weixing, Gerald Chan, and Zha Daojiong (eds), *China's international relations in the 21st century* (Lanham: University Press of America, 2000).

Ikenberry, John G., *After victory: institutions, strategic restraint, and the rebuilding of order after major wars* (Princeton: Princeton University Press, 2001).

Johnston, Alastair I., 'China and international environmental institutions: a decision rule analysis,' in Michael B. McElroy et al (eds), *Energizing China: reconciling environmental protection and economic growth* (Harvard University Committee on Environment, 1998).

Kent, Ann, *China, the United Nations, and human rights* (Philadelphia: University of Pennsylvania Press, 1999).

Kim, Samuel S. (ed), *China and the world: Chinese foreign relations in the post-Cold War era*, 4th ed (Boulder: Westview, 1998).

Kim, Samuel S., 'Human rights in China's international relations,' in Edward Friedman and Barrett L. McCormick (eds), *What if China doesn't democratize? Implications for war and peace* (Armonk, NY and London: M.E. Sharpe, 2000).

Lampton, David M. (ed), *The making of Chinese foreign and security policy in the era of reform* (Stanford: Stanford University Press, 2001).

Lieberthal, Kenneth, *Governing China: from revolution through reform* (New York and London: W.W. Norton, 1995).

Lo, Carlos Wing-hung and Chung Shan-shan, 'China's green challenges in the twenty-first century,' in Joseph Y.S. Cheng (ed), *China's challenges in the twenty-first century* (Hong Kong: City University of Hong Kong Press, 2003).

Lubman, Stanley B., *Bird in a cage: legal reform in China after Mao* (Stanford: Stanford University Press, 1999).

Nathan, Andrew and Robert Ross, *The Great Wall and the empty fortress: China's search for security* (New York and London: W.W. Norton & Co., 1997).

Peerenboom, Randall, *China's long march toward rule of law* (Cambridge: Cambridge University Press, 2002).

Potter, Pitman B., *The Chinese legal system: globalization and local legal culture* (London; New York: Routledge, 2001).

Raustiala, Kal and Anne-Marie Slaughter, 'International law, international relations and compliance,' in Walter Carlsnaes, Thomas Risse, and Beth A. Simmons (eds), *Handbook of international relations* (London; Thousand Oaks; New Delhi: Sage Publications, 2002).

Shapiro, Judith, *Mao's war against nature: politics and the environment in revolutionary China* (Cambridge: Cambridge University Press, 2001).

Smil, Vaclac, *China's environmental crisis: an inquiry into the limits of national development* (Armonk, New York; London: M.E. Sharpe, 1993).

Solomon, Russell (ed), *Rights, rules & responsibility in international conduct* (Palmerston North, New Zealand: Dunmore Press, 2000).

Svensson, Marina, *Debating human rights in China: a conceptual and political history* (Lanham: Rowman & Littlefield, 2002).

Swaine, Michael D. and Alastair Iain Johnston, 'China and arms control institutions,' in Elizabeth Economy and Michel Oksenberg (eds), *China joins the world: progress and prospects* (New York: Council on Foreign Relations Press, 1999).

Turner, Karen, James V. Feinerman, and R. Kent Guy (eds), *The limits of the rule of law in China* (Seattle: University of Washington Press, 2000).

Wan Ming, *Human rights in Chinese foreign relations: defining & defending national interests* (Philadelphia: University of Pennsylvania Press, 2001).

Yearbook of international organizations 2003–2004 (Munich: K.G. Saur, 2003).

Zhang Kunmin and Wang Cao, 'China's sustainable development strategy and international cooperation on environment,' in Tao Zhenghua and Rüdiger Wolfrum (eds), *Implementing international environmental law in Germany and China* (The Hague; London; Boston: Kluwer Law, 2001).

Zhang Yongjin and Greg Austin (eds), *Power and responsibility in Chinese foreign policy* (Canberra: Asia Pacific Press, 2001).

Zhou Wei, 'The study of human rights in the People's Republic of China,' in James T.H. Tang (ed), *Human rights and international relations in the Asia-Pacific region* (London and New York: Pinter, 1995).

E. NEWSPAPERS AND MAGAZINES

Asia Times
The China Business Review
The Economist
Far Eastern Economic Review
The Guardian
International Herald Tribune
South China Morning Post
The Standard
Taipei Times
Times

F. OTHER REFERENCES

Cleminson, F.R., 'Multilateral on-going monitoring and verification (OMV) of compliance: nurturing cost-effectiveness,' the Sixth ISODARCO Beijing Seminar on Arms Control, Shanghai, 29 October–1 November 1998.

Crossen, Teall, 'Responding to global warming: a critique of the Kyoto Protocol compliance regime: an annotated bibliography,' a paper accessed through the Internet, April 2005.

Harding, Harry, Book review on Elizabeth Economy and Michel Oksenberg (eds), *China joins the world: progress and prospects* (New York: Council on Foreign Relations, 1999), *The China Quarterly*, No. 161 (March 2000), pp. 304–305.

Kamm, John, 'Engaging China on human rights,' a speech made at The Brookings Institution, Washington DC, 14 October 2004.

Medeiros, Evan S., Report on the 3rd US-China conference on arms control, disarmament and non-proliferation, East Asia Nonproliferation Program, Center for Nonproliferation Studies, Monterey Institute of International Studies, October 2000.

'The People's Republic of China and the international human rights system,' Office of the United Nations Office of the High Commissioner for Human Rights, January 2005.

G. WEBSITES

Biological and Toxin Weapons Convention, http://www.opbw.org/
Chemical Weapons Convention, http://www.opcw.org/
Comprehensive Test Ban Treaty Organisation, http://www.ctbto.org/
Friends of Nature, http://www.fon.org.cn/
Ministry of Foreign Affairs of the PRC, http://www.fmprc.gov.cn/
Missile Technology Control Regime, http://www.mtcr.info/english/partners.html/
Non-proliferation of Nuclear Weapons Treaty, http://www.un.org/Depts/dda/WMD/treaty/
Nuclear Threat Initiative, http://www.nti.org/db/china/
United Nations Office of the High Commissioner for Human Rights, http://www.unhchr.ch/html/
US-China Economic and Security Review Commission, http://www.uscc.gov/
US Congressional-Executive Commission on China, http://www.cecc.gov/
Universities Service Centre for China Studies, the Chinese University of Hong Kong, http://www.usc.cuhk.edu.hk/
World Trade Organisation, http://www.wto.org/
Zangger Committee, http://www.zanggercommittee.org/

Index